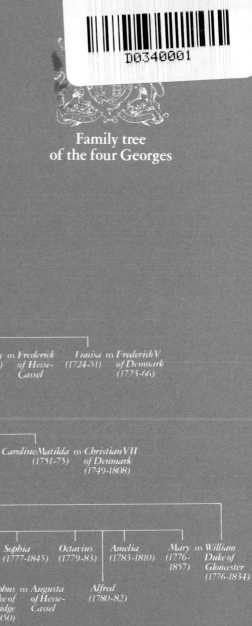

Family tree
of the four Georges

Elizabeth m Frederick
        Elector Palatine

Ernest m Sophia
ector of   (1630-1714)
anover
529-98)

Ernest
Duke of York

EORGE II m Caroline of Ansbach
683-1760) | (1683-1737)

Caroline   George   William Augustus   Mary m Frederick   Louisa m Frederick V
(1713-57)   (1717-18) Duke of Cumber-   (1723-72) of Hesse-   (1724-51) of Denmark
                       land (1721-65)   Cassel   (1723-66)

        Henry m Lady   Louisa   Frederick   Caroline Matilda m Christian VII
        Duke of Anne   (1749-68) (1750-65)   (1751-75) of Denmark
ve   Cumberland Horton   (1749-1808)
        (1745-90)

Elizabeth m Frederick   Augustus   Sophia   Octavius   Amelia   Mary m William
(1770-1840) of Hesse-   D. of Sussex   (1777-1845) (1779-83) (1783-1810) (1776- Duke of
          Homburg   (1773-1843)   1857)   Gloucester
                                                                                            (1776-1834)

sta   Ernest m Frederica   Adolphus m Augusta   Alfred
-1840)   Duke of Princess   Duke of of Hesse-   (1780-82)
              Cumberland of Solms- Cambridge Cassel
              later K. of Braunfels (1774-1850)
              Hanover
              (1771-1851)

BLOOD ROYAL

Friends of the Library

Presented by

DALE FISK

Concordia College — Portland

Christopher Sinclair-Stevenson

Blood Royal

The Illustrious House of Hanover

DOUBLEDAY & COMPANY, INC.
GARDEN CITY, NEW YORK
1980

ISBN: 0-385-09663-1
Library of Congress Catalog Card Number 74–33662
Copyright © 1979 by Christopher Sinclair-Stevenson
Printed in the United States of America
All Rights Reserved
First Edition in the United States of America

FOR MY FATHER

Acknowledgments

The sources which I have consulted for each chapter will be found at the end of the text on pp. 235 39. But I also owe a considerable debt of gratitude to a great many more books which I have failed to mention. I do not choose to burden such an impressionistic essay with a ponderous bibliography and detailed footnotes; it is intended to be lighthearted and, I hope, entertaining, much as my model, Nancy Mitford's *The Sun King*, was. Even so, my thanks to biographers and historians of the period are sincere.

Perhaps I should express even more fervent gratitude to my editor, David Machin. He has been inordinately patient about the delivery of a script, and unceasingly tactful in his encouragement. Finally, I trust that my wife will believe me when I say that she has helped and inspired me when I thought the book would never be finished.

C.S.-S.

Contents

Introduction

This study of the first four Georges and their age is not a work of scholarship, I must emphasise that from the start. I have written a highly impressionistic book, which attempts to convey some images of the eighteenth century and the first part of the nineteenth century. It is a partial view. I have exercised the writer's prerogative, to tell what I wish to tell, and damn the consequences. I began with the feeling that the first four Georges had become fixed in history. They were faintly absurd, certainly unattractive, both physically and in their characters, they contributed little or nothing to the gaiety of nations, let alone to the development of civilisation, of democracy, of the arts. And yet they presided over one of the most remarkable periods in British history. When George I came to the throne, the union between England and Scotland was barely a decade old, the tensions within the kingdom were almost tangible, a repetition of the strifes which had bedevilled the seventeenth century was entirely possible, England was exhausted from Marlborough's wars and the centuries-old conflict with the French. And yet by the death of George IV, the British Empire was more than a dream: it had become a fact. And the nation had progressed in many, far deeper and more significant ways. A political system which was based on two parties had arisen. The loss of the American Colonies and the establishment of what was to become the most powerful state in the western world set the seal on democracy attainable without wholesale slaughter. The dominance of Napoleon Bonaparte had been crushed. And, in other spheres, a great flourishing in the arts had taken place. In painting, architecture, music and literature, extraordinary outbursts of genius had occurred. It would be reasonable to claim that the nineteenth century—the age of Victoria, Queen and Empress—saw the arrival of far more colossal changes, but they surely grew from the seeds sown and nurtured in the previous century.

The four Georges, often disagreeable, reprehensible, irascible, idiotic, disgraceful though they may have been, possessed many qualities, even if they were those of *laissez-faire*. They allowed things to happen, to put it at its crudest. They were, admittedly, blessed with extraordinary talents among their advisers—Walpole, the two Pitts, Fox and Canning—though they survived the Butes, the Norths, the Pelhams and the other political nonentities who rose briefly into the firmament and were consumed in the flames of the political sun. But they cannot escape some portion of the credit which posterity owed to the eighteenth century. They were not mere Germanic buffoons, lacking the finer sensibilities, and given almost extensively to venereal pursuits. It was a sexually uninhibited age, and it would have been strange if they had not conformed; as it was, George III was remarkable for his sobriety and his uxoriousness. The Hanoverians, too, were not the philistines which contemporary and subsequent critics so often have dubbed them. George II patronised Handel at a crucial stage in his career, George III was a great collector, and George IV was arguably the most intelligent and artistic monarch ever to sit upon the English throne. His monuments

—the Brighton Pavilion, Carlton House Terrace, the reconstituted Windsor Castle—speak for themselves and for him.

This book, then, though no act of piety, is an attempt to strike a balance, to give some credit where such credit is due, to place the four Georges and their families and courts in their setting, and to bring out some of their qualities as well as their defects. I have, as I say, concentrated on those aspects of a century and a quarter which intrigue and interest me. I do not claim to have produced a deep analysis, certainly not of the political and intellectual changes; instead I have lighted on matters of social relevance. The study of architecture, or fashion, or gambling, or the relationships between different members of a family, of funerals and coronations, is not totally worthless.

Prologue

Vivat Rex

The King in his Royal Robes of crimson velvet, furr'd with ermine and border'd with a rich broad, gold lace, wearing the collar of the order of St. George . . . and on his head a cap of estate, turn'd up with ermine, adorned with a circle of gold, enrich'd with diamonds.

Description of George I's coronation

The entire ceremony was one pleasant muddle from beginning to end.

Description of George III's coronation

George I was crowned King in Westminster Abbey on October 20, 1714. Those who had been present at the three previous coronations agreed that the inauguration of the Hanoverian dynasty lacked a certain style and splendour. The Queen could hardly be present as she was incarcerated at Ahlden, and though the Princess of Wales had arrived in time she did not take part in the procession. There was, consequently, less opportunity for ceremonial, though public interest could hardly have been more intense.

The Abbey contained a number of prominent Jacobites, and there was considerable speculation as to how they would behave. Francis Atterbury, Bishop of Rochester, could not be excluded, and Henry St. John, Viscount Bolingbroke, was observed to bow three times almost down to the ground when the King enquired who he was. Lady Cowper later noted in her diary:

One may easily conclude this was not a Day of real Joy to the Jacobites. However they were all there, looking as cheerful as they could, but very peevish with Everybody that spoke to them. My Lady Dorchester stood underneath me; and when the archbishop went round the Throne, demanding the consent of the People, she turned to me and said, "Does the old Fool think that Anybody here will say no to his Question, when there are so many drawn swords?"

But Lady Dorchester was unusually outspoken. A former mistress of James II, when she espied the Duchess of Portsmouth, one of Charles II's mistresses, and Lady Orkney, who had fulfilled the same function for William III, she exclaimed, "Good God! Who would have thought we three whores would have met together here."

Drawn swords or no, the Tory peers gave every appearance of enthusiasm for the new monarch as he was crowned. The coronation service proceeded on its leisurely way. The Bishop of Oxford delivered himself of an interminable sermon, mingling piety with politics (Dr. Tennison, the Archbishop of Canterbury, was far from well, and a new Primate of England might be required any day), congratulating God on having selected so propitiously the hour of Queen Anne's death, when "the unsettled posture of affairs abroad would not permit the Pretender's foreign friends to send any forces to encourage an insurrection, and the unreadiness of his surprised abettors here would not permit them to appear in such a manner, as to invite an invasion," and deploring the faintest possibility of the Old Pretender ascending the throne of England. Warming to his theme, the Bishop referred darkly to

"the maxims of French tyranny" and "the principles of
Popish superstition," looked back in sadness to the reigns of
Charles II and James II—"if those Princes chastised us
with whips, this would have done it with scorpions, who
would have come with a spirit, not only of popery and big-
otry, but also of resentment and revenge"; and was convinced
that, with the accession of George I, a new era of lasting happiness was on the point of being ushered in. Outraged refer-
ences to Louis XIV were given a touch of irony by the presence, in the Abbey, of two gentlemen in robes of crimson
velvet edged with miniver. These were supposed to represent
the Dukes of Aquitaine and Normandy.

There were a few discordant notes. The Venetian and
Sicilian ambassadors quarrelled over the seats they had been
allocated in the gallery set aside for foreign diplomats. Lady
Cowper took her friend Lady Nottingham to task for shouting out the words of the Litany with rather too much gusto.
And, when the King's Champion rode into Westminster Hall
to deliver his challenge, one lady was heard to declare that
James III was the rightful king of England. But there was a
feeling of relief in the air. The Whigs were in ecstasies, and
even High Tories like Robert Harley and Bolingbroke appeared to condone the Hanoverian succession by their presence in the Abbey. The Treasurer of the Household scattered coronation medals with a liberal hand, eight new peers
were created, the banquet in Westminster Hall was lavish,
even the sun shone. Lady Wentworth's comment was ill-
spelled but convinced: "All hear are in great raptures of the
King and say he is the Wysest and the Richis Princ in
Yoarup. I hope he will prove soe."

The Coronation of George III a month short of forty-seven
years later, was considerably less dignified and free of incident. As Jocelyn Perkins's *The Coronation Book* puts it,
"never was the English mind, with all its total incompetence
to grasp details of ceremonial, displayed in such utter baldness

and nakedness, as in the frantic efforts of the Deputy Earl-Marshal and the Lord Great Chamberlain." First, there was a strike of workmen who were to erect the decorations. Then Lord Effingham, the Deputy Earl-Marshal, completely forgot about the Sword of State and the canopy; the Lord Mayor lent his own sword, but the loss of the canopy delayed the start of the procession until midday. In the Abbey, the Bishop of Salisbury droned on, becoming so muddled that he alluded to the extraordinary number of years the King had already sat on the throne, and the coronation service took six hours to complete.

Being the latter end of September, the Procession was compelled to make its return journey in a dusky twilight, which rendered all surrounding objects dim and indistinct. The Hall was enveloped in almost complete darkness; and, as it was not lit up until the arrival of the royal pair, the main body of the Procession entered in a manner by no means dignified, the nodding plumes of the Knights of the Bath conveying to many minds a very forcible suggestion of a funeral and hearse!

During the banquet, Lord Talbot, the Lord High Steward, came into his own. Already in a state of high nervous tension, he proceeded to argue furiously with the Barons of the Cinque Ports, the Knights of the Bath, and the Aldermen of the City of London:

These three sets of functionaries on entering the Hall, ready to do full justice to the good cheer awaiting them, found that they had been shamefully ousted from their places, in defiance of all ancient precedent. The aldermen indeed, with characteristic regard for the needs of the inner man, were fully equal to this emergency; and by dint of many hard words, and not a few bullying threats, they forced Lord Talbot to admit them a place far above their own proper rank.

The Knights of the Bath were less persistent and less fortunate. Their plumes nodding ever more funereally, they were banished to the Court of Requests and a lonely, and inferior, dinner. But it was the Barons of the Cinque Ports who suffered the most. Talbot lost his temper completely and raged at them: "If you come to me, as Lord Steward, I tell you it is impossible; if as Lord Talbot, I am a match for any of you!"

The unfortunate Barons were afforded some small consolation by Lord Talbot's next manoeuvre. He was due to accompany the King's Champion during the latter's traditional arrival in Westminster Hall, and had spent many weary hours practising and training his horse to back out of the Hall once the challenge had been delivered. The horse was too literally minded, and proceeded to back into the Hall and to present its rump to the startled King. It was a theatrical coup of enormous popularity. Laughter was unrestrained, and several ladies succumbed to hysterics. It was all, as one observer put it sharply, "a terrible indecorum, such as one might expect at Bartholomew Fair." Only the King seemed unmoved by the goings-on. Bishop Newton wrote approvingly,

The King's whole behaviour at the coronation was justly admired and commended by every one, and, particularly, his manner of ascending and seating himself on the throne after his coronation. No actor in the character of Pyrrhus, in the "Distressed Mother" [a contemporary tragedy by Ambrose Phillips] not even Booth himself, who was celebrated for it in the *Spectator*, ever ascended the throne with so much grace and dignity.

Finally, though, George complained to Lord Effingham, who did not ease the situation by his answer: "It is true, sir, that there has been some neglect; but I have taken care that the *next* coronation shall be regulated in the greatest manner possible."

Thomas Gray was an eye-witness and left a vivid account of the scene in Westminster Hall:

The instant the Queen's canopy entered, fire was given to all the lustres at once by trains of prepared flax that reached from one end to the other. To me it seemed an interval of not half a minute before the whole was in a blaze of splendour. It is true that for that half minute it rained fire upon the heads of all the spectators, the flax falling in large flakes; and the ladies, Queen and

all, were in no small terror, but no mischief ensued. It was out as
soon as it fell, and the most magnificent spectacle I ever beheld
remained. The King bowing to the Lords as he passed, with the
crown on his head, and the sceptre and orb in his hands, took his
place with great majesty and grace. So did the Queen with her
crown, sceptre and rod. Then supper was served in gold plates.
The Earl Talbot, the Duke of Bedford, and the Earl of
Effingham in their robes, all three on horseback prancing and
curveting like the hobby horses in the "Rehearsal" [the play by
George Villiers, 2nd Duke of Buckingham], ushered in the
courses to the foot of the *haut-pas*. Between the courses The
Champion performed his part with applause. The Earl of Den-
bigh carved for the King; the Earl of Holderness for the Queen.

Unremarkably, Horace Walpole was less charitable in his
description:

For the Coronation, if a puppet show could be worth a million,
that is; the multitudes, balconies, guards, and processions made
Palace Yard the liveliest spectacle in the world. The Hall was the
most glorious. The blaze of lights, the richness and variety of
habits, the ceremonial, the benches of peers and peeresses, frequent and full, was as awful as a pageant can be, and yet, for the
King's sake, and my own, I never wish to see another . . . The
Champion acted his part admirably, and dashed down his gaunt-
let with proud defiance. His associates, Lord Effingham, Lord
Talbot, and the Duke of Bedford, were woeful.

It all ended late in the evening:

Their Majesties returned to St. James's a little after ten o'clock at
night; but they were pleased to give time for the peeresses to go
first, that they might not be incommoded by the pressure of the
mob to see their Majesties. After the nobility were departed,
the Hall doors were thrown open according to custom, when the
people immediately cleared it of all the moveables, such as the
victuals, cloths, plates, dishes, etc., and, in short, everything that
could stick to their fingers.

Decorum had not triumphed—though witnesses of George
III's coronation would have been vastly more shocked if they

could have foreseen the disgraceful events which were to occur on July 19, 1821, when George IV was to preside over the expenditure of nearly a £ ¼ million: the designing of a gallimaufry of absurd costumes and robes, the scandal of Queen Caroline and her attempt to storm the Abbey, and a near-riot in Westminster Hall. The coronations of the Hanoverian Georges were not edifying spectacles, and that of George III was no exception. When, later in his reign, the American colonies were lost, all too many people looked back to 1761, shook their heads sadly, and recalled that the great diamond had fallen from the crown in Westminster Hall. The reign had commenced unpropitiously.

Part One

GEORGE I

1738–1820; King, 1760–1820

The Brunswicker who is "fort doux" and makes her [his mother] love him because he is so ugly.

The Electress Sophia

The Elector is grossly selfish, sly, and deceitful . . . Suspicion, pride and avarice make this Elector what he is.

Elisabeth Charlotte, Duchesse d'Orléans

His views and affections were singly confined to the narrow compass of the Electorate; England was too big for him.

Lord Chesterfield

Take what you can get, was the old monarch's maxim. He was not a lofty monarch, certainly; he was not a patron of the fine arts; but he was not a hypocrite, he was not revengeful, he was not extravagant. Though a despot in Hanover, he was a moderate ruler in England. His aim was to leave it to itself as much as possible, and to live out of it as much as he could. His heart was in Hanover. He was more than fifty years of age when he came amongst us: we took him because we wanted him, because he served our turn; we laughed at his uncouth German ways, and sneered at him. He took our loyalty for what it was worth . . . There are stains in the portrait for the first George, and traits in it which none of us need admire; but, among the nobler features are justice, courage, moderation—and these we may recognise ere we turn the picture to the wall.

William Makepeace Thackeray

In private life he would have been called an honest blockhead, and fortune which made him a King only prejudiced his honesty and shortened his days.

Lady Mary Wortley Montagu

I

Pudding Time

> When George in pudding-time came o'er
> And moderate men looked big, sir,
> I turned a cat-in-pan once more
> And so became a Whig, sir.
> > *"The Vicar of Bray"*

Had the Queen lasted a month longer; had the English
Tories been as bold and resolute as they were clever and
crafty; had the Prince whom the nation loved and pitied
been equal to his fortune, George Louis had never talked
German in St. James's Chapel Royal.
> *William Makepeace Thackeray*

In April 1713, Lord Halifax entertained a number of distinguished Whig politicians to dinner, and to an exposition of
what might lie in the immediate future. Queen Anne, swollen,
dropsical and ruled by emotion, could not live much longer.
The Tories would certainly triumph at the imminent election. There were moves afoot to ensure that James Francis
Edward Stuart should be the next crowned king of England

and Scotland. Halifax and his cronies were convinced that dramatic action was essential, that indeed George Lewis, the son of the Electress Sophia of Hanover, should come immediately to England, "as an infallable remedy against present evil." He could be provided with a false passport and thus travel incognito, "with a valet de chambre and two footmen, without his Order of the Garter, without liveries . . . in the pacquet boat."

The Whigs maintained pressure on the Electress to such a pitch that she abandoned her previous position of non-interference and instructed her envoy, Schutz, to apply to the Lord Chancellor, the Earl of Harcourt, for the necessary writ of summons to be issued for George Lewis to take his seat in the House of Lords as Duke of Cambridge. Harcourt was disturbed, and the Queen was outraged. As Robert Harley put it, it would be tantamount to placing "her coffin before Her Majesty's eyes." The Queen's Chief Minister went further:

It will infallibly change the argument and shift the dispute. It will no more be between a Popish Pretender and the Serene House of Hanover, but people will immediately change it into a contest between the present possessor and the future successor. It is the mutual interest of the Queen and the Elector to have a firm friendship and that the world should know it so; if the world should get it into their heads that the Queen, so much beloved, is hardly used, God knows what may be the consequence.

The Queen did indeed feel herself hardly used, and under delicate prompting from Harley and Bolingbroke she reacted with vigour. Schutz was informed that he was no longer *persona grata* at the court, and Anne sat down to write three letters, to George Lewis, to his son George Augustus, and to his mother the Electress Sophia. One passage culled from the letter to George Lewis gives a vivid impression of the Queen's emotions:

As rumour increases that my cousin the Electoral Prince has resolved to come over to settle in my lifetime in my dominions, I do not choose to delay a moment to write to you about this and to communicate to you my sentiments upon a subject of this importance. I then freely own that I cannot imagine that a prince who possesses the knowledge and penetration of your Electoral Highness can ever contribute to such an attempt, and that I believe you are too just to allow that any infringement should be made upon my sovereignty which you would not choose should be made upon your own; I am firmly persuaded you would not suffer the smallest diminution of your authority, I am no less delicate in that respect, and I am determined to oppose a project so contrary to my royal authority however fatal the consequences may be.

George Lewis at once backed away from any possible confrontation, recalled the offending Schutz, and wrote a pacifying rejoinder. The effect on the Electress Sophia, however, was catastrophic. Her ambition to succeed to the English throne was strong, and now she perceived a barrier to all her plans. She was the essential link between the Stuarts and the Hanoverian Guelphs.

The intrusion of an apparently insignificant German princely family on to the diplomatic and dynastic battlefield of Europe demands explanation. Sophia herself was the daughter of the tragically romantic Winter Queen, Elizabeth of Bohemia, who had married Frederick V, Elector of the Palatinate; she was, therefore, the granddaughter of James I of England and VI of Scotland. There was no doubt in her mind that she, and then her son George Lewis, were the true heirs to her cousin Anne. In order to validate her claim still further, she had instructed the eminent Leipzig philosopher, Gottfried Wilhelm Leibnitz, to delve away in the archives at Modena, whose ruling Duke represented the Italian Guelphs. Leibnitz's task was to trace back the family tree of Ernest Augustus, first Elector of Hanover, and to reveal the purity of the line. He performed his task to perfection and soon began to make public some startling, and somewhat suspect, discoveries. It was eminently clear to Leibnitz that Ernest Augustus could be linked through the Emperor Otho of Germany, and his father Henry the Lion (who in turn had married Henry II of

England's daughter Matilda) to Guelph, Prince of the Scyrri, one of Attila the Hun's allies. Admittedly, the immediate predecessors of Ernest Augustus's great-grandfather, Ernest of Zell, were less than distinguished, but they were at least legitimate.

Ernest Augustus had died in 1698, and Sophia and George Lewis prepared for their destinies. Sophia herself was a realist. Although she longed for the words "Sophia, Queen of Great Britain" to be inscribed on her tomb, she knew that the odds against her surviving her cousin Anne were heavy. She once wrote in this vein to an English diplomat, Stepney:

If I were thirty years younger, I should have a sufficiently good opinion of my birth and of my religion to believe that I should be appreciated in England. But as there is little probability of my surviving two people much younger, although more subject to ordinary dangers than myself, it is to be feared that at my death my sons would be regarded as strangers, the eldest of whom is much more accustomed to claim a high prerogative as sovereign than the poor Prince of Wales [James Francis Edward], who is too young to profit by the example of the King of France, and who apparently would be so glad to recover that which the King, his father, has so inconsiderately lost, that they would be able to do with him just what they wished. I am not so philosophical nor so thoughtless that you should think I do not like to hear a crown spoken of, and that I do not give due consideration to the weighty judgment you have given on this subject. It seems to me that in England there are so many parties that one can be sure of nothing.

But, however sensible she may have been about her own accession to the English throne, the Electress Sophia was fervently partisan in the cause of her son. Now, the arrival of Queen Anne's letter seemed to destroy her aspiration at the stroke of a pen. Her cousin was, if anything, more forthright than in her letter to George Lewis:

It is of importance, with respect to the succession of your family, that I should tell you such a proceeding will infallibly draw along with it some consequences, that will be dangerous to that succession itself, which is not secure any other ways, than as the Prince, who actually wears the Crown, maintains her authority and prerogative.

Sophia was heartbroken. "This affair will make me ill, I shall never get over it," she wrote. "I shall have this gracious letter printed so that all the world may see that it will not have been by my fault if my children lose the three Kingdoms."

She was taken ill the day after the arrival of the fatal letter, but two days later seemed to have recovered. She went out into the grounds of her beloved Herrenhausen for her usual evening walk, but only managed to reach the first fountain. Then, she sank into the arms of Princess Caroline and one of her ladies-in-waiting, murmured, "I feel very unwell, give me your hand," and died. She was eighty-four years old, and had nearly outlived her younger cousin Anne. Now her son George—no longer George Lewis, as the evaporation of his second name was considered prudent and tactful because of English hatred for Louis XIV of France—was the Protestant heir to the British crown.

But there was still a Catholic heir waiting in the wings, and he had the support not only of the French but of a considerable number of English and Scottish Tories. It is impossible to unravel the tortuous strands of Robert Harley's diplomatic manoeuvrings, but what is certain is that a group of prominent Tories in Queen Anne's final ministry were not averse to the thought of a Stuart on the throne. The Duke of Ormonde, Lord Landsdowne, the Earl of Mar, the Duke of Buckingham and Sir William Wyndham all held office, and all were subsequently to show where their true loyalties lay. Anne herself felt increasingly sharp pangs of conscience about her exiled half-brother, and increased doubts about the suitability of her cousin George. And it was noticeable that the Pretender's birthday on June 10 was always an occasion for the populace to show its enthusiasm for the Stuart succession.

Two events, however, had conclusively altered any hope of a reversal of the Act of Settlement: the death of the Duke of Hamilton, and the signing of the peace with France at the Treaty of Utrecht. Marlborough's wars had been dragging on with appalling loss of life and devastation of country, and English support had waned severely since the glorious days of Blenheim and Ramillies. In the autumn of 1712, an ambassador extraordinary had been sent to Versailles. The choice had fallen on the Duke of Hamilton, one of the grandest of the Scottish grandees, who had been bitterly opposed to the Act of Union between England and Scotland, and who was considered to be the leader of the Jacobite faction in Scotland. The impression given by the appointment was crystal clear: Hamilton was going to Versailles, certainly to negotiate a peace treaty, but also to prepare the way for James's return on the death of Anne.

Hamilton never reached France. On November 15, he fought a duel with Lord Mohun, a strong Whig supporter, and both principals were killed. The Duke's second, a Colonel John Hamilton, swore that Mohun's second, the notoriously fiery General Macartney, had thrust his sword into the Duke's body as he lay wounded, though other eyewitnesses disputed this account. In any event, Macartney wisely fled the country, and Hamilton was replaced by the staunchly Whig Duke of Shrewsbury as ambassador extraordinary to Versailles. When the terms of the peace treaty were made public, they were seen to contain one vital clause: Louis XIV at last reneged on his promise to support the Jacobite court in France, and James was forced to find refuge at Bar-le-Duc, in the independent duchy of Lorraine.

Even then, the Tories did not abandon their hope of a Stuart succession, and it was Henry St. John, Viscount Bolingbroke, that most extraordinary of eighteenth-century statesmen, who was the prime mover. Many years later, after his quarrel with James, Bolingbroke disputed the fact that there had been any plot to restore the Stuarts: "There was no design on foot during the last four years of Queen Anne's reign to set aside the succession of the House of Hanover, and to place the crown on the head of the Pretender to it . . . deny the fact absolutely." But this was very far from the truth. Bolingbroke had been in close correspondence with the exiled Jacobite court for some time, and wielded all possible influence on the moderate Harley to pack his administration with Tories sympathetic to James. He went still further when he engineered Harley's dismissal on July 27, 1714. Already the Whig Duke of Argyll had been stripped of his appointments, and the Schism Act, which forbad any control to Dissenters over the education of their children, had been pushed through. But, even now, complete power eluded Bolingbroke. Harley had been dismissed, but he still had many supporters and dependants in the administration; he was, moreover, in close contact with the Elector's adviser, Baron Bothmer, assuring him of his undying loyalty to the Hanoverian succession. The final stumbling block to Bolingbroke's ambitions was, however, the Queen herself. Anne could not stomach his immorality, and refused to bestow upon him the coveted Lord Treasurer's white staff. As Erasmus Lewis wrote to Swift, "His character is too bad to carry the great ensigns, for the man of Mercury's bottom is too narrow, his faults are of the first magnitude."

Bolingbroke enjoyed exactly two days of power as Secretary of State without the presence of Harley as Lord Treasurer above him. But he had alienated too many factions. The Whigs would not serve with him, nor would Sir Thomas Hanmer's Hanoverian Tories. Harley's friends abhorred what they saw as the blackest treachery; the Dissenters knew that their only hope of salvation lay with the Hanoverian succession; the majority of English church-goers had been deeply, and irrevocably, shocked by the Pretender's declaration that he would never alter his religious beliefs.

Even so, Bolingbroke pressed on with his grand design. The Duke of Ormonde was Commander-in-Chief, Harcourt was Lord Chancellor, and Sir William Wyndham was at the Exchequer; Bishop Atterbury would be made Lord Privy Seal. There was a nucleus of the right men in the right positions. But Bolingbroke sought wider support, and he even threw out feelers to the younger, and perhaps more ambitious, Whigs. He decided to give a dinner party at his house in Golden Square, and sent out invitations to General Stanhope, Robert Walpole, Pulteney and Craggs—though Walpole was out of town and could not attend. It was an extraordinary manoeuvre, and one doomed to failure. Bolingbroke might declare his passionate attachment to the Protestant succession, but his guests were unimpressed. Stanhope took a particularly firm stand, criticising Bolingbroke's friends, demanding the inclusion of Marlborough and Orford in any administration, and insisting on the removal of the Pretender from Lorraine.

Stanhope then made himself abundantly clear. "Harry," he said,

you have only two ways of escaping the gallows. The first is to join the honest party of the Whigs, the other to give yourself up entirely to the French King and seek his help for the Pretender. If you do not choose the first course, we can only imagine that you have decided for the second.

The dinner party broke up. It had not been a success.

The violent quarrel between Harley and Bolingbroke, and the former's subsequent attempt to warn the Queen of the inherent dangers in his rival's personal plans, had sapped the last remnants of resistance Anne could summon. She was unable to sleep, and it was noticed that her mental faculties were deteriorating when she asked the same question three times during a meeting of the Council on July 28. She was worse on July 29, and by the following day was virtually paralysed. The Council was hastily summoned to Kensington Palace.

The Jacobites heavily outnumbered the Hanoverians, who contributed only three—the Duke of Shrewsbury, the Bishop of London, John Robinson, and Lord Dartmouth, but the

proceedings of the Council were interrupted by two unex-
pected arrivals. The Dukes of Argyll and Somerset had already informed Bothmer of the Queen's imminent death, and
they had then driven to Kensington Palace. They had not
been invited, but they nevertheless insisted on their rights as
members of the Privy Council, and joined the deliberations.
Stanhope, in a letter to the Emperor Charles VI, described
the extraordinary scene:

She recovered a little about 11 o'clock and the Council, which
had assembled, profited by this interval of health to persuade the
Queen to nominate the Duke of Shrewsbury for the High Treasurer, instead of the five Commissioners proposed, who would
have been subordinate to Lord Bolingbroke as first Minister. The
Council continued its sitting and gave all necessary commands
for keeping public order and assuring the taking possession to
Monsignor the Elector.

The Council worked on until midnight, and relays of mes-
sengers rode out of the gates of Kensington Palace on their
way to lords-lieutenant, mayors and governors, to the Tower
of London and to Edinburgh Castle, and to Bothmer. The
news went forth that the Queen was dying and that the name
of her successor was George. Stanhope wrote to the Emperor: "They [the doctors] are of the opinion that the Queen
cannot live a dozen hours . . . this accident, sudden and un-
foreseen, came like a thunderbolt to the Jacobites." "I venture to assure your Imperial Majesty," continued Stanhope,
"that, if the doctors prophesy truly, Monsieur l'Electeur of
Hanover will be proclaimed King and will take possession of
the realm as peaceably as any of his predecessors have done."
Bolingbroke, mercurial as ever, appeared to agree whole-
heartedly with every proposal, although his innermost feelings must have been very different. He later wrote blithely to
Swift: "The Earl of Oxford [Harley] was removed on Tuesday, the Queen died on Sunday. What a world this is, and
how does fortune banter us." But he was probably truer to
himself when he told Atterbury: "I am not in the least intimi-

dated from any consideration of the Whig malice and power. The Grief of my soul is this, I can see plainly that the Tory Party is gone."

On July 31, Bothmer was advised of all developments, and a letter, to which all the Privy Councillors appended their signatures, was carried across to Hanover. In the early hours of the following morning Queen Anne died, at half-past seven. The Duke of Shrewsbury and a few other members of the Council, who had been hastily summoned, arrived too late. Dr. Arbuthnot penned the truest epitaph:

My dear mistress's days were numbered even in my imagination, and could not exceed certain limits; but of that small number a great deal was cut off by the last troublesome scene of this contention among her servants. I believe sleep was never more welcome to a weary traveller than death was to her.

The Council moved to St. James's, and the three black boxes which had been in the keeping of the Lord Chancellor, the Archbishop of Canterbury and Kreyenberg, the Hanoverian Resident, and which contained the details of the Regency Council, were opened and verified. In accordance with the Act of 1706, the seven chief officers of state, including Shrewsbury and Harcourt, were nominated, but there were in addition eighteen members appointed by the new King. Shrewsbury featured on this list, too, as well as the Dukes of Somerset, Bolton, Devonshire and Roxburgh, the Earls of Orford, Anglesea and Nottingham, Lord Cowper and Lord Townshend. Of the Duke of Marlborough there was no mention, and, more curiously, Lord Sunderland, Lord Wharton and Lord Somers, who had designed the Act of Settlement, were omitted. Joseph Addison was appointed Secretary of State.

The news was given a mixed reception. The Dissenters were overjoyed. By a curious quirk of fate, the day of the Queen's death was also the day on which the Schism Act should come into force, but it automatically lapsed. Mr. Brad-

bury, the dissenting minister of Fetter Lane, had begun his
sermon when he saw a man drop a handkerchief from the gallery. It was the signal agreed with Bishop Burnet, and as
Bradbury announced the accession of George I a wave of joy
swept through the building.

The Jacobites, not surprisingly, were somewhat less over-
come with delight. Atterbury offered to proclaim James at
Charing Cross in his lawn sleeves. There were disturbances at
York and Exeter, and in Scotland there were more positive
signs of trouble ahead, but it was all too late. According to
Carte,

the night before the Queen died, when the Council broke up the
Duke of Buckingham came to the Duke of Ormonde, clapped his
hand on his shoulder, and said, My Lord, you have twenty-four
hours' time to do our business in and make yourself master of the
kingdom.

The twenty-four hours passed.

Without further delay, the Proclamation was read outside
St. James's Palace, and in all the principal towns throughout
the country. The heralds, preceded by the sound of trumpet
and kettledrum, delivered the sonorous words:

We therefore, the Lords Spiritual and Temporal of the Realm,
being here assisted with those of Her late Majesty's Privy Council, with numbers of other principal gentlemen of quality, with
the Lord Mayor, Aldermen and Citizens of London, do now
hereby with one voice and consent of tongue and heart, publish
and proclaim that the High and Mighty Prince George Elector
of Brunswick-Luneburg is now by the death of our late sovereign of Happy Memory, become our only lawful and rightful
liege Lord, George, by the Grace of God King of Great Britain,
France and Ireland. God save the King.

An address was prepared by the Scottish chief, including
Cameron of Lochiel, Macleod of Macleod, Glengarry, Chis-
holm and Macdonald of the Isles; and in Dublin the same rit-
ual blossomed forth, though a sour note was struck when the

Lord Chancellor of Ireland, Sir Christopher Phipps, a pronounced Jacobite, had to be stripped of his seals of office.

In London, the Imperial Resident noted, "the people showed great and sincere joy," though there was even more excitement when the Duke of Marlborough arrived on August 4. Bolingbroke was hissed, though he tried to ingratiate himself with the crowds by lighting a substantial bonfire in Golden Square. The French Ambassador requested military protection. The public funds rose by 3 per cent the day of the Queen's death. Bothmer wrote to Hanover, to say that "all went very well for him here."

Bothmer, who had manipulated events so expertly, now found himself in a position of considerable importance, besieged by office-seekers, visited by foreign diplomats eager to congratulate and ingratiate themselves with the new dynasty. His main task was to prepare for the arrival of his master from Hanover, and he and Kreyenberg instituted a search among the late Queen's papers. A vague request, without seal or signature, was found, indicating that she wished to be buried without ceremony beside her husband in Henry VII's Chapel, and her body was removed without more ado on August 22. A sealed packet was found in her closet at Kensington Palace, with firm instructions in her own handwriting that it should be destroyed on her death. It was thought to contain letters from the Pretender, but this was pure supposition as the Duke of Somerset duly consigned the packet to the flames, and no one could catch more than a fleeting glance at the writing.

Parliament met the day after the Queen's death, but was not opened formally by the Regents until August 5. Harcourt read the Speech on behalf of the Council: "It having pleased Almighty God to take to himself our late most gracious Queen, of blessed memory, we hope that nothing has been omitted, which might contribute to the safety of these realms, to the preservation of our religion, laws, and liberties, in this great conjuncture . . ." The Lords then adjourned, but the Commons were intent on useful oratory. They sent their congratulations to the new King,

whose princely virtues give us a certain prospect of future happiness in the security of our religion, laws, and liberties, and engage us to assure Your Majesty, that we will, to our utmost, support your undoubted right to the Imperial Crown of this Realm, against the Pretender and all other persons whatsoever.—Your faithful Commons cannot but express their impatient desire for Your Majesty's safe arrival and presence in Great Britain. In the meantime, we humbly lay before Your Majesty the unanimous resolution of this House, to maintain the public credit of the nation, and effectually to make good all funds which have been granted by Parliament, for the security of any money which has been, or shall be advanced for the public service, and to endeavour, by every thing in our power, to make Your Majesty's reign happy and glorious.

The Tories fell over one another in offering loyal greetings, voting money, doing anything which might absolve them of any collective guilt. Suddenly, a general calm descended. On September 4, Thomas Strafford wrote to Robethon, the Elector's envoy, from The Hague: "Nothing can go quieter than things do in Great Britain, and we have prospect of the gloriousest reign we ever had." Even Bolingbroke remarked on the atmosphere in a celebrated letter to Sir William Wyndham: "The thunder had long grumbled in the air; and yet when the bolt fell, most of our party appeared as much surprised as if they had had no reason to expect it. There was perfect calm and universal submission through the whole kingdom."

The recipient of all the loyal greetings and inheritor of the kingdom still sat at Herrenhausen. He had been kept in touch with every new development, both by his agent in London, and by the special envoys dispatched to Hanover by the Council, and subsequently by the Regents. Bolingbroke's friend, Lord Clarendon, had been in Hanover at the end of July, and had not made a good impression. He was snubbed by George and the Electoral court, subjected to embarrassingly close questioning on the role that Bolingbroke had played, and left with the firm impression that he was considered of no consequence. In revenge, Clarendon noted that the Elector "knows very little of our Constitution." It is not certain whether Clarendon or Lord Dorset was the bearer of the news, but George was apprised of Queen Anne's death at Herrenhausen late at night.

A rumour was put about that he was reluctant to accept the throne, though Pollnitz, who knew the Court of Hanover intimately, did not agree:

Many people were pleased to say that the Elector hesitated a good while whether or no he should accept of the august dignity which was offered him, but for my part I fancy that the voyage to England was more the subject of the Council's deliberation than the question whether the crown should be accepted.

He was not the most imaginative or ambitious of men—one biographer says bluntly, "To imagine for a moment that George I possessed any exalted views regarding either the supremacy of the Protestant religion or the economic and progressive development of Europe is to credit a mollusc with the aspirations of an eagle"—but he was hardly liable to cast away a crown which had been gained without expending an ounce of engergy, let alone a drop of blood.

At last, on August 31, he left Hanover, reputedly in an elegiac mood and with these words: "Farewell, dear place, where I have spent so many happy and peaceful hours; I leave you, but not for ever, for I shall hope to see you again frequently"; he kept his promise all too well. He travelled slowly to The Hague, and eventually went on board the yacht *Peregrine*, which had been lying at anchor off Orange Polder. The weather was appalling but the royal yacht, escorted by a fleet of ships under the command of Lord Berkeley, finally set sail, and arrived off Greenwich at six o'clock on the evening of September 18. He was greeted by dense fog, a mass of dignitaries and officials, and some execrable

verse, specially composed for the occasion. Mr. John Tickell
hailed him as "great Brunswick" and went on:

> Mature in wisdom, his extensive mind.
> Takes in the blended interests of mankind.
> O'er the vast deep, great Monarch, dart thine eyes,
> A watery prospect bounded by the skies.

Mr. Eusden, soon to become Poet Laureate, did even better:

> Hail, mighty GEORGE! auspicious smiles thy Reign,
> Thee long we wish'd, Thee at last we gain.
> Thy hoary Prudence in green Years began,
> And the bold Infant stretch'd at once to Man.
> How oft, Transported, the great *Ernest* smil'd
> With the Presages of his greater Child.

George made some important decisions without delay. Ormonde was dismissed and the Duke of Marlborough was appointed Captain-General in his place. Lord Oxford was allowed to kiss his hand, but was then ignored. George I knew,
or thought he knew, who his enemies were.

The state entry into London was fixed for the following
Monday. Tindal describes the scene:

The King of France and Prince of Wales made their entry with
great pomp and magnificence. There were in the King's coach
the Prince and the Duke of Northumberland, Captain of the
Life-Guard in waiting. Above two hundred coaches of the nobility and gentry, all with six horses, preceded the King's. When he
came to St. Margaret's hill in Southwark, he was met by the Lord
Mayor, aldermen, recorder, sheriffs, and officers of the City of
London; in whose name Sir Peter King, recorder, made a con-
gratulatory speech. The Lord Mayor delivered the sword to the
King, who returned it to him, and he bore it in the procession
bare-headed. The royal pomp continued till his arrival at his palace of St. James's, and was favoured by as fair a day as was ever
known in that season of the year.

George was not impressed by his first view of his new residence at St. James's, particularly when he had to pay Lord

Chetwynd, the Ranger of the Park, for the present of a brace
of carp "out of my canal, in my own Park."

Thackeray, waspish as ever, gives one description of the
royal arrival:

He brought with him a compact body of Germans, whose society he loved, and whom he kept around the royal person. He had
his faithful German chamberlains; his German secretaries; his
negroes, captives of his bow and spear in Turkish wars; his two
ugly, elderly German favourites, Mesdames of Kielmansegge and
Schulenberg, whom he created Countess of Darlington and
Duchess of Kendal. The Duchess was tall, and lean of stature,
and hence was irreverently nicknamed the Maypole. The Countess was a large-sized noblewoman, and this elevated personage
was denominated the Elephant. Both of these ladies loved Hanover and its delights; clung round the linden-trees of the great
Herrenhausen avenue, and at first would not quit the place.
Schulenberg, in fact, could not come on account of her debts;
but finding the Maypole would not come, the Elephant packed
up her trunk and slipped out of Hanover unwieldy as she was.
On this the Maypole straightway put herself in motion, and followed her beloved George Louis.

More precisely, one observer noted: "The happy day is
come: His Highness the Elector has arrived in his Kingdom."

II

A Royal Scandal

Do you think I could ever abandon you whatever happens? If you were ever reduced to that state, nothing would stop me from following you and I would want to die with you. But for God's sake, let us not abandon ourselves to such morbid thoughts, perhaps we shall be happier than we think. Let us love one another all our lives and find comfort in one another for all the unhappiness brought on us.

Sophia Dorothea to Philip von Königsmarck

He was a noble Swede, in the Flower of his Age, admirably well made, tall, handsome, with flowing hair and sprightly Eyes; in one Word, an equal mixture of Mars and Adonis.

Aurora von Königsmarck on her brother Philip

The love affair between Sophia Dorothea, wife of George Lewis, Elector of Hanover and future King of England, and Count Philip Christopher von Königsmarck, has always had a strong effect on writers of the romantic school. Here was the beautiful young woman, ignored by her bear-like husband, plotted against by her husband's mistress, finding solace and true love in the arms of a dashing, handsome, slightly raffish soldier of fortune (but one of noble birth). It was an irresistible tale of passion, death and incarceration waiting for the pen of an Anthony Hope. Unfortunately, as such stories so often are, the saga of Sophia Dorothea and Philip von Königsmarck has become encrusted with the patina of age and exaggeration. Rex Whistler's drawings for A. E. W. Mason's *Königsmarck* sum up the popular ideal. A pretty girl, with a parasol and a small pomeranian dog, receives a bunch of flowers from a somewhat effeminate, periwigged young man, by a garden urn supported by symbolic putti; the girl, still pretty and now naked, lies on a bed, waiting to receive the young man, equally naked, wigless, and if anything even more androgynous, who looms over her while he turns out the lamp; a shadowy figure climbs from a rowing-boat and slinks through a secret door into the palace; the young man gasps out his last breath, while a gargantuan lady brandishes a candle and lavishes orders on a number of nervous-looking soldiers. It is the story of Sophia Dorothea and Königsmarck presented as a pretty strip-cartoon. It is some of the truth, but far from the whole truth.

The chief characters in the first major scandal to set the Hanoverian Court by the ears (it was the first of many—the Hanoverian dynasty was to display a great propensity for scandal) were an ill-assorted collection, and they deserve individual investigation and analysis.

Sophia Dorothea's father, George William, was the second son of William, Duke of Lüneburg. In his youth, he had led a rackety life, touring Europe in search of adventure, and showing a marked fondness for Venice, in particular the decadent Serenissima's seemingly endless supply of carnivals and loose women. George William enjoyed himself, and introduced his youngest brother Ernest Augustus to the delights of the wicked world at a tender age (of the other two brothers, Christian Lewis died in 1665 without leaving any mark, and John Frederick was eccentric enough to be a fervent supporter of Louis XIV and, worse, to embrace the Catholic faith in spite of the fact that his great-grandfather had studied under Luther at Wittenberg), but it was eventually borne in upon him that his subjects would prefer him to stay at home, and to marry, rather than bankrupting himself abroad. A suitable wife was found in Sophia, daughter of Frederick, the Elector Palatine, and granddaughter of James I of England, and preparations for the marriage began.

George William, however, considered that he had fulfilled his obligations to his countrymen, and embarked again on his life of pleasure with increased determination. In Venice, he attached himself "to the first courtesan he met, a Greek woman who had no other claim to beauty except the clothes she wore." But he had some conscience, and suddenly realised that he could not marry Sophia. Instead he suggested that his favourite brother, Ernest Augustus, should sacrifice himself on the altar (John Frederick was extremely annoyed that he had not been offered the chance, and had to be pacified). Ernest Augustus agreed, so too did Sophia, and George William gave a solemn undertaking not to marry. What he could not promise was that, henceforth, he would never fall in love.

While Ernest Augustus and Sophia lived an amiable existence at the episcopal palace of Osnabrück, George William, now Duke of Celle on the death of his eldest brother, embarked on a spirited love affair. The object of his affections was Eléonore d'Olbreuse, the daughter of a French Huguenot Marquis who had settled with his family at Breda in Holland. Eléonore had one unusual characteristic. Perhaps out of modesty, perhaps out of cunning, she refused to surrender her virtue unless the Duke agreed to marry her. And George William had sworn that he would never marry. Finally, Eléonore gave way and what Sophia disapprovingly termed a marriage of conscience, "without candles or witnesses," took place on November 11, 1665. After the signing of the "anti-contract," "the two lovers went to bed together without further ado." Ten months later, a daughter, Sophia Dorothea, was born at Celle to George William and his anti-bride, who was now called Madame de Harburg.

Sophia Dorothea's childhood was dominated by her father's attempts to ensure her and her mother's future. Louis XIV of France was prevailed upon to issue a Certificate of Naturalisation on behalf of the little girl, thus giving tacit approval to the unsolemnised union between George William and Eléonore. George William also began to buy up pieces of land for his daughter's future dowry, and purchased the island of Wilhelmsburg on the Elbe for his mistress. After he had assisted the Emperor Leopold to fight off a French invasion, he persuaded the Vienna chancery to make Eléonore a Reichsgräfin. Sophia Dorothea was engaged to Augustus Frederick of Wolfenbüttel, and in April 1676 George William at last morganatically married the new Countess of Wilhelmsburg. Four months later, Sophia Dorothea's fiancé was dead from wounds received at the siege of Philipsburg.

Sophia Dorothea was, by now, a considerable heiress, and her legitimisation had removed her last vestige of unsuitability. The Duke of Wolfenbüttel was reluctant to let her dowry slip away and suggested his second son as a prospective suitor, but Ernest Augustus suddenly decided that she was the ideal wife for his favourite son, George Lewis, provided that the financial arrangements were satisfactory: 100,000 crowns a year and the ceding of two fortresses seemed not unreasonable. His wife Sophia, still nursing a profound contempt for Eléonore and for the protracted papering over of the cracks in Sophia Dorothea's birth certificate, was less amenable. When John Frederick, the third of the four brothers, died in 1679 and Ernest Augustus automatically became Duke of Hanover, Sophia saw her opportunity. Suddenly, her husband was a duke in more than mere title: he had land and property, and influence in the complicated games of statecraft which exercised the Empire and the German principalities. Surely, her son could do better than the child of a morganatic marriage. George Lewis was packed off to England to stay with his Stuart cousins, and to try for the hand of the Duke of York's daughter, Anne.

It all came to nothing. Anne was not impressed by her serious, down-to-earth, unsophisticated cousin. He could speak no English, and his manners smacked more of the barracks than of the court. George Lewis returned to Hanover in the spring of 1681. On September 12, the following year, his engagement to his first cousin, Sophia Dorothea, was agreed. Sophia Dorothea signed the marriage contract on October 24, and the wedding took place on November 21.

Sophia Dorothea was barely sixteen when she left the settled and happy life of her father's court at Celle for the maelstrom of Hanover. Her unhappiness, which grew from month to month, was inevitable. Her father-in-law, Ernest Augustus, was kind to her, as he was to any pretty woman, and her mother-in-law endeavoured to mask her disapproval. But George Lewis and Sophia Dorothea were mutually antipathetic. He preferred campaigns and battles, and was allergic to his wife's gaiety and wit, which he misconstrued as barbs aimed at his slowness and lack of social graces. She, on the other hand, disliked the strict protocol of the court at Hanover. They shared the matrimonial bed only on rare occasions, and after the birth of two children, a son and a daughter, hardly at all. It was a situation which was seized upon by one of the most important participants in the ensuing drama.

Clara Elizabeth, Countess Platen, was a born intriguer. The daughter of an insignificant and penniless Count from Hesse, she and her sister Catherine Marie had both made good marriages. The younger girl had married John Busche, governor to Ernest Augustus's younger son, and Clara Elizabeth had opted for George Lewis's governor. Platen was ambitious himself but needed the persistent goading of his power-crazy wife. Soon he was a minister, and she was Ernest Augustus's mistress. Even Sophia recognised her status, and before long she was the most influential person in Hanover. Her husband was satisfyingly complaisant and did not appear to worry about however many lovers his voracious consort took, provided that his own advancement was not affected. Even after her overblown but striking looks vanished and she took to painting her face with layers of powder and enamel, her hold over Ernest Augustus continued. And her position was only strengthened when her sister became George Lewis's mistress.

The arrival of Sophia Dorothea introduced an immediate threat, but Goerge Lewis's obvious indifference towards his wife reassured Countess Platen. An attempt to re-establish Catherine Marie as George's mistress failed, but her abilities as a procuress were more successful with the appearance of the thin and tall Ermengarda Schulenburg, who was to remain with George even after he became King of England. Sophia Dorothea was appalled by her husband's infidelity and remonstrated with him. George Lewis lost his temper and nearly strangled her in his rage. A series of balls and parties, given to celebrate the birth of a daughter to Sophia Dorothea in March 1687, were mere pretence. Almost exactly a year later, another ball was given. One of the guests was a young Swedish officer, Count Philip Christopher von Königsmarck.

There were two Königsmarck brothers, Charles John, the elder, and Philip Christopher. They were brave, handsome, amoral and highly sexed. Charles had sown his wild oats indiscriminately from an early age, and been involved in a sensational murder case. While in London, he had encountered an eleven-year-old heiress, Lady Ogle, who had been recently widowed. He proposed marriage, but her guardians were unimpressed by his qualifications. Instead, they promised her to a man who had no real need of financial inducement, one of the richest magnates in the country, Thomas Thynne of Longleat. The match had no opportunity to prosper.

Thynne's coach was ambushed in Pall Mall, and he died soon after. The three attackers were arrested, but the authorities cast interested eyes in the direction of the amorous Count von Königsmarck. He too was arrested and stood trial. Influence was brought to bear and the King of Sweden's name was bandied about. The three confederates were found guilty and hanged, but Charles was acquitted. Wisely, he decided to leave England without delay, and departed to fight the Turks. He was killed in the Morea in 1686, and his young brother inherited the title of Count and his brother's money and possessions.

Philip had also been in London, but engaged in more intellectual pursuits, as well as attending the famous Foubert's Academy in order to acquire grounding in the essential arts of dancing, riding and fencing. However, his brother's imbroglio put paid to the idea of his going up to Oxford, and he decided to try out his new-found social attributes at Versailles. From there he went briefly to Celle—his mother was an intimate friend of Eléonore, and she had once hoped that her elder son might marry Sophia Dorothea—before emulating his brother's example in the struggle against the Turks.

When he was still in his twenties, he visited Hanover for the first time. Like his brother, Philip was an amorist through and through; he fought hard on the battlefield, and he fought equally hard in the bedchamber. A hedonist with an inexhaustible lust for pleasure, he found the atmosphere of Hanover much to his liking. Ernest Augustus, besotted with the memory of Venice permanently *en fête*, had decided that Hanover should mirror the gaiety of the Adriatic city. The carnival season in Hanover lasted from December to Easter, almost as if the continuous celebrations of pagan winter were being recaptured. The ducal Leine Palace and the great summer château of Herrenhausen were full to the brim with distinguished guests, and Countess Platen's semi-royal residence of Monplaisir was also included on what can only be called the tourist route. The masquerade ruled. There were other forms of entertainment, but the masked rout, very much in the Venetian tradition, was immensely popular, affording as it could and did endless opportunities for silken dalliance and wholesale lechery.

Königsmarck's initial taste of Hanoverian high life was cut short by the news that his regiment had been disbanded, and he left abruptly for Hamburg. He returned in time for the ball on March 2, 1688, at which all the instigators of Sophia Dorothea's tragedy were present: her mother and father, her father-in-law and mother-in-law, her husband, the father of her Wolfenbüttel fiancé, and Countess Platen. Philip was introduced to Sophia Dorothea, but his thoughts were more closely concentrated on a Danish girl, Charlotte Rantzau, to whom he was on the point of becoming engaged (the engagement was quickly broken off, and Charlotte died shortly afterwards). Soon, though, he took a house near the Leine Palace, and was joined by his two sisters: Aurora, who was to write his biography, and Amelia, whose husband Count Lewenhaupt was a general in the Duke of Celle's army.

Ironically, Philip's first liaison was not with Sophia Dorothea, but with Countess Platen. Always ambitious, if not unscrupulous, he realised that preferment could be influenced by his expertise in the bed of the Duke of Hanover's former mistress. Perhaps the Countess was too old, or too painted, but in any event the relationship was brief. Instead, Königsmarck found himself greatly drawn to Sophia Dorothea. As a friend of her brother-in-law Charles, who had always sympathised with her over George Lewis's less-than-conjugal behaviour, Philip had the *entrée* to her intimate set and, as an experienced man of the world, knew only too well how to lend an attentive ear to her stories of neglect and unhappiness. It is difficult, without concrete evidence, to judge whether Königsmarck planned his liaison with Sophia Dorothea out of cynical self-interest, sexual passion, a sense of adventure, or love. Perhaps it was a mixture of all four. Certainly he was arrogant enough to think that he could form a close relationship with the wife of the future Duke of Hanover without endangering his own life. Certainly, he was foolish enough, or so carried away by passion, to believe that his dismissal of Countess Platen and his obvious attention on Sophia Dorothea would not be noticed by a small court, entirely given up to intrigue and gossip. Conceivably, he imagined that his Swedish citizenship would act as a safeguard, just as it had saved his brother from an English noose. Conceivably, he did not care. Young, handsome, dashing, he might have contemplated death on the battlefield, but this was love, sex, passion, call it what you like—and the reward for that was surely life.

In 1690, the great flow of letters between Philip von Königsmarck and Sophia Dorothea began to flow via her lady-in-waiting, Eleonore Knesebeck. But while Philip knew well what he wanted, Sophia Dorothea still had her doubts and scruples. Her position was extremely dangerous. George Lewis's temper had been experienced on a number of occasions, and she was only too painfully aware of Countess Platen and her web of deceit. Also, she had a remarkably strict morality for her time. But then, with Philip away at the wars, and the memory of him—sympathetic, glamorous, gently insistent—growing fonder by the day, she must have considered the more unbridled conduct of other European princesses and noblewomen who had not bothered to wait eight years before taking lovers.

And so the letters came and went. Those from Sophia Dorothea during the first year and a half of the correspondence have vanished, but it is possible to gauge the momentum of the affair from Königsmarck's lines from the front. Phrases like "I was in agony, thinking you have forgotten all about me," "I beg of you to give me a chance to see you and say just two words to you," and "God knows when I shall see you again, my life and my goddess" may owe something to the gallantry and exaggeration of letter-writing at the end of the seventeenth century, but one can imagine their effect on a young woman starved of affection. Königsmarck wrote from Flanders and he wrote from The Hague, whither he had gone as a diplomatic aide to Ernest Augustus. Sophia Dorothea still prevaricated. And Countess Platen endeavoured to implicate them both with the melodramatic evidence of small pavilions and abandoned gloves.

Eventually, Sophia Dorothea allowed her heart to rule her head. Sometime in the first months of 1691, the liaison, which had previously been conducted in an epistolary rather than bodily form, was consummated. The letters became even more frequent, and those from Königsmarck ranged from thinly veiled pleasure at the course of their love and its more intimate aspects to arrant jealousy. He seemed incapable of realising the dangers which at any moment might overwhelm his mistress, and failed to understand the doubts and fears which she sometimes expressed. Like the single-minded male animal that he was, he construed any scruple on her part as waning passion, and any suggestion that their meetings should be less frequent or more cautious as an indication that she had returned to George Lewis's bed. She, on the other hand, was desperately afraid that their love would be revealed or that, during Königsmarck's absences from Hanover, he might forget her and transfer his affections to a younger or more beautiful woman; she could expect nothing better from a self-confessed sexual athlete.

Two letters may suffice to give an impression of Königsmarck's ability to convey the most passionate sentiments, whether artificial or not. He wrote after one of his frequent misapprehensions of her caution,

I must say that never did a letter arrive more in time, for I was about to accuse you of the blackest treachery; but your letter convinces me that you are incapable of such a thing. It is true that I am not too happy with the cold airs you put on yesterday. That is why I spent such a miserable night. I was so wrought up I could not help crying. I was so agitated my fever returned and I was hot for three hours. Believe me, my divine beauty, that ever since I have known myself, I have never been in such a state.

Do you know what I thought? "God has sent me this illness to punish me, and as if this is not enough, He has also frozen my beloved's heart towards me. This is unbearable, I cannot bear it." I threw myself down on my knees, my eyes full of tears, and begged God, if it were true you did not love me any more, to take my life away. I would have welcomed death with all my heart, for I really thought you had turned cold to me.

My pen is not skilled enough to tell you what depth of sorrow I was in, nor can I describe what immense relief your letter gave me. I kissed it a thousand times, and then a thousand more. I hated myself for having thought you capable of inconstancy. I throw myself at your feet and ask your forgiveness, and I promise that in future I shall not be so quick to imagine anything like that.

But I beg of you, never be fickle and do believe that I too am constant. To convince you all the better that I adore no one but you, I will sign this with my blood. You must know that as long as you love me you will always be worshipped by

Königsmarck
Signed in blood.

Here was the full paraphernalia of melodrama: if there was any prospect of his sense of outrage and then relief being undervalued by the letter's recipient, then a few drops of the hero's blood would add the necessary emphasis. He was on safer ground in a subsequent letter:

The minutes seem like centuries, I cannot watch the daylight without hating it. Why can't the hours turn themselves into minutes? What would I not give to hear midnight strike? Make sure to have some rosemary water by, in case I faint with joy. What, tonight I shall embrace the loveliest woman in the world, I shall kiss her sweet lips, I shall gaze into the eyes that enslave me, I shall hear from your very lips that you are not indifferent to me, I shall embrace your knees, my tears will run down your cheeks, my arms will have the pleasure of holding the most beautiful body in the world.

And, after that night, he wrote again: "I slept like a king, and I hope you did the same. What joy, what pleasure, what enchantment have I not felt in your arms? God, what a night I have spent! It makes me forget all my worries, I am the happiest man on earth."

And so matters continued through 1692 and 1693. Königsmarck conducted a brief flirtation with the Duchess of Saxe-Eisenach, and was prodigal with excuses and denials when Sophia Dorothea taxed him with it. What was more disturbing was an impression Königsmarck had that some of Sophia Dorothea's letters were being opened and then resealed. Countess Platen was indeed not idle. She had hoped to turn Ernest Augustus against his daughter-in-law, but he was either too permissive or too aware of his former mistress's jealousy. Instead, she directed her attention towards the more vulnerable target of Königsmarck. He had distinguished himself at the siege of Namur and was generally popular with his superior officers, but he was also extravagant and the Countess was able to persuade Ernest Augustus that he was planning to buy a more lavish house where he could entertain Sophia Dorothea less surreptitiously. The reasoning was thin, but even Ernest Augustus must by now have become aware that the scandal might affect his own ambitions.

The Duke of Hanover had set his sights on an Elector's coronet, and his campaign was about to reach fruition. But in order to become an Elector he was forced to abide by the rules of primogeniture, so that his titles could become hereditary. His younger sons not unnaturally objected, and the whole family dissolved into plotting and counter-plotting. Ernest Augustus no longer had time to waste on a wayward daughter-in-law and her presumed lover. At the end of 1692, the Imperial edict was made known, and there were great celebrations in Hanover. Königsmarck, who had managed to snatch a few weeks with his mistress while George Lewis was away, wrote a searing letter:

Electoral Princess! Now we can call you that, for apparently the Electoral Prince invested you last night with this honourable title. Has his love-making more charm now that he has achieved higher rank? I cannot sleep for rage when I think that an Electoral Prince has robbed me of my charming mistress. This morning I would have offered you my congratulations on your new rank, but I doubted whether your husband had done his duty by you. If I am to judge his keenness to see you, the investiture will not start before ten o'clock in the morning.

Ironically, all his jealousy was pointless. The imperial edict was never confirmed, because too many powerful German rulers opposed the Duke of Hanover's election. Not until 1708, ten years after Ernest Augustus's death, was the Hanoverian representative permitted to take part in the Electoral College's deliberations.

Königsmarck's extravagance had reduced him to debt, but he continued to entertain lavishly—and to write incriminating letters to Sophia Dorothea. Her family made one last attempt to reconcile her with George Lewis. George did not object, as no mention was made of his abandoning Ermengarda Schulenburg, but Sophia Dorothea was appalled. There was, however, nothing she could do. Königsmarck, enraged, went off to Dresden in an attempt to claim some money he had once lent to the new Elector of Saxony. He was drinking heavily and, in his cups, became distressingly indiscreet about his liaison with Sophia Dorothea, and Countess Platen's with Ernest Augustus. He told all, and everything he told was duly reported back to Hanover. Countess Platen decided that, if Ernest Augustus would do nothing, she must act independently.

George Lewis had gone off to stay with his sister in Berlin. It was summer. The Hanoverian Court had moved to Herrenhausen. The Leine Palace was almost empty. It was there that Sophia Dorothea met Philip von Königsmarck for the last time. He intended to leave for Dresden on July 5, to resume his military career as a general in the Elector of Saxony's army. Whether he and Sophia Dorothea discussed plans for escape will never be known, though the legend has been established that they were about to elope. Certainly, he went to the Leine Palace on July 1 at some time before midnight. He was never seen again.

What occurred in the Leine Palace that summer's night remains a mystery. What is certain is that Countess Platen organised the murder of Königsmarck, assisted probably by four courtiers, one of whom almost certainly was the estate manager at Osnabrück, Montalban; later he received substantial sums of money from the ducal exchequer, but was himself to die early the following year. There remained only the question of the disposal of the body. Whether quicklime was used, or whether it was merely placed in a sack and thrown into the Leine river, in any case Königsmarck was no more.

The crucial day had been a Sunday. Monday passed without the alarm being given, but on Tuesday Königsmarck's secretary communicated his fears to his master's commanding officer and to the Elector of Saxony. Then, on the Wednesday, government officials arrived to seize Königsmarck's papers, which were highly incriminating. Hildebrand, the secretary, realised that Königsmarck's liaison with Sophia Dorothea must finally have proved too embarrassing to the court at Hanover, but he still hoped that he had been imprisoned rather than killed. He wrote at once to Aurora von Königsmarck, and she in turn started a campaign to uncover the facts behind her brother's disappearance. She was hampered by Ernest Augustus's decision to ban her from Hanover, and she received bland dismissals of her enquiries at Celle, but she had better luck at Dresden. The Elector was indignant that one of his generals should have been treated as a common criminal, and promised his full support. But the Hanoverian government maintained that they had no knowledge of the events surrounding the disappearance of Königsmarck, and reminded the Elector that he was still an officer in the Hanoverian army on July 1 and had therefore not come under the jurisdiction of Saxony.

Europe was agog for news. Ernest Augustus's enemies saw an admirable opportunity for further embarrassing the upstart Hanoverian dynasty, and the King of Denmark and the Duke of Wolfenbüttel pressed for an official enquiry. England's envoy in Dresden wrote to his counterpart in Hanover:

I have great curiosity to know what piece of mischief has been brewing at Hanover. If you dare not trust it at length, I must beg you to satisfy me in cipher, as likewise with the particulars of your Princess's ruin. Amours are fatal in these parts; we have had a scene of them here and may hereafter have more the like nature. But at present the Tragedy is removed to your Courts, and I fear Daggers and poison will be as familiar among you as they are in Italy . . . A servant or two of Count Königsmarck run frequently betwixt this place and Hanover, seeking out their master, but have no tidings . . . I have been told his sister raves like Cassandra and will know what is become of her brother; but at Hanover they answer like Cain, that they are not her brother's keeper and that the Body should be found (which I believe as little as that of Moses) . . . I knew him in England, at Hamburg, in Flanders and at Hanover for a dissolute debauchee whom I would always have avoided . . . If he has been so black as we think he is, his Fate (be what it will) is not to be pitied.

Ernest Augustus and his compliant son-in-law, the Elector of Brandenburg, took their case to the Emperor, and pressure was applied on the Elector of Saxony. Gradually, interest in the case began to subside, and Augustus of Saxony agreed to accept the Hanoverian explanation that nothing concrete was known about Königsmarck's disappearance but that he was in all probability dead. Even Aurora gave up her campaign, and instead became the Elector of Saxony's principal mistress until she retired to the Abbey of Quedlinburg. One of their sons was to become famous throughout Europe as Maurice de Saxe.

But there was one person who could not forget Königsmarck, and whose future life was to be cruelly changed by his death. Sophia Dorothea, as soon as she heard the news of the seizure of her lover's papers and correspondence, knew that she was lost. Ernest Augustus, whether or not he was personally implicated in Countess Platen's activities on the night of July 1, was now determined to act with the greatest stringency. She was an embarrassment to him and to his brother George William. George Lewis wanted her disposed of with the utmost speed. The Platens acted out of vengeance and self-interest, nervous that her continued presence at court might reveal their own part in the murder of Königsmarck.

The only solution was divorce. Count Platen devised a simple plan. George Lewis wrote to his wife, requesting her to resume her duties as wife in act as well as name. Sophia Dorothea, predictably, refused, and compromised her position still further by demanding that she should be allowed to join her parents at Celle. This was enough for Platen, for Ernest Augustus, and for George William.

On July 17, Sophia Dorothea left Hanover for the last time. It had been decided that she should live permanently at the castle of Ahlden, some twenty miles away from her father's court at Celle. Deprived of her last friend, her faithful lady-in-waiting, and guarded by a troop of dragoons, she went into exile. All that was left to do was for the bureaucrats of Hanover and Celle to draw up the necessary documents governing the divorce proceedings, the apportioning of Sophia Dorothea's financial assets, and the assurance that she could never remarry. More eyebrows were raised in diplomatic circles throughout Europe, as it became plain that divorce and incarceration appeared to be inseparable in Hanover, and renewed questions about Königsmarck's disappearance were posed. There was even a belated sense of outrage at Celle over Hanoverian insistence that Sophia Dorothea should be prohibited from remarrying. But nothing now could be accomplished in reopening the case. On December 28, the final papers were signed by the Consistorial Court of Hanover, and Sophia Dorothea also signed them.

The English envoy in Hanover reported to London:

The Carnival here is very provoking, but they cannot live without it, they are a sort of people that can rejoice even in their own
disgraces . . . I think them as little in their senses as at Dresden.
The Duke of Celle has been at Hanover half of the time and the
other with his Duchess at Celle. The divorce was finished but the
day before their frolics began here. The sentence was pronounced upon malicious desertion . . . Those who don't like the
proceeding say there is a nullity in the manner of it, but those
persons were no competent judges, and that the Princess may appeal to the Emperor whenever she pleases. She is still confined.

On the point of an appeal, he was quite wrong, since Sophia
Dorothea herself had undertaken not to appeal against the divorce settlement. But, in his final sentence, the English envoy
effectively summed up the remainder of her life. Sophia
Dorothea finally took up residence at Ahlden on February
28, 1695, at the age of twenty-eight. Except for a brief period, when her mother managed to persuade the authorities
that Sophia Dorothea was in danger at Ahlden because it
might lie in the path of an invading French army, she was to
remain a prisoner there for thirty-two years, more than half
her life.

Those thirty-two years were to see the death of Ernest
Augustus and the accession of George Lewis to the Duchy of
Hanover; the final granting of the Electoral coronet; the
death of Countess Platen, blind and forgotten; the death of
George William; the marriages of Sophia Dorothea's two
children, George to Caroline of Ansbach and Sophia
Dorothea to Frederick William of Brandenburg; the death of
William III of England and of the Electress Sophia of
Hanover and of Anne of England; and George Lewis's coronation as George I of England in Westminster Abbey. And,
in 1722, Eléonore died, aged eighty-five. For all that those
years held for Sophia Dorothea, she might better have died
with her lover in 1694. Lonely, deprived of her children and
her confidante, losing touch with events in the outside world,
her few vain attempts to come to some manner of arrange-

ment with George Lewis ignored or rebuffed, she still maintained her dignity and forbearance, and remembered those few months of uncomplicated passion with Philip Christopher von Königsmarck.

Sophia Dorothea, Duchess of Ahlden, died on November 13, 1726. She predeceased George Lewis by only six months. The King of England had time enough to arrange the burning of his wife's papers—in particular a will leaving all her possessions to her two children—and the burial of her body in as surreptitious and contemptuous ceremony as could be conceived, before his stroke on the road to Osnabrück. Some said that Sophia Dorothea had cursed him, some that a last letter from her had induced the stroke. His son, the new George II, attempted to rehabilitate his mother's memory, but when he read her letters to Königsmarck he ordered them to be destroyed. He never referred to her again.

III

Jacobites

You may soon have your wish to enjoy the gallant sights of armies, encampments, standards waving over your brother's cornfields, and the pretty windings of the Thames stained with the blood of men.

Alexander Pope

I am come home, sir, and I will entertain no notion at all of returning to that place whence I came, for I am persuaded my faithful Highlanders will stand by me.

Charles Edward Stuart

On Saturday, August 27, 1715, John, Earl of Mar, welcomed a number of distinguished and influential guests to a hunting party at Braemar. It was the traditional month for such gatherings, but this one had a special significance. Invitations had gone out to the great Highland magnates, the Dukes of Gordon and Atholl, though they both seemed to have pressing engagements elsewhere, sending instead their eldest sons, Huntly and Tullibardine. But, it was reliably reported, the noblemen and chieftains who joined in the chase round by

Glen Cluny and back to the Glen of Quoich included George
Keith, Earl Marischal, and the Earls of Erroll, Southesk,
Seaforth, Linlithgow, and Carnwath; Viscount Kilsyth, and
Lords Drummond, Duffus, Ogilvy and Rollo; Lyon of Auchterhouse, Gordon of Auchintoul, Glengarry, General Hamilton; and two men more important for their connections than
for themselves, Auldbar, the nephew of the great Claverhouse, and Campbell of Glendaruel, who brought apologies
from his notorious kinsman Breadalbane.

A casual observer might have construed the gathering as
nothing out of the normal, merely another manifestation of
the Highland gentleman's love of the chase. But the casual
observer would not have known of Lord Mar's somewhat
precipitate departure from London August 1. "Bobbing
John," as he was to be nicknamed, had emerged from the
King's levée and, together with General Hamilton, had chosen to board a collier bound for Newcastle. Joined also by
Colonel John Hay, the titular Earl of Inverness, and a couple
of servants, the little group had sailed on to the Fife coast.
Mar had crossed the Tay on August 18, and arrived at
Braemar two days later. It was the King's business that
brought him north, but it was not that of George I; Mar, already snubbed by the recently arrived Hanoverian, had decided that the time was right to change his allegiance.

When the hunt was over, the moment for oratory had arrived. Rae, the official historian of the 1715 rising, commented acidly:

Having thus got his Friends together, he address'd himself to
them in a publick Speech, full of invectives against the Protestant
Succession in General, and against King George in particular;
wherein, to gloss his Actions with a seeming Reflection as of Sorrow for what was past, he told them, That tho' he had been In-
strumental in forwarding the Union of the two Kingdoms in the
Reign of Queen Anne, yet now his Eyes were open'd and he
could see his Error, would therefore do what lay in his Power to
make them again a Free People, and that they should enjoy their

ancient Liberties, which were by that cursed Union (as he call'd it) delivered up into the Hands of the English . . . and to establish upon the Throne of these Realms the Chevalier St. George (the Pretender), who, he said, had the only undoubted Right to the Crown, had promis'd to hear their Grievances, and would redress their Wrongs.

According to Mar, the rising was not only lawful in the eyes of God and man, it could not fail. The French, ever ready to embarrass the English, had promised arms and money; already, funds amounting to £100,000 were available; there would be a simultaneous rising in England; and, to set the seal on Mar's initiative, he was able to brandish a hastily completed and unsigned draft of his commission from James Stuart as major-general of the army of Scotland.

A week later, the eleven most fervent Jacobite leaders met again at Aboyne, the Marquess of Huntly's castle, and on September 6, the standard was raised at Braemar. The Lord Justice Clerk received information that as many as 600 people were present, though other accounts lower the total to sixty. There were more speeches and ceremonial, and copies of Mar's commission were distributed. The rising was now an established fact. Only the superstitious paid any attention to the sight of the golden ball on the top of the standard falling to the ground.

Unrest in Scotland had been growing over the decades ever since the Act of Union in 1707. The twenty-five articles of the treaty had been bitterly contested as Lords Seafield and Stair had steered them through the Scottish Parliament, and entrenched opponents of this appalling catastrophe talked bitterly of past English atrocities. Cromwell's victories at Dunbar and Worcester, Claverhouse's gallant death at Killiecrankie, the massacre at Glencoe, the collapse of the Darien Scheme, the affair of the *Worcester*, when anti-English mob fervour had led to a hideous miscarriage of justice and three dangling bodies on Leith Sands, even Flodden, where the flower of Scottish chivalry had been scythed down, all these stations of the Caledonian cross were revived and discussed and used as propaganda.

But, nevertheless, Scotland had been officially joined to England on May 1, and Queen Anne had processed with 400 coaches to St. Paul's, to give thanks for the miracle. In Scotland, there had been a marked lack of rejoicing. The Scottish Parliament had inevitably dissolved itself, and the elders of the Kirk called for a day of atonement for the country's humiliation. Even the famous Equivalent, the sum of £400,000 which was to be paid as compensation for past sufferings and present losses, was slow in arriving. The Earl of Mar received a letter from Edinburgh, the first of many: "The Equivalent is so much despaired of here that among the vulgar the greatest part believe it is gone to Spain, and some believe that the bridge of Berwick is fallen with the weight of it, and all is lost." When it did appear, on August 5, cynics were not surprised to discover that only a quarter was in bullion, the remaining three-quarters being paid in suspect Exchequer bills.

Within months, the first Jacobite invasion was being mounted at Dunkirk and Saint-Omer. Louis XIV and his Ministers had, foolishly, been impressed by a document dreamed up by John Ker of Kersland, a notorious troublemaker with a glib tongue and even glibber pen. Ker had no doubt that all Scotland would rise:

They are resolved never to agree to the Union, because it hurts their consciences, and because they are persuaded that it will bring an infinite number of calamities upon this nation, and will render the Scots slaves to the English. They are ready to declare unanimously for King James.

Further evidence was provided by Colonel Hooke who returned from a secret mission to Scotland with a document signed by ten of the most influential noblemen, including Lords Erroll, Panmure, Kinnaird and Stormont, and stating categorically that "the whole nation will rise upon the arrival of its king." All that was needed was an army of 8,000 men, weapons for the Scottish clansmen, a large sum of money, ammunition and artillery, and "majors, lieutenants and serjeants to discipline" the presumably unruly Scottish commanders.

Yet another Scot of dubious reputation, Simon Fraser, claimed that Lochiel, Keppoch, Glengarry, Appin, Clanranald and Macdonald of Sleat were all eager and ready to raise their men in the Stuart cause; and the French reminded themselves that a rising in Scotland would alleviate the pressure in Flanders. The expedition was immediately put in a state of readiness. It was to prove an utter fiasco. The naval commander, Forbin, and the Comte de Gacé, in command of the troops, were at daggers drawn, and Forbin, in any case, considered the entire scheme a piece of arrant lunacy. James Stuart, who was to be in nominal command, caught measles. The equinoctial gales were blowing, and Whitehall's spies had already passed back news of the ships and men being mustered at the Channel ports. At one moment, orders went out from Versailles cancelling the expedition, but these were in turn countermanded, and Forbin's flagship set sail on March 6.

The troubles besetting the whole enterprise were, in point of fact, only beginning. Gacé and his staff instantly succumbed to seasickness, and Forbin gloated over their misery: "I can do nothing, the wine's drawn and you must drink it. Suffer, feel as uncomfortable as you please; I'm quite content, and don't pity you at all. You have your wish. Why are you so dissatisfied?" The gales continued unabated and three of the ships broke their cables. James wrote to his mother, Mary of Modena, on the 9th: "Here I am on board at last. My body is very weak, but my spirit is so strong that it will make up for the weakness of the body. I hope not to write to you again until I do so from the place in Edinburgh, where I expect to arrive on Saturday."

He was not even to set foot on Scottish soil. Burntisland, at the mouth of the Forth, had been chosen for the landing, but the pilots miscalculated, and Forbin eventually dropped anchor near the Isle of May, north-east of North Berwick. He noted in his diary:

In vain we made Signals, and fired our Cannon; nobody appeared . . . At daybreak we discovered the English fleet anchored at four leagues distance from us. The sight of them caused me considerable uneasiness. We were shut in a sort of bay, with a cape to be doubled before we could gain the open sea.

Forbin decided to run for it, losing one ship in the fight which he could not entirely avoid. Eventually, the English fleet hove to off Buchanness and returned to Leith. Forbin, now even more certain that the expedition had no future, set sail for Dunkirk. The arrival of the mauled fleet was watched from the quayside by some English prisoners of war:

We saw the person called the Pretender land on the shore, being a tall, slight young man, pale smooth face, with a blue feather in his hat, and a star on his cloak; at his first going off they mightily huzzaed him with *Vive le Roi*, but were very mute at his coming back.

In England, there were few repercussions. Arrests were made, the Habeas Corpus Act was suspended, a number of Scottish grandees were obliged to deposit bonds as surety of their future good behaviour. Queen Anne ordered a special medal to be struck. The Earl of Mar showed great zeal in a campaign directed against Roman Catholics and those who had opposed the Act of Union.

Seven and a half years later, a new monarch sat on the throne of England and Scotland, and the Earl of Mar was a disillusioned man. He was also vacillating and incompetent. The rebellion moved slowly, and Perth did not fall to Mar's troops until September 14. True, Inverness had been taken by Macintosh of Borlum, but an attempt to seize Edinburgh Castle had failed through a combination of drunkenness and inefficiency.

The government forces, based at Stirling and outnumbered two to one by the rebels, were commanded by the Duke of Argyll, the chief of the hated Campbells. He was not optimistic. He wrote to Townshend, the Secretary of State for Scotland: "I must end with insisting on considerable reinforcements, for without it, or a miracle, not only this country will be utterly destroyed but the rest of his Majesty's dominions put in the extremest danger."

Mar himself reached Perth on September 28, but he failed to make a good impression. The Master of Sinclair, who despised him, was particularly sharp:

We were drawn out to the North Inch to receive him, and from that time did he daily take more and more upon him to act like our General, and did all of himself, without consulting anybody, as if he had been another Moses, meek and spotless, sent from Heaven with a divine commission to relieve us miserable wretches out of bondage . . . He spent a number of weeks in Perth, issuing edicts which he had not the power fully to enforce, practising feints against an enemy not equal to his own army by nine-tenths, in order to cover a petty village warfare and fortifying a camp which the moment his antagonist was in sufficient force to attack, he behoved of necessity to abandon.

The campaign had reached a most curious juncture. By October, the Jacobites held almost the whole of Scotland, with the exception of Campbell country in the west, Sutherland's territory in the north, and the country around Glasgow and south of Edinburgh. Reinforcements were coming in almost by the hour, and Macintosh of Borlum was engaged in a highly successful march eastwards, capturing Leith, threatening Edinburgh, and finally moving on into the Border country. And yet Mar made no move. He was faced with a chronic lack of money and the threat of mutiny unless the Highlanders were paid. Sinclair commented:

While everyone was building castles in the air, and making themselves great men, most of our arms were good for nothing; there was no method fallen on, nor was the least care taken to repair those old rusty broken pieces, which, it seems, were to be carried about more for ornament than use, though gunsmiths were not wanting; but this was either because he who took upon him the command expected no powder from the beginning, or because what was everybody's business was nobody's.

On November 1, Macintosh, with some reluctance, marched into England. He had already joined up with the Lowland lords under Lord Kenmure, and with the North Country Jacobites led by Thomas Forster, Member of Parliament for Northumberland. By November 9, the army had reached Preston. The inhabitants were unimpressed: "The horse and ye footmen did not draw their swords nor show their colours, neither did any drums beat. Only six Highland bagpipes played." A strange apathy seems to have overcome the rebels, and General Wills, the government commander, found comparatively little resistance. They surrendered on November 13. It was a pitiful end to the rising in the north. As Argyll's biographer, Robert Campbell, put it, "none but fools would have stayed to be attacked in that position, and none but knaves would have acted when there as they did."

The battle of Sheriffmuir was fought on the very same day as the surrender of Preston. Mar, with the news that the Duke of Ormonde's rising in the west of England had failed, realised that he had, at last, to take some action. Desertions were increasing. The Frasers had gone, and 200 of Gordon of Glenbucket's men followed them. The army was looking increasingly bizarre:

There were country gentlemen from Angus and Aberdeenshire, riding on stout horses, with sword and pistol, each dressed in his best laced attire, and each attended by servingmen, also armed, and also on horseback. Then there were Highland gentlemen in the more picturesque garb of their country, with obeisant retinues of clansmen on foot. The mass of the army was composed of Lowland peasants, with arms slung over their plain gray clothes, and of mountaineers, nearly naked, or at least wearing little more than one shirt-like garment. Two squadrons of cavalry, which Huntly had brought with him, excited, under the name of light-horse, the derision of friends and foes; being composed of stout bulky Highlandmen, mounted on little horses, each with his petit blue bonnet on his head, a long rusty musket slung athwart his back, and not one possessed of boots or pistols, those articles so requisite to the idea of a trooper. On arriving at Dunblane, this puissant body of cavalry took two hours to dismount; and it is the opinion of one who observed them, that, if attacked by an enemy, they would have been as long before they were in readiness to receive him.

The cold was bitter as the two armies were drawn up and deployed. Argyll was still heavily outnumbered, but Mar showed no talent for generalship; Sinclair described him as "stunned, finding there was something more requisite than lies, for it was not with us he was to have to do, but with the enemy and blows must decide it." The Highlanders charged gallantly, but Argyll had the benefit of more seasoned troops and, above all, of dragoons. The result was a complete stalemate, both right wings gaining ground. Argyll was allowed to reform his army and march away towards Dunblane, without many of the rebels even being engaged in the fighting. Sinclair cavalry were not used, nor were the Macphersons. Rob Roy Macgregor marched his clan away because he could not judge who had won. The Camerons, the Stuarts of Appin, the Gordons, and the majority of Seaforths all ran away.

Technically, neither side had won, though Argyll returned the following morning to remove the spoils of battle. But, in effect, as Rae put it, "by this battle the heart of the Rebellion was broke." A month after Sheriffmuir, James Stuart landed at Peterhead, but he had come too late, and with no reinforcements. He took up residence in the old palace of Scone, and his coronation was fixed for January 23, 1715. It was never to take place. James left Perth on January 29, and sailed from Montrose on February 4. It was only forty-five days after his landing at Peterhead. His presence had, if anything, dispirited his supporters:

When we saw the man whom they called our king, we found ourselves not at all animated by his presence; if he was disappointed in us, we were tenfold more so in him. We saw nothing in him that looked like spirit. He never appeared with cheerfulness and vigour to animate us. Our men began to despise him; some asked if he could speak. His countenance looked extremely heavy. He cared not to come abroad amongst us soldiers, or to see us handle our arms or do our exercise. Some said the circumstance he found us in dejected him; I am sure the figure he made dejected us; and, had he but sent us five thousand men of good troops, and never himself come among us, we had done other things than we have now done.

It was a biting assessment, perhaps unfair, but understandable. The Highlanders felt themselves betrayed, and were to feel it even more strongly as the last flickers of rebellion gradually died out or were forcibly extinguished. Curiously, though, the government reserved the full force of revenge for the English rebels. Lord Kenmure was executed, and the estates of the most prominent leaders were declared forfeit. The Act of Attainder dissuaded many from returning to Scotland, and the government troops committed many acts of pillage and petty vengeance. But not one Scot was hanged, and, when the prisons eventually delivered up their wretched, ragged inmates and the Act of Pardon was passed, only Rob Roy Macgregor was exempted from the general amnesty. Indeed, the government seemed unaware of how close they had come to disaster. Years later, Thackeray played the conditional game, letting his imagination run riot on what might have happened if Edinburgh Castle had fallen:

Edinburgh Castle, and town, and all Scotland were King James's. The north of England rises, and marches over Barnet Heath upon London. Wyndham is up in Somersetshire; Packington in Worcestershire; and Vivian in Cornwall. The Elector of Hanover, and his hideous mistresses, pack up the plate, and perhaps

the crown jewels in London, and are off *via* Harwich and Hel-
voetsluys, for dear old Deutschland. The king—God save him!
—lands at Dover, with tumultuous applause; shouting multitudes,
roaring cannon, the Duke of Marlborough weeping tears of joy,
and all the bishops kneeling in the mud. In a few years, mass is
said in St. Paul's; matins and vespers are sung in York Minster;
and Dr. Swift is turned out of his stall and deanery house at St.
Patrick's, to give place to Father Dominic, from Salamanca.

But it was only supposition. And yet the glimmer of hope
never died. There was a third attempt in 1719, which ended
with Marischal's little army, supplemented by bemused
Spanish mercenaries, being trapped in the Pass of Glenshiel
and forced to surrender, and there were periodic Jacobite
scares, but the 1720s and 1730s passed by in an atmosphere of
comparative calm and peace. Then, on July 22, 1745, a small
boat, the *Du Teillay*, was sighted off South Uist in the Outer
Hebrides. There were eleven passengers on board. The elev-
enth was a handsome young man of twenty-five. William
Murray, Marquess of Tullibardine, noticed an eagle hovering
overhead. "Sir," he said, "I hope this is an excellent omen, and
promises good things to us. The King of birds is come to welcome Your Royal Highness upon your arrival in Scotland."

Charles Edward Stuart's first glimpse of his inheritance
must have been as depressing as his father's back in 1708. The
rain poured down on the bleak coastline of Eriskay, the only
shelter was a tacksman's cottage, and the only nourishment a
dish of flounders. The following day, Clanranald's younger
brother, Alexander Macdonald of Boisdale, came over from
South Uist and promptly advised the whole party to return
to France. His brother would certainly not come out, nor, he
thought, would Macleod or Macdonald of Sleat. But Charles
would have none of it and, when he had sailed on to Loch na-
Nuagh, between Arisaig and Moidart, he began to attract
supporters at last. Kinlochmoidart, Glenaladale and Young
Clanranald all seemed to be bewitched. Charles received them
in a pavilion which had been erected on the deck of the *Du*

Teillay, and the effect he had on his reluctant guests was extraordinary. One of the Macdonalds recorded his impression:

About half an hour after there entered the tent a tall youth of a most agreeable aspect, in a plain black coat, with a plain shirt, not very clean, and a cambric stock fixed with a plain silver buckle, a fair round wig out of the buckle, a plain hat with a canvas string having one end fixed to one of his coat buttons; he had black stockings and brass buckles in his shoes; at his first appearance I found my heart swell to my very throat.

Whether it was the simplicity of his clothes, or the effect of plain black and white, or the youth and good looks of Charles, he was irresistible. Even Cameron of Lochiel was won over. He had suggested that Charles should send his companions back, and himself remain in hiding while the clan chief deliberated on the best course of action. This was not at all what Charles was expecting, and he reacted vigorously:

Soon, with the new friends I have, I will raise the royal standard and proclaim to the people that Charles Stuart is come over to claim the crown of his ancestors—to win it, or die in the attempt. Lochiel, who my father has often told me was our firmest friend, may stay at home, and from the newspapers learn the fate of his prince.

Lochiel, not surprisingly, could only agree to follow Charles, and his example was followed by Keppoch and Glencoe. On August 9, the *Du Teillay* sailed for France, on August 18 John Murray of Broughton was appointed Secretary of State, and the following day the royal standard was raised.

The ceremony was to take place in Glenfinnan; 150 Macdonalds were already there when the prince and his party arrived, but there was no sign of the Camerons. Then the distant sound of the pipes was heard, and at last Lochiel's men marched into the glen. The standard, of red, white and blue silk, was unfurled by Tullibardine, and James VIII was proclaimed, a commission appointing Charles as Regent was read and a manifesto of intent delivered. Finally, Charles himself, in fawn and scarlet, spoke briefly but effectively. He now had an army of 1,200 men.

Sir John Cope was the commander of the government troops in Scotland, and these amounted ostensibly to 3,000, but when he marched north from Stirling he took only two regiments, two companies of Black Watch, four mortars, a few small field guns and a ponderous wagon train. He moved far too slowly, and was completely outmanoeuvred by Charles's men, who were intent on seizing Edinburgh. The rebels were in sight of the capital by September 16, and consternation grew among supporters of the government. Lord Provost Stewart was less active than he might have been, and an atmosphere of pessimism grew:

A great many of the trained-bands were of the opinion that the city was not tenable; that the sudden flight of the dragoons [the notorious Coltbridge Canter] made it evident that they were of the same opinion; and that if standing out for an hour or two, which was all that could be done, would bring the lives and properties of the inhabitants into certain hazard without doing real service to the cause intended to be served it was certainly more desirable to capitulate on the best terms that could be got.

In the event, no resistance was offered, and Charles rode on to Holyroodhouse; the number of people wearing the knotted white ribbons of the Jacobites increased remarkably, and a mere twenty-five left to join Sir John Cope. Only the Castle held out, hopeful that the government troops would be able to sweep away the Highland rabble without difficulty. This, however, Cope proved quite unable to do. He was soundly defeated at Prestonpans, and eventually withdrew as far as Berwick.

Charles spent six weeks in Edinburgh, while his council of advisers made up their minds about an invasion of England. As was always the case when Jacobites talked rather than fought, there were disputes and disagreements. Lord George Murray despised what he thought of as the Irish clique, many of whom had sailed with the prince on the *Du Teillay*, and was not prepared to be overruled. Rather than run the risk of an encounter with Field-Marshal Wade near Newcastle, he was in favour of a descent to Carlisle, and finally persuaded the doubters. But even after the fall of Carlisle, Lord George's touchiness remained a problem. He felt that he should have drawn up the terms of surrender, but instead this duty had been given to Murray of Broughton and the Duke of Perth. An exchange of letters between him and the prince ensued:

Sir,—I cannot but observe how little my advice as a general officer has any weight with your Royal Highness, ever since I had the honour of a commission from your hands. But as I ever had a firm attachment to the royal family, and in particular to the king, my master, I shall go on as a volunteer, and design to be this night in the trenches as such, with any other that will please to follow me, though I own I think there are full few on this post already. Your Royal Highness will please order whom you think fit to command on this post and the other parts of the blockade. I have the honour to be, Sir, Your Royal Highness's most faithful and most humble servant.

(signed) George Murray

I think your advice ever since you joined me at Perth has had another guess weight with me than that what any general officer could claim as such. I am therefore extremely surprised you should throw up your commission for a reason which I believe was never heard of before. I am glad of your particular attachment to the King, but I am very sure he will never take anything as a proof of it but your deference to me. I accept your demission as lieutenant-general and your future services as a volunteer.

Charles P. R.

Lord George Murray may have been arrogant and prickly, but he was also an experienced soldier and commander, and someone whose services Charles could not afford to dispense with. The Irish clique would have been only too happy to see the back of him, but the Duke of Perth realised that this would be disastrous. He went so far as to offer his resignation, and Murray of Broughton agreed to resign from the council. Lord George's fit of pique was soothed, temporarily.

The army proceeded south, via Preston, Wigan, Manchester and Macclesfield, and reached Derby on December 4. It was to go no further. Charles wanted to push on to London, but the clan chiefs were becoming nervous. They were far from home in increasingly hostile country; the Duke of Cumberland lay between them and London; no one of any consequence had declared for the Stuarts; and their own men were far from ready for a pitched battle.

The council met on the 5th, and both the chiefs and the Duke of Perth put their case with force. The Chevalier de Johnstone recorded the final arguments:

The chiefs of the clans answered the Prince, that our army, being without the incumbrance of baggage, and the Highlanders extremely agile and hardy (as they had often proved since they entered England by marching twenty miles a day without leaving any stragglers) would, by having merely the start for a few hours of the Duke of Cumberland, prevent him from ever overtaking us. With bad roads, his army could scarcely march twelve miles in a winter day without leaving the half of the soldiers behind. We had, therefore, little to fear from this army. As for the army of Marshal Wade, we had no greater reason for fearing it now, than when we entered England: nay, nothing was more desirable than that we should fall in with it, because, by beating it, we should retire gloriously from England with arms in our hands, which would console the Highlanders, whose hopes would be disappointed by their retreat.

It was all special pleading, and almost certainly the wrong decision. It was not well received:

The Highlanders, conceiving at first that they were on the march to attack the army of the Duke of Cumberland, displayed the utmost joy and cheerfulness, but as soon as the day allowed them to

see the objects around them and they found that we were retrac-
ing our steps, nothing was to be heard throughout the whole
army but expression of rage and lamentation. If we had been
beaten, the grief could not have been greater.

Except for a skirmish at Clifton, the return march passed
off without incident, and by the beginning of January Stirling was under siege. But General Hawley was in pursuit, and
the two armies clashed near Falkirk. Johnstone described the
tactics of the clansmen:

The cavalry closing their ranks . . . put spurs to their horses and
rushed upon the Highlanders at a hard trot, breaking their ranks,
throwing down everything before them and trampling the Highlanders under the feet of their horses. The most singular and extraordinary combat immediately followed. The Highlanders,
stretched on the ground, thrust their dirks into the bellies of the
horses. Some seized the riders by their clothes, dragged them
down and stabbed them with their dirks, several again used their
pistols, but few of them had sufficient space to handle their
swords . . . The resistance of the Highlanders was so incredibly
obstinate that the English . . . were at length repulsed and forced
to retire. The Highlanders did not neglect the advantage they
had obtained, but pursued them keenly with their swords, running as fast as their horses, and not allowing them a moment's
time to recover from their fright.

The result of Falkirk was not dissimilar to that of
Sheriffmuir. Neither side seemed to win the day, but it was
the Jacobite army that retreated. Charles himself was furious,
though resigned:

After all this I know I have an army that I cannot command any
further than the chief officers please, and therefore if you are all
resolved upon it I must yield; but I take God to witness that it is
with the greatest reluctance, and that I wash my hands of the
fatal consequences which I foresee but cannot help.

The final confrontation came on April 16, at Culloden.
The English troops, armed with the bayonet, made short

shrift of the courageous but undisciplined rebels. Johnstone was appalled by the sight:

The left wing . . . was not twenty paces from the enemy, who gave their first fire at the moment the flight began to become general, which spread from the right to the left of our army with the rapidity of lightning. What a spectacle of horror! The same Highlanders, who had advanced to the charge like lions, with bold, determined countenances, were in an instant seen flying like trembling cowards in the greatest disorder. It may be said of the attack of the Highlanders, that it bears great resemblance to that of the French; that it is a flame, the violence of which is more to be dreaded then the duration. No troops, however excellent, are possessed of qualities which will render them constantly invincible.

While Charles reluctantly left the battlefield, Cumberland's dragoons began their war of attrition. Johnstone looked back on the scene of revenge and savagery:

The Duke of Cumberland had the cruelty to allow our wounded to remain amongst the dead on the field of battle, stripped of their clothes, from Wednesday, the day of our unfortunate engagement, till three o'clock in the afternoon of Friday, when he sent detachments to kill all those who were still in life. A great many, who had resisted the effects of the continual rains which fell all the time, were then dispatched. He ordered a barn, which contained many of the wounded Highlanders, to be set on fire and the soldiers stationed round it drove back with fixed bayonets the unfortunate men who attempted to save themselves, into the flames, burning them alive in this horrible manner, as if they had not been fellow-creatures.

No doubt, reports of brutality were exaggerated, but innumerable instances of cruelty were noted by impeccably unbiased observers. General Hawley, smarting after his very modified success at Falkirk, encouraged his own soldiers with complete impartiality to kill anyone who moved.

The wanderings of Charles Edward Stuart are well documented and have often been described. He was finally taken off in September. The Chevalier de Johnstone has the last word:

In the month of October he landed at Morlaix, having escaped death a thousand times during the space of five months, and having exposed himself to a thousand times more danger than if he had supported his cause with courage and perseverance, at the head of his faithful Highlanders, as long as he could hope to make head against the English. He should only as a last resource have embraced the resolution of skulking and running about the Highlands without attendants, after the passes had been forced and all possibility of opposing the enemy was destroyed. But our situation was not desperate. All that we can say is that this Prince entered on his expedition rashly and without foreseeing the personal dangers to which he was about to expose himself; that in carrying it on he always took care not to expose his person to the fire of the enemy; and that he abandoned it at a time when he had a thousand times more reason to hope for success than when he left Paris to undertake it.

With Charles Stuart's final departure from Scotland, the last spark of Jacobite optimism had been effectively extinguished. He was to remain a political pawn for the rest of his life, but he had ceased to be of any consequence. The weary years of exile, the scandals and sottishness, the attempts to beget an heir, all these were the dying fall. His death, from apoplexy, in Rome on January 31, 1788, at the age of sixty-seven, was almost an anti-climax. His cause had perished in 1746, and he with it. The Hanoverian dynasty was completely secure after Culloden.

Scotland did not suffer from the collapse of Jacobitism. After the initial acts of revenge, the executions and burnings, the seizing of property and the hangings, were over, the only real victim was seen to be the clan system. The chieftains took to wearing extravagant peacock versions of the old Highland costume; they sipped tea in Edinburgh drawing-rooms; they observed the extraordinary intellectual flowering; they became absentee landlords. Their clansmen also lost their sense of identity, of belonging to a unified tribe. Their tragedy was yet to come. But, ironically, when the Highland Clearances became one of the major scandals of the nine-teenth century, it was not the English but the Scottish gran-dees and landowners who encouraged their tenants into star-vation and exile without a care in the world. And it was the English, above all George IV, who suddenly decided that the Jacobites had been wrong, but very definitely romantic.

Part Two

GEORGE II
1683–1760; King, 1727–1760

He had something of humanity, and amongst many other royal and manly virtues, he possessed justice, truth and sincerity.

William Pitt, Earl of Chatham

How the king made away with his father's will under the astonished nose of the Archbishop of Canterbury; how he was a choleric little sovereign; how he shook his fist in the face of his father's courtiers; how he kicked his coat and wig about in his rages, and called everybody thief, liar, rascal, with whom he differed; you will read in all the history books; and how he speedily and shrewdly reconciled himself with the bold minister, whom he had hated during his father's life, and by whom he was served during fifteen years of his own with admirable prudence, fidelity, and success.

William Makepeace Thackeray

He always was what he appeared to be. He might offend but he never deceived.

Lord Charlemont

The King used often to brag of the contempt he had for books and letters; to say how much he hated all that stuff from his infancy; and that he remembered when he was a child he did not hate reading and learning merely as other children do upon account of the confinement, but because he despised it and felt as if he was doing something mean and below him.

Lord Hervey

When will England ever have a better prince?

John Wesley

IV

The Eldest Son

I always hated the rascal, but now I hate him worse than
ever.

George II on Frederick, Prince of Wales

He had a father that abhorred him, a mother that
despised and neglected him, a sister that betrayed him, a
brother set up to pique, and a set of servants that neither
were of use to him, nor were capable of being of use to
him, nor desirous of being so.

Lord Hervey on Frederick, Prince of Wales

A father's dislike for his eldest son is a universal characteristic
of the human race which has greatly exercised generations of
psychoanalysts. It is, unfortunately, a perfectly natural trait.
A father will be jealous of his son, because the latter is
younger, or because he may have usurped his mother's love
for her husband, or because he will inherit the money, property or even title which the father cannot take with him to
the grave. Usually, however, when such a relationship exists,
it is disguised or in some respect sublimated. The Hanoverian

Kings made no such attempt to disguise, let alone sublimate, their feelings toward their eldest sons. The Stuarts had been, perhaps, unusual in their devotion for their children. James I and Charles I had both demonstrated considerable affection, Charles II was notoriously generous towards his frequent offspring, though they, being bastards, had no claim on the succession, and James II had supervised the upbringing and education of his young son with great care, though it was obscured by excessive religiosity. The Hanoverians had few such stirrings of paternal love. Even George III, basically a kind man, had firm ideas on the treatment that should be meted out to his sons. When asked by their tutor, the Bishop of Chester, what special instructions the King had, he answered without hesitation, "If they deserve it, let them be flogged; do as you used to do at Westminster." The Bishop took him at his word, and laid on with a will, thus helping to ensure that the royal sons would react equally violently against certain disciplines as soon as they were grown up (the strictness shown by Queen Victoria towards the hapless future Edward VII, and by George V towards his sons, produced very much the same results).

But the most obvious, and most bitter, example of a father's loathing for his eldest son is provided by the relationship between George II and Frederick, Prince of Wales. In a greatly magnified sense, it was a repetition of George I's dislike for his eldest son, whom he saw as a permanent threat, dynastically and politically. He had more or less abandoned his children to be brought up by their grandparents, and refused to allow them any access to their disgraced and exiled mother. When the future George II and his clever, cultured wife Caroline established what was in reality a rival court at Somerset House, they also collected around them Opposition politicians already anticipating the next reign and their return to office. George I showed his displeasure by avoiding any contact with his son, by refusing to appoint him to the Privy Council or to any high rank in the army, by blocking attempts to create him Regent during his father's frequent absences in Hanover, and by quarrelling with him on almost every conceivable topic or policy. Schulenburg wrote to Leibnitz in 1714: "The father treats the son with excessive rigour, not wishing to satisfy his most insignificant wish"; though he felt impelled to add, "On the other hand the son behaves in such a manner that the king has good reason to complain." Five years later, nothing had changed, except for the worse. An eye-witness at one of their rare encounters reported: "The King spoke not one word to him either good, bad or indifferent, but made a sign to him to rise with his hand, nor did the Prince stay in his presence above two minutes."

It might be imagined that George II, having received such cold and unpaternal treatment at the hand of his father, might have resolved to expend slightly more charity and affection on his son. Such was very far from the case.

Frederick, Prince of Wales, is remembered almost solely for the brutally dismissive epitaph: "Poor Fred who was alive and is dead." Some historians put him down as half-witted, infantile, malicious, certainly of no importance whatsoever. And yet he was intelligent enough to be interested in Bolingbroke's views on statecraft, and to draw up an extremely sensible plan for his eldest son's education. Lady Mary Wortley Montagu, who was not given to empty adulation, sent an admiring description to Lady Bristol:

I am extremely pleased that I can tell you without either flattery or partiality that our young Prince had all the accomplishments that it is possible to have at his age. With an air of sprightliness and understanding and something so very engaging and easy in his behaviour that he needs not the advantage of his rank to appear charming. I had the honour of a long conversation with him last night before the King came in. His governor retired on purpose that I might make some judgment of his genius by hearing him speak without constraint; and I was surprised at the quietness and politeness that appeared in every thing he said: joined to a person perfectly agreeable and the fine fair hair of the Princess.

Frederick had been brought up and educated in Hanover, and like his father spoke English with a strong German accent. He was sickly as a boy, and had suffered from the attentions of the court doctors who prescribed a regime of asses' milk. His mother had been greatly alarmed by the news of this fashionable treatment, expressing fears that it might affect her son's sexual potency. But Frederick seems to have survived unimpaired, and soon launched himself on the round of wholesale whoring which was an essential part of any young Hanoverian Prince's upbringing. He had a mistress at the age of sixteen, and was already looking forward to his arranged marriage to Princess Wilhelmina of Prussia.

George I died in 1727, and Frederick's life changed dramatically. At the time, his relations with his parents were amicable, perhaps because he rarely saw them. Some indication of this is given in a letter he wrote to his sister Anne:

I am sure that you share the grief I have felt since the death of our dear grandfather. I should be lacking in filial duty of the most ungrateful of men if it had not caused me great sorrow, for he treated me with especial affection and friendship. I was so overcome by sadness when they told me the news, I could not leave my bed for two days and fainted twice. My only consolation in this sad affliction is the knowledge of my dear parents' goodness. I flatter myself that I shall always conduct myself in a manner deserving of their esteem and friendship for me. I pray you dear sister, as you are by them, to remember me often to Their Majesties.

But the "dear parents" showed a strange reluctance to see their son. Two years before, while George I was still alive, George and Caroline had attempted to bar Frederick from the succession. The Lord Chancellor noted in his diary:

The Prince of Wales and his wife were for excluding Prince Frederick from the throne of England, but that after the king and prince, he should be Elector of Hanover, and Prince William his brother King of Great Britain; but that the king said it was unjust to do it without Prince Frederick's consent, who was now of an age to judge for himself, and so this matter now stood.

Now Frederick was twenty-one, and his arrival in England could not be delayed much longer. But still his father prevaricated, until the discovery of a romantic but hare-brained scheme of Frederick's to marry Wilhelmina without more ado made him realise that it might be safer to have his son in London where he could be protected from such foolishness.

Lord Hervey, who was to chronicle the reign of George II so minutely and so one-sidedly, wrote about the King's resolve:

It was in this winter [1728], just before the Parliament met, that the King was prevailed upon to send for his son from Hanover. His ministers told him that if the Prince's coming was longer delayed an address from Parliament and the voice of a whole nation would certainly oblige His Majesty to send for him and consequently that he would be necessitated to do that with an ill grace which he might now do with a good one. These persuasions prevailed and the King, as children take physic, forced himself to swallow this bitter draught for fear of having it poured down his throat in case he did not take it quietly and voluntarily.

Frederick set off in early December in fierce wintry weather. The roads were appalling, the harbour at Helvetsluys was iced over, and the North Sea was seasonably rough. No one appeared to care about his arrival, and he finally arrived at St. James's Palace in an ordinary hackney coach. Hervey recorded the King's first reactions:

When first the Prince came over he was in great favour with his father, but it lasted not long. The King was pleased with him as a new thing, felt him quite in his power, condemned him as rival, made him no great expense and looked upon his being there with so little court paid to him as an escape from a danger which he had dreaded, and yet was obliged to expose himself to. Sir Robert

Walpole told me one day that the King, speaking to him of his son soon after his arrival, said with an air of contempt and satisfaction: "I think this is not a son I need be much afraid of." But this relation I look upon as apocryphal and give it as such.

The King gave Frederick an allowance of £2,000 a month, so that his annual income, including the revenues from the Duchy of Cornwall, amounted to some £34,000 a year. Frederick's friends were not slow in pointing out to him that his father had received £100,000 a year when he was Prince of Wales. The rift was beginning to show already. Hervey thought that Frederick was as much to blame as his father: "The Prince, on this occasion, as on all like occasions afterwards, between anger and timidity went to just such lengths with those who were against the Court as served to irritate his father and not far enough to attach them to his service." Certainly, Frederick was easily influenced, and the obvious magnet towards which Walpole's enemies were drawn. Hervey had some hard things to say about his shortcomings in an extended, often unfair, but interesting portrait:

The Prince's character, at his first coming over, though little more respectable, seemed much more amiable than it was upon his opening himself and being better known. For though there appeared nothing in him to be admired, yet there seemed nothing in him to be hated—neither nothing great nor nothing vicious. His behaviour was something that gained one's good wishes, though it gave one no esteem for him. For his best qualities, whilst they prepossessed one the most in his favour, always gave one a degree of contempt for him at the same time, his carriage, whilst it seemed engaging to those who did not examine it, appearing mean to those who did; for though his manners had the show of benevolence from a good deal of natural or habitual civility, yet his cajoling everybody, and almost in an equal degree, made those things which might have been thought favours, if you more judiciously or sparingly bestowed, lose all their weight. He carried this affection of general benevolence so far that he often condescended below the character of a Prince, and as people attributed this familiarity to popular and not particular motives, so it only lessened their respect without increasing their good will, and instead of giving them good impressions of his humanity, only gave them ill ones of his sincerity. He was indeed as false as his capacity would allow him to be, and was more capable in that walk than in any other, never having the least hesitation, from principle or fear of future detection, in telling any lie that served his present purpose. He had a much weaker understanding, and, if possible, a more obstinate temper, than his father; that is, more tenacious of opinions he had once formed, though less capable of ever having right ones. Had he had one grain of merit at the bottom of his heart, one should have had compassion for him in the situation to which his miserable poor head soon reduced him, for his case, in short, was this: he had a father that abhorred him, a mother that despised and neglected him, a sister that betrayed him, a brother set up to pique, and a set of servants that neither were of use to him, nor were capable of being of use to him, nor desirous of being so.

A less biased observer, Schutz, in a letter to Lord Egmont in November 1731, brings out many of the same flaws though he sees them in a kindlier light:

He has no reigning passion. If there be, it is to pass the evening with six or seven others over a glass of wine and hear them talk of a variety of things. He loves plays and plays to win that he may supply his pleasures and generosities, which last are great; but so ill-placed that he often wants the wherewithal to do a well-placed kindness. He has had several mistresses and now keeps one, an apothecary's daughter of Kingston; he is not nice in his choice and talks more of feats this way than he acts. He can talk gravely according to his company, but is sometimes more childish than becomes his age. He thinks he knows business, but attends to none. He likes to be flattered. He is good natured and if he meets with a good Ministry may satisfy his people. He is extremely dutiful to his parents who do not return it in love. They let him do as he will but keep him short of money.

The combined accounts offer a picture of normal human frailty. Here is a young man who is naturally affectionate but starved of parental love, who is generous and is kept short of money, who is undiscriminating in his friendships and more of a sexual boaster than a sexual athlete, something of a gambler, with a quick temper inherited from his irascible little father, influenced by flattery and not averse to lying in order to extricate himself from some difficulty; weak, certainly, but desperately unsure of himself, and trying to disguise his inadequacy and lack of self-confidence through the time-honoured palliatives of drinking, gaming and womanising: by no means an attractive amalgam, but hardly unique in its degradations, as many contemporary critics and commentators might have one believe.

Frederick, though, fatally lacked discretion where women were concerned. He took up with the daughter of an oboe player, and paid court to an opera singer. Then there was the unfortunate incident reported by one of the royal pages:

My man, John Cooper, saw the Prince last night let into the Park through St. James's Mews alone, and the next morning a grenadier told him the Prince was robbed last night of his watch, twenty two guineas and a gold medal by a woman who had run away from him. The Prince bad the grenadier run after her and take the watch which with the seals were the only things he valued, the money she was welcome to he said and he ordered him when he got the watch to let the woman go. But the grenadier could not find her, so I suppose she dropped the watch in the Mall.

Most seriously, he fell in love with Anne Vane. She was far from pretty, indeed Lord Egmont called her "a fat ill-shaped dwarf," and Horace Walpole was cutting about her lack of virtue. "She had no other charms," he wrote, "than being a maid of honour [to the Queen] who was willing to cease to be so at the first opportunity." She had already had a liaison with Lord Harrington, who was more than twice her age, and she had then become rather too friendly with Lord Hervey. Hervey was Frederick's most intimate friend and adviser, and may well have felt something more than mere affection for him, but Frederick wasted no time in paying court to Miss Vane, or "Vanella" as he called her. Hervey, when he found out, was outraged, and never forgave Frederick. He was supplanted in the latter's favour by George Bubb Dodington, later Lord Melcombe, and his allusions to the Prince in his memoirs became viciously antagonistic.

Vanella was established in a fine house in Grosvenor Street, and shortly afterwards gave birth to a son who was christened Fitz-Frederick Vane and acknowledged by the Prince. The affair did not raise Frederick in the esteem of his father. Hervey noted with satisfaction that "the coldness between the Prince and his parents at this time increased so much that it furnished conversation to the whole town, though it so far put an end to all that ever used to pass between him and his parents that the King never spoke to him, and the Queen very slightly." A year later, Hervey witnessed a dreadful confrontation. The Princess Royal, who was married to the Prince of Orange, had been visiting the King and Queen and had now left once more for Holland. The Queen appeared greatly affected by the parting:

Lord Hervey found her and the Princess Caroline together, drinking chocolate, drowned in tears, and choked with sighs. Whilst they were endeavouring to divert their attention by beginning a conversation with Lord Hervey on indifferent subjects, the gallery door opened, upon which the Queen said, "Is the King here already?" and, Lord Hervey telling her it was the Prince, the Queen, not mistress of herself and detesting the exchange of the son for the daughter, burst out anew into tears, and cried out, "Oh! my god, this is too much." However, she was soon relieved from this irksome company by the arrival of the King, who, finding this unusual and disagreeable guest in the gallery, broke up the breakfast, and took the Queen out to walk.

"Whenever," added Hervey,

the Prince was in a room with the King, it put one in mind of stories one had heard of ghosts that appear to part of the company and are invisible to the rest; and in this manner, wherever the Prince stood, though the King passed him ever so often or ever so near, it always seemed as if the King thought the place the Prince filled a void space.

Frederick was able to irritate the King seemingly without trying. He supported the grossly inferior Bononcini against George II's favourite Handel. The Opposition continued to flock to his house, and he was increasingly influenced by Bolingbroke. Even his dismissal of Vanella and the transference of his affections to the middle-aged Lady Archibald Hamilton caused nothing but trouble. Miss Vane was not amused, and enlisted the help of none other than Lord Hervey, who set to with eagerness to compose a letter which should cause Frederick the maximum embarrassment. It was something of a small masterpiece.

After the inevitable reminders of what she had sacrificed in her love for the Prince, she turned to more specific matters:

I have resigned everything for your sake but my life; and, had you loved me still, I would have risked even that too to please you; but as it is, I cannot think in my state of health of going out of England, far from friends and all physicians, I can trust, and of whom I stand in so much need. My child is the only consolation I have left. I cannot leave him, nor shall anything but death make me quit the country he is in. Your royal highness may do with me what you please; but a prince who is one day to rule this country will sure, for his own sake never show he will make use of power to distress unreservedly; that one who has put herself without conditions into his hands has the hardest terms imposed upon her, though she never in her life did one action that deserved anything but your favour, your compassion and your friendship; and it is for these reasons I doubt not but your royal highness will on this occasion, for your own sake if not for mine, do everything that will hinder you from being blamed and me from being more miserable than the reflection of what is past must necessarily make one who has known what it was to be happy, and can never expect to taste that font again.

Frederick was amazed, and failed to recognise the style of the man with whom he had once collaborated in a disastrous

play, though he was certain that Vanella was not the author
of the letter. He, foolishly, and she, with malice afore-
thought, showed copies of it to their friends, and the gutter
press enjoyed a field day. Verse doggerel with titles such as
"The Foresaken Whore" and "Vanella or the Amours of the
Court" had ready buyers, and a major public scandal broke.
It was clearly time for Frederick to marry, and a suitable
match was found in Princess Augusta of Saxe-Gotha.

The wedding, a private affair, took place on Tuesday,
April 27, 1736. Augusta made a good impression by curtsey-
ing particularly low before the King. According to Lord Egmont, "she is much pitted with smallpox, and had a great
colour from the heat of the day and the hurry and surprise
she was in. But she has a peculiar affability of behaviour and a
very great sweetness of countenance, mixed with innocence,
cheerfulness and sense." Hervey was less complimentary, saying that "her person, from being very ill-made, a good deal
awry, her arms long, and her motions awkward, had, in spite
of all the finery of jewels and brocade, an ordinary air, which
no trappings could cover or exalt."

There were squabbles over who should sit on which variety of chair, almost as if they were at Louis XIV's Versailles,
and even about the ceremonial of serving coffee. The marriage ceremony itself was at nine o'clock in the evening. Hervey noted the scene:

It was performed in much the same manner as that of the Princess Royal had been, only there was no gallery built. Consequently there could be no procession in form, and they were
married in that Chapel to which the King constantly goes on a
Sunday. At supper nothing remarkable happened but the Prince's
eating several glasses of jelly, and every time he took one turning
about, laughing, and winking on some of his servants. The King
went after supper to the Princess's apartment whilst the Queen
undressed the Princess, and when they were in bed everybody
passed through their bed-chamber to see them, where there was
nothing remarkable but the Prince's nightcap, which was some
inches higher than any grenadier's cap in the whole army.

Hervey awaited the following morning with prurient interest:

There were various reports on what did and did not pass this night after the company had retired. The Queen and Lord Hervey agreed that the bride looked extremely tired with the fatigues of the day, and so well refreshed next morning, that they concluded she had slept very sound; and Her Majesty did not forget to descant at the same time with her usual enjoyment on the glasses of jelly and the nightcap, saying that one made her sick, and the other, if it had not been her son, would have made her laugh.

The first years of Frederick's married life provided further scandal. First, he was discovered to be the author of a somewhat feeble fairy tale in the style of Perrault, in which the noble and heroic Prince Titi has to suffer a pair of appalling parents, "*le roi Guinguet*," "haughty, fierce, partial in his affections, ungovernably rash and insatiably avaricious," and "*la reine Tripasse*," who completely dominated her husband. They showed distinct favouritism to Titi's younger brother and generally behaved like George and Caroline. The fact that Titi lived happily ever after was Frederick's rather feeble attempt at wish-fulfilment.

Far more dramatic was the affair of the Prince's £100,000. It had always rankled with him that his father had received this sum of money annually when he was Prince of Wales, and he now determined to have the case debated in Parliament. Walpole was sympathetic but felt bound to oppose the demand, suggesting instead that £50,000 should be given to the Prince, and a further £50,000 voted as a jointure to his wife. Queen Caroline was vehemently opposed to any such measure, and she exploded to Hervey, who reported the scene with his customary relish.

All you other great and wise people were for it, and so one was forced to give way; but I knew *canaille* my good son so well that I was sure he would only be more obstinate on any step taken to soften him. You know as well as I that he is the lowest stinking

coward in the world and that there is no way of gaining anything of him but by working upon his fear. I know, if I was
asleep, or that he could come behind me, he is capable of shooting me through the head, or stabbing me in the back.

Walpole got his majority, having spent a mere £990 on
two essential votes, and the enmity between Frederick and his
two parents was now past repair. It was still further exacerbated when the news that Augusta was pregnant was sent to
Queen Caroline on July 5, 1737. The King ordered the baby
to be born at Hampton Court rather than at St. James's, and
Frederick and Augusta reluctantly moved in. Frederick,
however, was determined that his child should not be born in
such a hostile atmosphere, and made his plans accordingly.
Lord Hervey describes the farcical scene with great verve:

On Sunday, the 31st of July, the Princess was taken in the evening, after having dined in public that day with the King and
Queen, so very ill, with all the symptoms of actual labour, that
the Prince ordered a coach to be got ready that moment to carry
her to London. Her pains came on so fast and so strong, that her
water broke before they could get her out of the house. However, in this condition. M. Dunoyer, the dancing-master, lugging
her downstairs and along the passages by one arm, and Mr.
Bloodworth, one of the Prince's equerries, by the other, and the
Prince in the rear, they, with much ado, got her into the coach
. . . the Princess begging, for God's sake, the Prince would let
her stay in quiet where she was, for that her pains were so great
she could not set one foot before the other, and was upon the
rack when they moved her. But the Prince, with an obstinacy
equal to his folly, and a folly equal to his barbarity, insisted on
her going, crying "Courage! courage! ah, quelle sottise!" and
telling her, with the encouragement of a toothdrawer, or the
consolatory tenderness of an executioner, that it would be over in
a minute.

And so the heavily laden coach set out for London at a full
gallop. Hervey gives the fullest obstetrical details which his
much-vaunted delicacy could allow:

Notwithstanding all the handkerchiefs that had been thrust one after another up Her Royal Highness's petticoats in the coach, her clothes were in such a condition with the filthy inundations which attend these circumstances that when the coach stopped at St. James's the Prince ordered all the lights to be put out that the people might not have the nasty ocular evidence which would otherwise have been exhibited to them of his folly and her distress . . . Her Royal Highness was put to bed between two tablecloths. At a quarter before eleven she was delivered of a little rat of a girl, about the bigness of a good large toothpick case.

This was the extent to which Frederick's hatred for his father had reached, that he could endanger the lives of his wife and first child in his insane desire to put as many miles between himself and Hampton Court as soon as possible. George was incensed by the whole affair and wrote sternly to his son on September 10. The letter ended with a command and a threat: "It is my pleasure that you leave St. James's with all your family, when it can be done without prejudice or inconvenience to the Princess. I shall for the present leave to the Princess the care of my granddaughter, until the proper time calls upon me to consider her education." Queen Caroline was equally determined, declaring, "I hope, in God, I shall never see him again." Frederick and Augusta moved to Kew on September 12. Less than two months later, on November 9, Queen Caroline was taken desperately ill. She suffered appallingly at the hands of the physicians, and died on Sunday, November 20. Frederick had attempted to see her, but his father had refused to allow him in, raging at his son,

I always hated the rascal, but now I hate him yet worse than ever. He wants to come and insult his poor dying mother; but she shall not see him; you have heard her, and all my daughters have heard her very often this year at Hampton Court, desire me, if she should not be ill and out of her senses, that I would never let that villain come near her; and whilst she had her senses, she was sure she would never desire it. No, no! he shall not come and act any of his silly plays here, false, lying, cowardly, nauseous, puppy.

The King never really recovered from his wife's death, and he continued to refuse to see his son. The news, in May 1738, that Augusta had given birth to a boy, George Frederick William, was ignored. It was not until 1742, when Walpole had fallen and been replaced by Wilmington, that Frederick was allowed to return to St. James's. Even then, it was an empty reconciliation. George refused to give his son any command in the war against the French, or in the campaign against the Jacobite rebels in 1745, and Frederick led an aimless existence, going to the theatre, playing cricket, indulging in the pursuits of a country gentleman. But as the 1740s neared their end, he began to think about his inheritance. The King was ageing, surely he would be king before long.

It was never to be. Frederick had been planning his garden at Kew during January and February 1751, out in all weathers. He caught a chill, which developed into pleurisy or pneumonia, but was up and about again by March 8. He went to the House of Lords in the heavy robes of the Prince of Wales, returned to Kew to work in the gardens, and then drove to Carlton House. He was feverish and tired, and was obviously very ill. He was removed to Leicester House. On the evening of March 20, he drank a cup of coffee, ate some bread and butter, and was suddenly seized by a paroxysm of coughing. He managed to utter four words: "Je sens la mort." His valet cried out, "The Prince is going." He was dead before his wife could reach him.

The King's reaction was churlish. Muttering, "Why, they told me he was getting better!," he hurried off to tell his mistress, Lady Yarmouth. A few months later, he was to say, "This has been a fatal year in our family. I have lost my eldest son, but I was glad of it." He gave orders that Frederick's funeral should not be a lavish affair. He did not attend it himself, nor did any other member of the Royal Family.

Smollett, in his *History of England*, provided the kindest obituary:

His Royal Highness expired on the 20th of March to the un-
speakable affliction of his Royal Consort and the unfeigned sorrow of all who wished well of their country. This excellent
Prince who now died in the forty fifth year of his age was possessed of every amiable quality which could engage the affection
of the people—a tender and obliging husband, a fond parent, a
kind master, liberal, generous, candid and humane; a munificent
patron of the arts, an unwearied friend to merit, well disposed to
assert the rights of mankind in general and warmly attached to
the interest of Great Britain. The Nation could not but be
afflicted at seeing a Prince of such expectations ravished from
their hopes; and their grief was the better founded as the King
had already attained an advanced age and the heir apparent,
George, now Prince of Wales, was a minor.

  But Frederick, Prince of Wales, though he deserved better,
will always be remembered by that Jacobite jingle

> Here lies poor Fred, who was alive and is dead.
> We had rather it had been his Father,
> Had it been his brother, better'n any other,
> Had it been his sister no one would have missed her,
> Had it been the whole generation, all the better for the nation,
> But as it's just poor Fred, who was alive and is dead,
> There's no more to be said.

George I, by D. Stevens

George II, by R. Pine

Above   George Frederick Handel, by Bartholomew Dandridge

Left   John Gay, by Sir Godfrey Kneller

Queen Charlotte, by P. E. Stroehling

V

Profane and Sacred

To play Macheath was the height of my ambition.
Michael Kelly

I did think I did see all Heaven before me, and the great
God himself!
George Frederick Handel

On February 15, 1728, John Gay wrote in high excitement to
his friend, the redoubtable Dean of St. Patrick's in Dublin,
Jonathan Swift:

I have deferred writing to you from time to time till I could give
you an account of the Beggar's Opera. It is Acted at the Playhouse in Lincoln's Inn fields, with such success that the Playhouse hath been crowded every night; tonight is the fifteenth
time of Acting, and 'tis thought it will run a fortnight longer. I
have ordered Motte [a bookseller] to send the Play to you the
first opportunity. I made no interest either for approbation or
money nor hath anybody been pressed to take tickets for my
Benefit, notwithstanding which, I think I shall make an addition
to my fortune of between six and seven hundred pounds.

In fact, *The Beggar's Opera* ran for a record sixty-two nights, and John Rich, the theatrical manager who had spotted the potential in Gay's exuberant conflation, cleared almost £4,000. A *bon mot* was coined: *The Beggar's Opera* had made Gay rich and Rich gay; and, arguably, the first musical comedy had appeared on a London stage.

The première of *The Beggar's Opera* had been on January 29, three weeks before the first performance of George Frederick Handel's new opera, *Siroe*. Based on a libretto by Metastasio about Cyrus of Persia, it was a final effort by Handel to save the British Academy. This well-intentioned institution had been founded back in 1719 under the patronage of George I, who himself had contributed £1,000. The Duke of Newcastle and Lord Burlington were directors; John Jacob Heidegger was in charge of production, Giovanni Bononcini was lured away from Italy to compose operas for the music-lovers of London, and Handel left the opulence of Cannons, the Duke of Chandos's great house, for what was to prove one of the most disquieting periods of his life. At first all had gone well, and Handel's early *Radamisto* was a resounding success. But quarrels and dissension soon drowned the strains of music. The inflation and final bursting of the South Sea Bubble turned the public's attention away from opera; Bononcini was unmasked as a ruthless borrower of other composers' airs; Heidegger began to concentrate on the production of masquerades; George wished to be amused rather than uplifted. True, there was the occasional flash of Handelian brilliance, in *Tamerlane* and *Admeto*, both considerable successes, but the Academy was finally torn asunder by the great rivalry between the two sopranos, Cuzzoni and Faustina Bordoni. *Siroe* was Handel's last fling on behalf of the Academy, and it was a failure. London was tired of serious opera, it wanted to be entertained. *The Beggar's Opera* ideally caught the mood of the moment, and Handel's next work, *Tolomeo*, was virtually ignored. It was not the last time that the seemingly disparate talents of Gay and Handel were to be involved.

The Beggar's Opera was the talk of the town, though few could have expected such a triumph. Swift had suggested the theme as long ago as 1716, as Alexander Pope recorded:

Dr. Swift had been observing once to Mr. Gay, what an odd pretty sort of thing a Newgate Pastoral might make. Gay was inclined to try at such a thing for some time, but afterwards thought it would be better to write a comedy on the same plan. This was what gave rise to "The Beggar's Opera." He began on it, and when first he mentioned it to Swift, The Doctor did not much like the project. As he carried it on, he showed what he wrote to both of us; and we now and then gave a correction, or a word or two of advice; but it was wholly of his own writing. When it was done neither of us thought it would succeed. We showed it to Congreve, who, after reading it over, said: "It would either take greatly or be damned confoundedly."

The Duke of Queensberry voiced a similar, unhelpful opinion: "This play is either a very good thing or a very bad thing."

With hindsight, it is easy enough to account for the instant impression made by *The Beggar's Opera*. Here was something totally original. It had political satire, aimed in the main at Walpole. It had some distinctly proletarian and ignoble, nevertheless romantic characters in Captain Macheath, the dashing highwayman, Polly Peachum, Lockit, and assorted prostitutes and pickpockets: analysed seriously, they were all thoroughly reprehensible, but Gay invested them with such simple charm, even sentimentality, that they rose above the squalid atmosphere of thieves' kitchen or Newgate. It had some very good tunes, plundered from any number of sources, not only traditional airs, but Purcell, Jeremiah Clarke, Bononcini, Pepusch, Henry Carey, even Frescobaldi, and, ironically, poor Handel himself, who was enraged by the appearance of his grand march from *Rinaldo*. Above all, it had dash and colour and rather obvious humour, and no pretensions whatsoever. It set out to entertain, to coax the occasional tear or belly-laugh, to set the foot tapping. "Over the Hills and Far Away," "Lillibullero," "Green Sleeves" and the rest were hardly new-minted, but they became the popular song hits of the day. Colley Cibber was perhaps nearest the truth when he commented that "Gay had more skilfully gratified the public taste than all the brightest authors that ever wrote before him." And it was Cibber who had refused to mount it at Drury Lane.

Inevitably, *The Beggar's Opera* was attacked by the more sober element. Dr. Herring, a future Archbishop of Canterbury, denounced it from the pulpit, castigating Gay for his choice of hero. In Herring's view, Macheath was nothing better than a vicious criminal, and the fact that he actually got away with it compounded Gay's lack of morals a thousandfold. The magistrature was equally jaundiced and continued to criticise and condemn for decades to come. As late as 1776, a year which saw rather more crucial events, Sir John Hawkins, acting in the full majesty of Chairman of the Middlesex Justices, pontificated: "Rapine and violence have been gradually increasing since its first representation."

Dr. Johnson, as might be expected, took a saner line:

The play, like many others, was plainly written only to divert, without any moral purpose, and is therefore likely to do good; nor can it be conceived, without more speculation than life requires or admits, to be productive of much wit. Highwaymen and housebreakers seldom frequent the playhouse or mingle in any elegant diversion; nor is it possible for anyone to imagine that he may rob as safely because he sees Macheath reprieved upon the stage.

Swift took up an even more radical standpoint. He wrote in the *Intelligencer:*

He has, by a turn of humour entirely new, placed vices of all kinds in the strongest and most odious light, and thereby done eminent service, both to religion and morality. This appears from the unparalleled success he has met with. All ranks, parties, and denominations of men, either crowding to see his opera, or reading it with delight in their closets; even Ministers of State, whom he is thought to have most offended (next to those whom the actors represented) appear frequently at the theatre, from a consciousness of their own innocence, and to convince the world how unjust a parallel, malice, envy, and disaffection to the Government have made.

The Dean of St. Patrick's' special pleading could not countenance a word of criticism levelled against John Gay's strict moral sense:

In this performance, all the characters are just, and none of them carried beyond nature, or hardly beyond practice. It discovers the whole system of that commonwealth, or that *imperium in imperio* of iniquity established among us, by which neither our lives nor our properties are secure, either in the highways, or in public assemblies, or even in our own houses. It shows the miserable lives, and the constant fate, of those abandoned wretches: for how little they sell their lives and souls; betrayed by their whores, their comrades, and the receivers and purchasers of those thefts and robberies. This comedy contains likewise a satire, which, without enquiring whether it affects the present age, may possibly be useful in times to come; I mean, where the author takes the occasion of comparing the common robbers of the public, and their various stratagems of betraying, undermining and hanging each other, to the several arts of the politicians in times of corruption.

It is doubtful whether Gay himself would have shared Swift's view of *The Beggar's Opera* as "this excellent moral performance," and the general public did not care a fig. Questions of moral uplift did not seem particularly germane; they simply went along to Lincoln's Inn fields to enjoy themselves. The reputations of Walker, the first Macheath, and of Lavinia Fenton, who played Polly Peachum, were established, and the latter went on to marry the Duke of Bolton. The opera was staged throughout the country, as the editor of the 1760 edition of Gay's plays noted:

The famous "Beggar's Opera" appeared upon the stage early in the ensuing season; and was received with greater applause than was ever known . . . It spread into all the great towns of England; was played in many places to the thirtieth and fortieth time; and at Bath and Bristol fifty times . . . The ladies carried about with them the favourite songs of it in fans, and houses were furnished with it in screens . . . Furthermore, it drove out of England, for that season, the Italian opera, which had carried all before it for several years.

John Gay, whom the success of *The Beggar's Opera* compensated for years of comparative obscurity, decided to do what so many other writers, basking in the glow of sudden fame, have done and will continue to do. He wrote a sequel. It is almost always an unwise departure, and in Gay's case it was doubly so. The plot of *Polly* can only be called a farrago. Macheath has been transported to America, but he escapes and becomes a pirate chief, having first sensibly acquired a new name and a new, black, face. Polly, who has landed in America, hoping to find her lost love, is entrapped by a procuress, sold to a rich merchant (Walpole again, thinly disguised), and helped to escape *en travesti*. Of course, she is then captured by the pirates, and of course she and Macheath do not recognise each other. The pirates are engaged in attacking the English settlers, who are being helped by the Red Indians, the epitome of a bunch of noble savages. Polly ends by capturing Macheath, who is executed, and she has to console herself with the Indian prince.

In spite of such a muddled scenario, John Rich planned to produce *Polly*, again at Lincoln's Inn fields, but the Lord Chamberlain had other ideas. On December 12, 1728, Gay was advised that *Polly* "was not allowed to be acted, but commanded to be suppressed." There was an uproar at court. The Duchess of Queensberry badgered and bullied George II to such an extent that she was forbidden to show her face. She did not mince her words in her reply—"The Duchess of Queensberry is surprised and well pleased that the King hath given her so agreeable a command as to stay from Court, where she never came for diversion, but to bestow a great civility on the King and Queen"—and she and the Duke departed for Scotland. It was a grand gesture which did nothing to assist Gay. He had always relied on court preferment, though he had usually bitten the royal hand that fed him, and now he was as good as banished. *Polly* was published and ran through two editions, Gay receiving about £1,200, but it was not produced on the stage (and then in a bowdlerised version) until 1777, when its *réclame* had long since subsided.

Arbuthnot wrote sadly but acutely to Swift: "There is certainly a fatality upon poor Gay. As for hope of preferment, he has laid it aside . . . I have begged Gay not to buy an annuity upon my life; I am sure I should not live a week." Gay himself survived less than four years, dying on December 4, 1732, at Queensberry's house in Burlington Gardens. He was buried in Westminster Abbey two days before Christmas. He was only forty-seven, and without the *succès de scandale* and *d'estime* of *The Beggar's Opera* would have been totally forgotten.

By a curious irony of fate, it can be maintained that if *The Beggar's Opera* had not been such an astonishing success—so much so that Colley Cibber's daughter-in-law, as singers and actresses so often do during a long run, became bored with the role of Polly Peachum—Handel's greatest masterpiece, *Messiah*, might never have become England's favourite oratorio, indeed Handel might have returned to Germany. In the years following the failure of *Siroe* and *Tolomeo*, Handel remained faithful to opera, but there was a change in him, perhaps caused or at least influenced by the death of his mother, the only woman he ever loved or understood. James Quin, the fiery Irish actor who had refused the role of Macheath in the first production of *The Beggar's Opera*, advised him against excessive melancholy, and to inject some comedy into his pieces, but Handel paid no attention. Instead, a series of interconnected events ushered in a new phase in his thoughts on composition.

Years before, when Handel was acting the part of court musician at Cannons, he had staged a masque called *Haman and Mordecai*. This was now revived and made an immediate impression. Lord Egmont heard it at the Music Club and was impressed: "This oratorio of religious opera is exceedingly fine, and the company was highly pleased." The choirboys from the King's Chapel sang superbly, and both Pope's text and Handel's music were much admired. Handel decided to produce it for the theatre, and promptly brought down a storm of controversy upon his head. Many people thought it the height of impiety to represent such a religious theme in the licentious atmosphere of the theatre, and the Bishop of London banned the performance. Unfortunately, the Bishop was also Dean of the Chapel Royal, so that the choir boys who had sung at the Music Club were withdrawn.

Handel reacted by commissioning additional text from Samuel Humphreys, converting the original one act divided into six scenes into a full-length work, and renaming it *Esther*. It was produced at the King's Theatre on May 2, 1732, without costumes, scenery or indeed any action on the stage. Four days later, the Royal Family attended a performance. The first oratorio was launched.

Though the occasional opera continued to come from Handel's pen, he now concentrated in the main on this new musical genre. *Deborah*, again with a text by Humphreys, followed in March 1733, and Lord Egmont pronounced it magnificent. The Royal Family, with the exception of the Prince of Wales, who had taken against Handel for the unadmirable but understandable reason that his father favoured him, came to the first performance, but *Deborah* was not the great success it seemed. Handel, dragged willy-nilly into the quarrel between the King and his son Frederick, pilloried in the press for having raised the price of admittance to *Deborah* to unprecedented heights, and facing financial disaster, abandoned London for the calmer atmosphere of Oxford. There he produced his new oratorio, *Athalia*, and prepared an opera on the subject of Ariadne to a libretto by Colman. But he could not withstand the political pressures. The Prince of Wales had decided that Niccola Porpora should be the new leader of London's musical scene, and Porpora's *Ariadne* appeared two months before Handel's treatment. Frederick's faction crowded the theatre at Linclon's Inn, while King George and Queen Caroline, loyal to Handel, sat rather sadly in their box at the King's Theatre. Handel lost the struggle, and was forced to give up the lease on the King's Theatre to his creditors. Amazingly, he moved to the theatre at Lincoln's Inn and to the management of John Rich, who had first produced *The Beggar's Opera*, and then to Rich's new theatre at Covent Garden.

Between 1734 and 1741, Handel was in a state of almost permanent dejection. *Ariodante* and *Alcina* were produced, the oratorio *Alexander's Feast* marked the professional début of the tenor John Beard, *Atalanta* was composed for the Prince of Wales's marriage, *Giustino*, *Arminio* and *Berenice* came and went. Handel was in debt, his right side was partially paralysed, his great supporter, Queen Caroline, died. But his brilliance seemed undimmed. 1738 saw both *Saul* and *Israel in Egypt*; 1739, the setting to music of Dryden's *Ode for St. Cecilia's Day* and Handel's version of Milton's *L'Allegro*. But his two final operas, *Imeneo* and *Deidamia*, were failures, and London now virtually ignored him. He had a few friends—in particular, Mrs. Cibber and Sir Hans Sloane—but he was not far short of becoming a recluse. Then, apparently at the lowest ebb of his life, came *Messiah*.

In 1741, Charles Jennens sent Handel selected passages from the Bible which he considered an ideal basis for an oratorio. Jennens had collaborated with Handel before, in *Saul* and *L'Allegro*. He was a most peculiar man: conceited, ostentatious, irritable and spendthrift. Dr. Johnson did not care for him, describing him as:

a vain fool crazed by his wealth, who, were he in Heaven, would criticize the Lord Almighty; who lives surrounded by all the luxuries of an Eastern potentate—verily an English "Solyman the Magnificent"; who never walks abroad without a train of footmen at his heels, and, like Wolsey, with a scented sponge 'neath his nose, lest the breath of the vulgar herd should contaminate his sacred person.

Jennens considered himself far superior in talent and wit to Handel. He wrote to Lord Guernsey in 1738:

Mr. Handel's head is more full of maggots than ever. I found yesterday in his room a very queer instrument which he calls carillon (Anglice, a bell) and says some call it a Tubalcain, I suppose because it is both in the make and tone like a set of Hammers striking upon anvils . . . His second maggot is an organ of £500 price . . . His third maggot is a Hallelujah which he has trump'd up at the end of his oratorio [*Saul*] since I went into the Country, because he thought the conclusion of the Oratorio not Grand enough; tho' if that were the case 'twas his own fault, for the words would have bore as Grand Musick as he could have set 'em to: but this Hallelujah, Grand as it is, comes in very nonsensically, having no manner of relation to what goes before . . . I could tell you more of his maggots: but it grows late and I must defer the rest till I write next, by which time, I doubt not, more new ones will breed in his Brain.

According to Jennens, Handel was a slightly crazed, workmanlike composer, blessed with the opportunity of setting to music Jennens's superb texts, which admittedly owed something to the Bible and Milton but were even so masterpieces in their own right. On the subject of *Messiah* he had no doubts where the fullest credit should lie: "He has made a fine entertainment of it, tho' not near so good as he might and ought to have done. I have with great difficulty made him correct some of the grossest faults in the composition." Handel, more generous, in a letter to Jennens, referred to "your Oratorio *Messiah*."

Jennens delivered the text of *Messiah* to Handel in his house in Brook Street during the summer of 1741. The whole musical score was completed in the astonishingly short time of twenty-four days. Handel was totally enthralled. Newman

Flower, in his biography of Handel, tries to describe his probable state of mind:

It was the achievement of a giant inspired—the work of one who, by some extraordinary mental feat, had drawn himself completely out of the world, so that he dwelt—or believed he dwelt —in the pastures of God. What happened was that Handel passed through a superb dream. He was unconscious of the world during that time, unconscious of its press and call; his whole mind was in a trance.

It was when Handel had finished the second part of the oratorio, containing the Hallelujah Chorus, that, tears in his eyes, he made his passionate exclamation about seeing all Heaven before him.

Messiah was finished on September 14 . . . and Handel put it away in a drawer, so that he could concentrate on *Samson*, his next oratorio. He was in no mood to offer it to London. Then he received an invitation. The Lord-Lieutenant of Ireland and the governors of three charitable institutions in Dublin wrote suggesting that he should visit that city. Handel accepted, and he took *Messiah* with him. He also took Mrs. Cibber. Susanna Maria was the daughter of a Covent Garden furniture-maker and the sister of Thomas Arne the composer. She had first caught the public's attention in a pirated version of Handel's *Acis and Galatea* but had later become his firm friend. Her marriage to Colley Cibber's appalling son Theophilus had been a disaster, and she was determined never to sing the, to her, hackneyed role of Polly Peachum in *The Beggar's Opera* at Covent Garden again. Handel's invitation to Dublin was also a godsend to her.

Suddenly, everything seemed to be proceeding splendidly. William Neal, a music publisher and secretary of the Charities' Commission, also possessed a music-hall, recently built, in Fishamble Street, and Handel rushed between this and the house he had taken in Abbey Street. But although the Dublin press was flattering, there was some doubt in his mind over whether the Irish public would be equally welcoming. It was decided that Mrs. Cibber should test the climate of opinion by appearing in a play called *The Conscious Lovers*. She was an instant success.

The Handel season opened just before Christmas with a performance of *L'Allegro*, and this was followed by *Alexander's Feast* and *Imeneo*. Handel wrote in ecstacy to Jennens: "The music sounds delightfully in this charming Room, which puts me in such excellent Spirits (and my health being so good) that I exert myself on the Organ with more than usual success." The horrors of London were forgotten, but still there was no mention of *Messiah*. Then, in March 1742 the announcement was made: the first performance of Handel's new oratorio would be on April 13; gentlemen wishing to attend were requested to leave their swords at home, and ladies not to don hoops.

It was a triumph for Handel, and for Mrs. Cibber, who sang with great simplicity and consequent effect. Dibdin described the impression given by her voice: "She was deliciously captivating. She knew nothing in singing or in nature but sweetness and simplicity. She sang exquisitely, as a bird does, her notes conveyed involuntary pleasure and indefinable delight." In *Messiah*, she added radiance, even a touch of tragedy. She repeated her performance on June 3, and again, in spite of the exceptionally hot weather, there was no doubt that *Messiah* was Handel's masterpiece.

He left for London in August. *Samson* was performed, to great applause, in February, 1743, but *Messiah* was a comparative failure, being played only three times that year. Again there were arguments over the suitability of a sacred oratorio being played in a theatre, although George II had no doubts in his mind. He was so moved during the Hallelujah Chorus that he remained standing until the final note, and because no one could sit while the monarch stood, the entire audience rose to its feet. Thus, a tradition was born.

Messiah was performed twice in 1745, and then not until 1749. In 1750, Handel started the practice of producing the oratorio once a year in aid of Captain Coram's Foundling Hospital, of which the composer was a governor. The final performance of *Messiah* in Handel's lifetime was at Covent Garden on April 6, 1759. A week later, he was dead, at the age of seventy-four. He was buried in Westminster Abbey, having left £600 in his will for a suitable monument. The funeral service drew 3,000 people and was conducted with great pomp and ceremony. Croft's funeral anthem was sung by the combined choirs of the King's Chapels Royal, St. Paul's and Westminster Abbey. They should have sung at least one chorus from *Messiah*.

The careers of both Gay and Handel were materially affected by the attitudes of the court. George I had given Handel his first important post at Herrenhausen, and had been one of the prime movers behind the Royal Academy of Music. George II also extended his patronage, though he later withdrew it when Handel's star seemed no longer in the ascendant. Frederick, Prince of Wales, tried to ruin Handel, simply as a move to further his quarrel with his father; and Handel acted as music master to George II's daughters. George III, in 1776, was to inaugurate the "Concerts of Ancient Music" and to insist on an annual performance of *Messiah*, as well as frequent celebrations of a great part of Handel's musical output.

Gay, too, had been taken up by George and Caroline when, after the former's quarrel with *his* father, they set up a rival establishment in Leicester Fields, and had always depended to a great degree on royal patronage. And he, too, finally received proof of Hanoverian fickleness after the banning of *Polly*. He was credited, on no very firm evidence, with one sharp riposte. When Colley Cibber was made Poet Laureate, an anonymous burlesque, "Ode for the New Year," was published. It attacked George II and included some sharp lines on Queen Caroline's supposed misconduct with Sir Robert Walpole:

> O may she always meet success
> In every scheme and job,
> And still continue to caress
> That honest statesman Bob.

It was well known that Gay had hoped to become Poet Laureate himself, and his enmity for Walpole was an all-absorbing cancer in his soul. The lampoon came too late; Gay's value to the court had long ceased.

Gay and Handel dominated long periods during the second quarter of the eighteenth century, and their careers crossed in surprising, often ironic ways. Gay, in producing *The Beggar's Opera*, the first popular musical, had a few years of adulation and success which fizzled out sadly like one of the spent rockets in the background of Handel's "Music for the Royal Fireworks." Handel, in producing *Messiah*, the first popular oratorio, was reprieved like Gay's Macheath in the eyes of the public only in his last years. But the real similarity between *The Beggar's Opera* and *Messiah*, as different as two works of music can be, is that they remain relevant two and a half centuries after their composition.

VI

Dettingen

Our noble generals played their parts,
Our soldiers fought like thunder,
Prince William too, that valiant heart
In fight performed wonders.
Though through the leg with bullet shot
The Prince his wound regarded not,
But still maintained his post and fought
For glorious George of England.
Contemporary Broadsheet

The battle of Dettingen, which was to be suitably celebrated by Handel in his *Te Deum*, is a curiosity of military and political history. It was the last time that a reigning British monarch appeared on the battlefield and actually took part in the action; and it was fought by the opposing British and French armies, whose respective countries did not consider themselves to be in a state of war. Although the first eccentricity has preserved the name of Dettingen, it is the second which is the more important, and which requires elaboration.

The first half of the eighteenth century was dominated by a series of extremely complex diplomatic crises, all hinging on the successions to various thrones. Already, in 1718, the attenuated blood of the Spanish Habsburgs had run dry, and the wretched Charles XII had bequeathed to his mediaeval nation a French king and a European war, neither of which the Spanish either desired or understood. Fifteen years later, the War of the Polish Succession had broken out and been waged for two years until the abdication of Stanislaus Leszczynski and the recognition of Augustus III. Finally in 1740, the very same year which saw the accessions of Frederick the Great in Prussia and of the Empress Anne in Russia, the Emperor Charles VI of Austria died. Europe had waited for this moment for twenty years.

The real seed of the War of the Austrian Succession was sown in 1703. The Emperor Leopold I, realising that the Austrian Hapsburgs, like their Spanish cousins, were threatened by an absence of male heirs, promulgated a remarkable pact, allowing for female heirs to succeed, with the daughters of the Archduke Joseph taking precedence over the daughters of the Archduke Charles. In 1711, Charles became Emperor on his brother's death, and promptly drew up what came to be called the Pragmatic Sanction, words which were to feature in documents of state and diplomatic *aides-mémoire* for decades. The Sanction, basically a secret family agreement, overturned Leopold's pact and gave precedence to Charles's daughters over Joseph's. It also laid down for the first time the principle of the indivisibility of the Hapsburg possessions. In due course, the Emperor Charles persuaded his two nieces, Maria Josepha and Maria Amalia, to renounce their claims to the succession on their respective marriages to the Elector of Saxony and the Elector Charles of Bavaria.

But the Emperor did not cease there. Slowly, he gathered acknowledgment of the validity of the Pragmatic Sanction throughout his Empire. The Estates of Upper and Lower Austria gave formal recognition in 1720, Hungary followed

two years later, and the Austrian Netherlands in 1724. Philip
V of Spain was the first non-Habsburg European ruler to
recognise the Sanction. Russia followed suit in 1726, and in
the same year Prussia, Mainz and the Electorates of Bavaria,
Cologne, the Palatinate and Trier. For the next twelve years
the Emperor Charles struggled desperately to assure the succession for his daughter Maria Theresa. The participants in
the baffling game of European political chess came and went;
new alliances were formed and broken asunder; Spain de-
fected; Denmark joined the guarantors; the Elector of Bavaria and the Elector Palatine considered themselves absolved
from supporting the Sanction by Philip of Spain's action;
Robert Walpole promised England's adherence to Maria
Theresa's succession; the Elector of Saxony was bought off
with the throne of Poland.

The Pragmatic Sanction had become the Emperor's *idée
fixe*, the future for which he was prepared to mortgage the
present. Austria lost the Two Sicilies to Spain, and Lorraine
to France; Francis of Lorraine had to be bought off with
Tuscany and the hand of Maria Theresa; the Austrian exchequer suffered from protracted war and loss of trade. But, in
1739, Charles VI appeared to have gained his objective.
France, Sardinia, Spain and Naples all acceded to the Pragmatic Sanction. The following year, the Emperor died. The
country was near bankruptcy, the army was thin on the
ground and lacking both effective commanders and morale.
This was the parlous state of affairs which Maria Theresa
inherited. Within a few months, Frederick of Prussia had in-
vaded Silesia and, the following April, he crushed the Austrian army at Mollwitz. Suddenly, the guarantors to the Pragmatic Sanction were becoming forgetful of their assurances.
The German principalities saw easy pickings in the offing,
and the Elector of Bavaria had a glorious vision of himself as
Emperor. France sided with Bavaria; Hanover, and therefore
England, supported Maria Theresa. Walpole persuaded Parliament to donate £300,000 to Maria Theresa's depleted

treasury, and to place an army of 12,000 at her disposal. Within months, Walpole had been hounded from office.

England's position was humiliating. While the Bavarian army with their French "auxiliaries" were marching on Vienna, George II was forced to declare Hanoverian neutrality for one year. Silesia had been ceded to Prussia, and Frederick was already preparing to break the peace treaty whenever the opportunity arose. Prague had fallen. The whole of Bohemia, let alone Vienna itself, lay at risk. Then, amazingly, the Bavarians faltered. Vienna was saved, and the Hungarian irregulars whom Maria Theresa had summoned so dramatically to her cause swept into Bavaria. Linz and Munich were capitulating just as Charles of Bavaria was forcing his election as Emperor on the Diet at Frankfurt. His was a hollow crown.

During the winter of 1742–43, the Maréchal de Belleisle was forced to retreat from Prague, and there were Austrian successes in Italy. Then, in February 1743, George II and his Pragmatic Army moved at last. The new administration in Whitehall, nominally headed by Lord Wilmington, but effectively dominated by Lord Carteret and Henry Pelham, had dispatched an army of 16,000 men to Flanders in May 1742, but George II maintained the fiction that England and France were not at war. The commander of the Pragmatic Army, Lord Stair, counselled an attack on Dunkirk, but George would have none of it. Stair himself, now nearing seventy, had never faced such frustrations before. His military career stretched back to the battle of Steenkirk, and he had fought in Marlborough's four great battles, and had learned the art of war from the Duke and his great ally Eugene of Savoy. Stair was not a man given to foolhardiness or excess of bravado, and his plans were well considered and had the enthusiastic support of Carteret at the Foreign Office. Unfortunately he had to contend with the indecisiveness of his King, the obstruction of the Austrian general, d'Aremberg, who had arrived with some 12,000 troops, and the caution of General Wade, who was appalled by the plan to defeat the French at Dunkirk and then move rapidly on Paris.

The morale of Stair's men was at a low ebb. Provisions and equipment were at a premium, and the prolonged inactivity during a bitterly cold winter led to a breakdown in discipline which was harshly dealt with. The 16,000 Hanoverians gave a more solid aspect to the mixed army. One contemporary historian spoke with approbation:

The Hanoverians are proportionable well-bodied men, and extraordinary good soldiers, bearing the most severe shock with all the calmness imaginable, seldom the least disorder to be perceived in their ranks; they march with as little concern to action, as if they were going to a banquet, and generally smoke tobacco, which is their common maxim in all intervals through an engagement; they are of the Reformed Religion, and appear very devout, being seldom addicted to any profaneness, and have commonly prayers at the head of their lines twice a day, and sing hymns as they march to action; which intimates, that good Christians seldom fail of being good soldiers.

Finally, in February 1743, George agreed to move out of Flanders. The decision came none too soon. During Walpole's long peace Ministry, the English army had lost much of its *esprit de corps*. Officers felt that they could come and go as they pleased; Parliament might be sitting, or their country estates might require inspection. Stair wrote to Carteret in February: "I thought it hard to refuse them leave, when they said that their preferment depended on the interest of their friends at Court. They had no notion that it depended on their exertions here." Stair, remembering a very different approach in Marlborough's officers, was reduced to empty sarcasm.

· Slowly, very slowly, the Pragmatic Army moved towards the Rhine. By May 6, now joined by the cavalry which had ridden out from Brussels and with the shortage of provisions

even more acute, Stair had set up his headquarters on the
north bank of the river Main. The French army, led by the
Maréchal Duc de Noailles, was established near Spires on the
Upper Rhine, and Stair was certain in his own mind that he
must cross the Main and threaten the French without delay.
He eventually persuaded d'Aremberg of the wisdom of this
plan, and his troops began the passage of the Main on June 3.
But it was all to no avail. D'Aremberg took fright and withdrew the entire body of Austrian dragoons; Noailles refused
to give battle; and, worst of all, George, who had arrived in
Hanover two weeks before, sent a stream of anguished des-
patches, advising extreme caution, and ordering Stair to return across the Main.

Stair was appalled. He wrote despairingly to Carteret:

I am too careful of the King's interest to be rash, but I am sure of
two things, that the French are far more occupied with Bavaria
than with us, and that we are superior to them even in numbers.
The importance of giving an army to a person who is trusted is
now evident. Had my plan been followed, we should now be in a
position to fall on the head of the French army which, after
sending away a detachment to Bavaria, is now taking post along
the Rhine.

Stair went so far as to ignore George's appeals, but eventually, when it was clear that Noailles was in no mood for a
battle, he admitted defeat and repassed the Main. He had at
least made his point.

George arrived on June 19 to take command of the army,
and reviewed the English and Hanoverian troops centred on
Aschaffenburg; he studiously avoided Stair, preferring to
consult his Hanoverian officers. The position of the Pragmatic Army was highly dangerous. Noailles controlled the
supply routes from Franconia, and had thrown two bridges
across the Main at Seligenstadt. In the firm knowledge that,
sooner rather than later, Stair must retreat to his magazines at
Hanau, Noailles also established five batteries on the bank of

the Main, and sent a strong force of 20,000 under Gramont to confront the retreating army at Dettingen. Major Richard Davenport, for one, was glad that the period of fruitless inactivity was at an end. On June 22, he had written to his brother:

The outguards of each side have sometimes fired at one another across the river but there have not been above two or three of our people killed, and, I am told, about a dozen of theirs—most of which are hussars, who are very impudent fellows and will venture anywhere in search of plunder . . . I have slept three nights upon the ground, rolled up in my cloak without any covering except the sky, and my skin, or rather my hide—which is well tanned, has been wet with the dew of heaven, yet am I as well as ever I was, as—unluckily—are all my senior officers.

But now they were on the move. Even George's equipage of 13 Berlins, 35 wagons, 54 carts, and 662 horses was in retreat.

Gramont waited at Dettingen, ready to fall upon Stair's army as they crossed the bridge to Hanau, while Noailles himself concentrated on the flank and rear. Soon, as Fortescue says,

these troops were to block the Allies to the south, impenetrable woods shut them off from the east, the Main barred their way on the west, and Gramont stood before them at Dettingen on the north. Noailles had caught them, as he said, in a mousetrap, and might reasonably feel certain that they could not escape.

Major Davenport describes the prelude to the battle:

The day before yesterday [he was writing on June 29], we decamped in the night and marched towards Frankfurt, but were attacked by the French near Dettingen, a little village upon the river, where the pass between the river and a thick wood was not more than cannon shot across. The French had passed the river in the night, to the number, as is believed, of 30,000, and began to cannonade us, both from the other side of the water, upon our left flank and from a battery of thirteen 12-pounders in our front, and had placed a great body of infantry in the wood upon our right, all which poured a vast fire on us for above three hours.

There was considerable confusion in the allied army. The baggage wagons had to be manoeuvred out of the line of battle, the artillery took an unconscionable time coming into action, the interminable marching and counter-marching of eighteenth-century warfare proceeded as if everyone was on the parade ground. George himself was in a state of choleric excitement, prancing around on horseback and getting in the way of his frantic staff officers.

Just before noon, the allied army was at last ready for battle. Noailles's opportunity had passed. Gramont had flagrantly disobeyed orders and advanced without any clear idea of what he should do in his new position. Noailles himself was so thunderstruck by his carefully conceived plans now lying in ruins that he seemed incapable of improvisation. And the appallingly low standard of competence among the French officers revealed itself only too clearly.

As the English troops advanced, they gave a cheer, which appeared to disconcert the French still further. William Biggs, in his history of the war, commented somewhat grandiosely:

It is a general maxim with the British troops, when they enter an action, to begin with a huzza, as it has a great effect on animal spirits, especially that of soldiers in action, who always catch their courage or panic one from another, the sympathetic warmth or coldness of spirit running through their blood like wildfire, which either sinks or bears them with a kind of prophetic force to victory.

Still more effective was the accuracy of the musketry volleys. The French were quite unprepared. So, too, was King George. His horse bolted with him, and his increasingly nervous staff officers witnessed the extraordinary sight of the

short, purple-faced, pop-eyed, panting monarch disappearing
to the rear like an irate grampus at the gallop. His horse was
finally mastered, and George returned to the fray quite un-
perturbed. One eye-witness, Cornet Kendal, later recorded
his memory of the royal Hanoverian warrior:

The French fired at His Majesty from a battery of twelve cannon, but levelled too high. I saw the balls go within half a yard
of his head. The Duke d'Aremberg desired him to go out of danger; he answered, "Don't tell me of danger; I'll be even with
them!" He is certainly the boldest man I ever saw.

The French got into the corner of a wood to flank our right.
The King then drew his sword and ordered the Hanoverian
horse and foot, and some English, through the wood, and rode
about like a lion. He drew them up in line of battle himself, ordered six cannon to the right, and bade them fire on the flank of
the French. He stood by till they fired; they did great execution
killing thirty or forty at a shot. Then he went to the foot and ordered them not to fire till the French came close and were about
one hundred yards distant. Then the French fired upon us
directly, and the shot flew again as thick as hail. Then the King
flourished his sword and said: "Now, boys, for the honour of
England; fire, and behave bravely and the French will soon run."

The French, however, seemed reluctant to run. Their superiority in cavalry was their chief weapon, and at one stage
of the fighting the allied left-wing was in great danger. The
3rd Dragoons, for instance, were outnumbered ten to one
and, after a third desperate charge, virtually ceased to exist.
Trooper Thomas Brown saw the last remaining regimental
standard lying on the ground, and prepared to dismount and
recover it, when, in Fortescue's words,

a French sabre came down on his bridle-hand and shore away
two of his fingers. His horse, missing the familiar pressure of the
bit, at once bolted, and before he could be pulled up had carried
his rider into the rear of the French lines. There Dragoon Brown

saw the standard of his regiment borne away in triumph by a French gendarme. Disabled as he was he rode straight at the Frenchman, attacked and killed him; and then gripping the standard between his leg and the saddle he turned and fought his way single-handed through the ranks of the enemy, emerging at last with three bullet-holes through his hat and seven wounds in his face and body, but with the standard safe.

Major Davenport confirmed that it was the allied cavalry which bore the brunt:

It was particularly the English Horse that was exposed to this fire, of which the Horse Guards formed the right, till our cannon coming up with the Austrians and some of our Foot and after about an hour and a half of incessant firing on both sides, the enemy fled in great confusion, leaving us the field of battle and nine pieces of cannon with several standards and colours. Their Maison du Roy have suffered more than any of their troops.

The French Black Musketeers made one last hopeless charge at the Royal Dragoons on the far right of the allied line, but they were decimated, and a clear way to the French infantry lay open. Perhaps wisely, they fled, in total disorder, made worse by the rout of the French Household Cavalry, which could not withstand the charge of the Scots Greys. Stair was eager to pursue the enemy over and beyond the Main, but George, by now completely winded, refused to press home the advantage. The battle of Dettingen was over. The French had lost up to 5,000 killed, wounded or taken prisoner; the allies half that. British losses were as low as 265 dead and 561 wounded.

George was elated. Not only had he taken a definite part in the action himself, but his son the Duke of Cumberland had distinguished himself. The latter's horse, too, had run away with him, but it had had the good grace to go forwards in the direction of the enemy. Cumberland had also performed an act of self-sacrifice:

His Royal Highness's generosity was no less conspicuous on this occasion than his courage; having found a French officer in the field covered with gore, whose bravery he had noted in the action, he ordered him to the surgeons, and had his wounds dressed before his own; this hero disregarded his own safety, to show how much he honoured valour in a foe, which is always the maxim of brave men, to manifest that generous spirit, when their adversaries are no longer capable of defending themselves.

The future General Wolfe, then acting adjutant of the 12th Foot, put it more succinctly: "He behaved as bravely as a man could do."

There were two final episodes, curiously contrasted. George decided to revive the old practice of creating knights banneret actually on the field of battle, and was evidently so overcome with emotion that he included a mass of people from Lord Stair to Trooper Thomas Brown. Then the wounded were left to the tender mercies of Noailles. Stair sent a trumpeter to the Marshal with a message peculiarly representative of an earlier age of chivalry,

that his Majesty having thought proper to remove to Hanau, he had left an independent company in the field to take care of the wounded, who were strictly forbid to commit any hostilities; that therefore the Marshal might send a detachment to bury their slain, and hoped he would treat with humanity those who were left behind.

Noailles appears to have abided by the request, and all the wounded were in due course removed to the French field hospitals.

It was a bizarre end to a curious episode in British military history. George's army was almost unbelievably lucky to carry the day. And the Warrior King certainly did not know how to capitalise on his success. The Pragmatic Army lay idle at Hanau until the beginning of August, and played almost no part in the war for the rest of the year. The War of the Austrian Succession was to drag on until peace was ratified at

Aix-la-Chapelle in March 1748. Fontenoy and Lauffeldt, the
deaths of Philip of Spain and Charles of Bavaria, Saxe's cap-
ture of Brussels and the Jacobite rising all lay in the future.

The news of Dettingen was greeted in London as if it were
another Blenheim. Stair was succeeded by the dilatory Wade
and vanished into retirement, but George II was welcomed
home as a true hero. Horace Walpole wrote:

I expect to be drunk with hogsheads of Mayne-water and with
odes to His Majesty and the Duke, and with Te Deums . . . We
are all mad—drums, trumpets, bumpers, bonfires! The mob are
wild and cry, "Long live King George and the Duke of Cumberland, and Lord Stair and Lord Carteret, and General Clayton
that's dead."

Never before had the Hanoverian dynasty been so popular.
Handel composed his Dettingen *Te Deum*, and a great many
versifiers composed a stream of deplorable rhyming rubbish.
Colley Cibber's ode was superior to most:

> Tho' rough Selingenstadt
> The harmony defeat,
> Tho' Klein Ostein
> The verse confound;
> Yet in the joyful strain
> Aschaffenburg or Dettingen
> Shall charm the ear they seem to wound.

Horace Walpole recorded George's return to London in
November:

He arrived at St. James's between five and six on Tuesday. We
were in great fears of his coming through the city after the trea-
son that has been publishing for these two months; but it is incredible how well his reception was beyond what it had ever
been before: in short, you would have thought that it had not
been a week after the victory at Dettingen. They almost carried
him into the palace on their shoulders; and at night the whole
town was illuminated and bonfired. He looks much better than
he has for these five years, and is in great spirits.

The great British public enjoys a victory as much as anyone, and they had had nothing to celebrate since the end of the Marlborough wars. They did not care that Dettingen was little more than a fierce skirmish on the fringe of the real war, a skirmish which should have been lost, a skirmish which led to nothing. But the bells pealed out, and they rejoiced.

Part Three

GEORGE III
1738–1820; King, 1760–1820

He has a kind of unhappiness in his temper, which, if it not be conquered before it has taken too deep a root will be a source of frequent anxiety. When ever he is displeased, his anger does not break out with heat and violence; but he becomes sullen and silent and retires to his closet.

Lord Waldegrave

A better farmer ne'er brushed dew from lawn,
A worse king never left a realm undone.

Lord Byron

His attention was ever awake to all the occurrences of government. Not a step was taken in foreign, colonial or domestic affairs, that he did not form his own opinions upon it, and exercise his influence over it . . . on all, his opinion is pronounced decisively; on all his will is declared peremptorily.

Lord Brougham

He has no heroic strain, but loves peace, and has no turn for extravagance; modest, and has no tendency to vice, and has as yet very virtuous principles; has the greatest temptation to gallant with the ladies, who lay themselves out in the most shameful manner to draw him, but to no purpose.

George Lewis Scott

Though God knows I always adored my dear, dear Father, yet his sore illness has endeared him to us beyond the power of expression; his health is *our only object;* life indeed would be a burthen to us poor Girls without him.

Princess Sophia

VII

The Royal Brood

The damnedst millstone about the neck of any Government that can be imagined.

The Duke of Wellington

I am like poor Lear, but thank God I have no Regan, no Goneril, only three Cordelias.

George III

It is difficult to keep a sense of proportion when considering the children of George III and Queen Charlotte. Both in number and in notoriety, they have a somewhat overwhelming quality. In an age when sexual peccadilloes were the norm rather than the exception, they scandalised or titillated society, depending on the moral sensibilities of the observer. Their niece, Princess Victoria, when she came to the throne in 1837, determined to clean the Augean stables so amply filled by her uncles, and whatever reputation for kindness, or generosity or intellectual patronage which they might once have possessed, was overwhelmed by the record of dissipation, both venereal and financial. It is perhaps not surprising that their characters were less black than their copious detractors have made out. It is even more probable that their characters were deeply affected by their environment and by their upbringing.

George, later George IV, was born in 1762; Frederick, Duke of York, in 1763; William, Duke of Clarence, later to be William IV, in 1765; Charlotte in 1766; Edward, Duke of Kent, in 1767; Augusta in 1768; Elizabeth in 1770; Ernest, Duke of Cumberland, and later King of Hanover, in 1771; Augustus, Duke of Sussex, in 1773; Adolphus, Duke of Cambridge, in 1774; Mary in 1776; Sophia in 1777; Octavius in 1779; Alfred in 1780; and Amelia in 1783—fifteen children altogether were born to King George and Queen Charlotte within the space of twenty-one years. George III himself had had four brothers and four sisters. The Hanoverian dynasty seemed intent on establishing a complicated and huge network of marriages and intermarriages. Ironically, this was not to be the case. It would be left to Queen Victoria to set herself at the epicentre of the European royal marriage market.

Of George III's fifteen children, only the last three were to die in infancy or at a comparatively early age: Octavius in 1783, Alfred in 1782, and Amelia in 1810. The remaining twelve, with the exception of the Duke of Kent, who died in 1820, reached their sixties, and a high proportion their seventies. The Duke of Cambridge lived on until 1850, the Duke of Cumberland to 1851, and Princess Mary, a relic of a bygone age, did not die until 1857. The men survived in spite of lechery, and the women in spite of boredom.

George III was consumed with a desire for morality. Two of his brothers, the Duke of Gloucester and the Duke of Cumberland, had entered upon highly unsuitable marriages. Edward, Duke of York, died in Monaco of, according to Horace Walpole, "a putrid and irresistible fever." And Princess Caroline Matilda, who had been forced to marry the mad Christian VII of Denmark, sought solace with a German doctor. Even George himself had felt youthful stirrings of pas-

sion in the direction of Sarah Lennox, and perhaps his deep
devotion for the handsome and elegant Lord Bute was not entirely platonic.

But all this was now behind him. He was married to an ir-
reproachably respectable German princess, and he was determined that his ever-increasing family should be close-knit,
content, and above suspicion. He went further. Appalled by
the reprehensible behaviour of his brothers, he planned what
was to become the Royal Marriages Act. The Bill, which was
entrusted to Lord North, laid down stringent rules for
members of the Royal Family. No member of it could marry
without the consent of the King before the age of twenty-
five. If he or she were over twenty-five, and the King had refused his assent, the Privy Council and Parliament must be
advised of the Prince or Princess's intention a year before the
marriage could take place. The bill did not receive by any
means unanimous support—Charles James Fox deplored its
narrowness of vision—but North eventually ensured its passage into law. From 1772 onwards, therefore, any chance of
freedom of choice which George III's children might have
expected was totally dashed.

Such considerations, and the evil effects of the Royal Marriages Act, were, however, still in the future. First, the Princes and Princesses had to survive the rigours of childhood.
The King and Queen were particularly fond of Kew, and it
was there that their ideas on education and upbringing were
put into practice. The Queen took a strong interest in her
daughters, seeing that they were bathed every morning at six,
watching over their lessons and meals, and choosing their
clothes. Fanny Burney greatly approved of her royal mistress: "Her manners have an easy dignity, with a most engaging simplicity, and she has all the fine high breeding which
the mind, not the station, gives, of carefully avoiding to distress those who converse with her, or studiously removing the
embarrassment she cannot prevent." Queen Charlotte was
dull but dependable, and though she later became increas-

ingly estranged from her husband as his illness grew more alarming, George himself never ceased to rely on her. He wrote to the Prince of Wales in 1780 a touching eulogy:

I can with truth say that in nineteen years I have never had the smallest reason but to thank Heaven for having directed my choice among the Princesses then fit for me to marry, to her; indeed I could not bear up did I not find in her a feeling friend to whom I can unbosom my griefs.

The sting in the tail was probably not lost on the sensitive Prince, who was far from certain that his mother showed the same understanding for his problems.

The older Princes were compartmentalised in a most peculiar manner. The Prince of Wales and the Duke of York were given special treatment, living primarily in the Dutch House at Kew, but also with suites at Buckingham House. The future Dukes of Clarence and Kent were established in another house, and the future Dukes of Cumberland and Sussex, subsequently joined by their younger brother Adolphus, in a third. Each group had its set of governors and tutors, and George III gave firm instructions that discipline should be strict, and punishment severe. The King, when he appointed Dr. Hurd in 1776, put his point of view succinctly: "We live in unprincipled days, and no change can be expected but by an early attention to the rising generation."

In spite of occasional relaxations, hunting and riding, attendance at the Queen's no doubt excessively decorous card parties, visits to suitable plays, the emphasis was on learning, and very little else. The royal children were constantly reminded that their parents expected much of them, too much. The King wrote to the Prince of Wales and the Duke of York in 1778:

My dear sons, place ever your chief care on obeying the commands of your Creator. Every hour will shew you that no comfort can be attained without that. Act uprightly and shew the anxious care I have had of you has not been misspent, and you will ever find me not only an affectionate father but a sincere friend. May Heaven shower the choicest blessings on you both and on the rest of my children.

Such sermonising was no doubt kindly meant, for George III was a kind man at heart, but this was hardly a letter to strike the right response in the Prince of Wales, who was nearly sixteen years old and beginning to think of interests far removed from the commands of his Creator.

Soon, family ties were being strained to breaking point. The Prince of Wales wrote to his brother Frederick in 1781:

I am sorry to tell you that the unkind behaviour of both their Majesties, but in particular of the Queen, is such that it is hardly bearable. She and I, under the protestations of the greatest friendship, had a long conversation together. She accused me of various high crimes and misdemeanours, all wh. I answered, and in the vulgar English phraze gave her as good as she brought. She spoke to me, she said, entirely without the King's knowledge. Now I am thoroughly convinced from the language she used and the style she spoke in she must previously have talked the subject over with the King, who wanted to try whether I could be intimidated or not, but when she found I was not so easily to be intimidated she was silent.

According to the Prince of Wales, his mother abused both him and Frederick roundly.

William, on the other hand, gave his mother credit for, as he put it, "wishing to keep peace among the chosen ones of Israel." He kept his venom for his father: "I wish I could say as much for our worthy friend our near relation. What can be the use of his keeping us so close? Does he imagine he will make his sons his friends by this mode of conduct?"

The answer, of course, to these rather pathetic rhetorical questions was that the King lacked imagination. He revelled in the concept of a large, united family, and, devoid of subtlety or psychoanalytical expertise, only considered one means of keeping it intact. To give him his due, his patience was sorely, repeatedly, often outrageously tried. It all should have gone so well. In Benjamin West's famous portrait of Queen Charlotte and her children, we have an idealised picture of the ideal family. The older boys are handsome, the younger ones appealingly attractive, the girls are charming; there is even a dog strategically positioned. What could be more delightful? And indeed, when they were young, the children were exceptionally good-looking: tall, thin, with no hint of the disastrous corpulence and coarseness which were to encase all but one of the brothers in later life. The girls, too, really were as pretty as Gainsborough's portrait of the three eldest shows them. He, apparently, was positively bowled over by what he called a "constellation" of beauty.

But the children were growing up, and in the eighteenth century they grew up fast. Already the Prince of Wales was showing his fondness for wine and women. His passion for "Perdita" Robinson, an actress in Garrick's company at Drury Lane, was the talk of the town; more importantly, the recovery of some highly indiscreet letters cost the King £5,000, and annuities for life payable both to Perdita and to her daughter increased the bill sharply. The actress recalled her royal admirer with considerable affection: "The graces of his person, the irresistible sweetness of his smile, the tenderness of his melodious and manly voice, will be remembered by me till every vision of this changing scene shall be forgotten." Financial security clearly made the heart grow fonder.

Nor was Perdita the Prince's first conquest. Only months before, he had fallen in love with Mary Hamilton, one of his sisters' governesses. He presented her with a character sketch of himself which cries out for understanding, an understanding which he never received from his parents:

His sentiments and thoughts are open and generous, above doing anything that is mean (too susceptible, even to believing people his friends, and placing too much confidence in them . . .), grateful and friendly to excess where he finds a *real friend* . . .

rather too familiar to his inferiors but will not suffer himself to
be browbeaten or treated with Haughtiness by his superiors.
Now for his vices, or rather let us call them weaknesses—too
subject to give loose or vent to his passions of every kind, too
subject to be in a passion . . .

Here, vividly caught, is all his charm, vulnerability and in-
furiating weakness. His father would have preferred vice to
weakness.

George III, however exasperated he became with his eldest
son, always maintained a firm affection for the Duke of York.
Frederick was destined early for a military career, and he was
packed off to Hanover. Lord Cornwallis was not impressed:
"The Royal Person whom I saw does not give much hope,
further than a great deal of good nature and a very good
heart. His military ideas are those of a wild boy of the
Guards." His amorous ideas were equally wild, and his reception at the Prussian court rather went to his head, but he was
undeniably popular, a good conversationalist, and attractive
in his personality. He also had sensible views on the increasingly bad relations between his father and his elder brother.
He wrote to the Prince of Wales from Hanover:

For God's sake do everything which you can to keep well with
him, at least upon decent terms; consider he is vexed enough in
publick affairs. He may possibly be cross, but still it is your business not to take that too high. You know, my dearest brother, I
hate *preaching* full as much as you do, but . . . I know you will
excuse what I write because it comes from the heart.

If Frederick had been a better army commander, and if he
had not fatally involved himself with the notorious Mary
Anne Clarke, an involvement which culminated in the accu-
sation that she had been guilty of selling army commissions,
posterity might have looked more kindly on him. As it is, he
is chiefly remembered as the main—and ludicrous—character,
in the children's nursery rhyme "The Grand Old Duke of
York."

The martial enterprises of William, Duke of Clarence, were equally undistinguished. Just as Frederick inevitably went into the army, so William found himself in the navy. He was not pleased. His father had seen fit to despatch him as Midshipman William Guelph at the age of thirteen, and accompanied by a future Bishop of Bangor. Admiral Hood noted his "volatile turn of mind and his great flow of spirits," and even his brother Frederick thought him excessively rough and rude. He swore like a deckhand, was arrested for brawling, ran up debts, fell in and out of love with alarming rapidity, caught venereal disease in the West Indies, and generally displayed that sailorly bluffness which is so much admired by romantic souls. His father, needless to say, was neither romantic nor amused. He addressed a particularly sharp reprimand to his erring son:

I cannot too strongly set before your eyes that if you set yourself to indulge every foolish idea you must be wretched all your life, for with thirteen children I can but with the greatest care make both ends meet and am not in a situation to be paying their debts.

William's response was: "During the bloom of youth I am not allowed to enjoy myself like any other person of my age." And, after a short-lived liaison with the daughter of a Plymouth merchant, he was spirited off to Nova Scotia. He wrote to his eldest brother in 1788: "Fatherly admonitions at our time of life are very unpleasant and of no use; it is a pity he should expend his breath or his time in such fruitless labour. I wonder which of us two he looks on with the least eyes of affection?" The recipient would have had no doubts. Even when the Duke of Clarence settled down to a long period of extra-marital bliss with the actress Mrs. Jordan and an ever-lasting supply of Fitzclarence offspring—there was much malicious talk of "bathing in the river Jordan"—the Prince of Wales was the son who always bore the brunt of parental disapproval.

Not that George and Charlotte had much reason to admire

their fourth son, Edward, Duke of Kent. He was a rebellious child, given to smashing clocks, and a military career merely exacerbated his temper. Inevitably he took a mistress, less inevitably he turned violently against his older brother, the Duke of York. He felt that he was continually being passed over, that his prowess as a commander was never properly rewarded. In 1802, he was sent to Gibraltar as Governor-General and quickly earned himself the reputation of a sadist. The army at the turn of the century was hardly the place for milksops or officers with delicate sensibilities, but even the most hardened veteran revolted against the reign of terror which the Duke of Kent introduced. The number and severity of the floggings which he ordered became so lavish, and his paranoia about discipline so intense, that complaints poured into Horse Guards. Unfortunately, it was the Duke of York who presided there and who was forced to recall his own brother. The consolation of a field-marshal's baton was hardly enough.

Augustus, Duke of Sussex, erred in a different way. He had escaped the military life because of what was diagnosed as "convulsive asthma," though it was very likely a further manifestation of porphyria, which was to attack his father so tragically, and had therefore been allowed to improve his mind instead. He had a collection of over 5,000 Bibles, and was something of a classical scholar. He was inordinately proud of his singing voice—"I had the most wonderful voice that ever was heard," he once said. "Three octaves; and I do understand music. I practised eight hours a day in Italy. One may boast of a voice, as it is a gift of nature." Augustus, though, was also prone to exercising other parts of his anatomy. He was profoundly susceptible to female charms, and equally sentimental in their exploitation. He fell head over heels for Lady Augusta Murray, who was described by one contemporary as "coarse and confident-looking." Augustus was nineteen, Augusta—or "Goosy," as he insisted on calling her—was thirty.

Augustus had no intention of obeying the dictates of the Royal Marriages Act, any more than the Prince of Wales did when he married Mrs. Fitzherbert. He opted for a morganatic union, and promptly drew up a curious marriage document, which overlaid the phrases of the Common Prayer Book with his own, more sentimental effusions. "On my knees before God our Creator," it proceeded,

I, Augustus Frederick, promise thee, Augusta Murray, and swear upon the Bible, as I hope for salvation in the world to come, that I will take thee, Augusta Murray, for my WIFE, for better, for worse, for richer, for poorer, in sickness and in health, to love and to cherish, till death us do part, to love but thee only, and none other; and may God forget ME if I ever forget THEE! The Lord's name be praised! So bless me; so bless me, O God!

The marriage between Mr. Augustus Frederick and Miss Augusta Murray duly took place at St. George's, Hanover Square, but the news of the real participants soon leaked out, and George III took immediate action. The court of Arches duly decreed that the marriage was null and void under the terms of the Royal Marriages Act—and Augustus and Augusta paid very little attention. Sadly, their idyll did not last. Augusta, now calling herself the Duchess of Sussex, was abandoned by her husband, left only with the odd title of Countess d'Ameland. Augustus waited the shortest possible time after her death in 1830 before marrying Lady Cecilia Buggin, the widow of a lawyer and daughter of the Earl of Arran. Creevey clucked over the liaisons: "Old Sussex comes here on Monday and Ciss Buggin too. Was there ever such a low-lived concern?" Once it had been Gussy and Goosy, now it was Suss and Ciss. *Plus ça change* . . . The Duke of Sussex, however, retained some popularity. He had made an ass of himself in the matrimonial stakes, yet his heart was clearly in the right place. He was a radical in politics and a supporter of the Reform Bill. The populace approved.

They did not approve of Augustus's elder brother, Ernest;

indeed of all the sons of George III, Ernest, Duke of Cumberland, earned—and probably merited—the greatest obloquy. He was quite unlike his brothers in looks, always retaining his figure and actually looking the part of an army officer. He was also unusually taciturn, choosing to grumble in an epistolary form rather than in conversation. Convinced that he was "born to be the most unhappy of men," he railed against his father, his brother the Duke of York, who he was convinced had blocked his rise in the army hierarchy, and against fate. Undeniably courageous and indestructibly reactionary, he was always unpopular both with his family and with the public. When he was severely wounded in the fighting against the French in the Low Countries, he received no word of approbation: "Is it not hard to have lost the use of an eye doing my duty and not to have got as yet an answer from his Majesty though I have wrote four times?" He was suspected of fathering his sister Sophia's child. He passionately opposed Catholic Emancipation. He was within an ace of being murdered by his valet, and when the unhappy servant committed suicide the gossip was that Ernest had killed him. Even his marriage was unfortunate. In 1815 he settled on Frederica, Princess of Solms-Braunfels, who had not only been married twice previously, but had also once been engaged to his younger brother Adolphus.

Adolphus was his parents' favourite son, and the only one who remained untarnished by rumour. His liaisons were discreet, his debts non-existent, his popularity was high. He spoke languages with ease, and was both musical and intellectual. He was an excellent Governor-General in Hanover, and he married suitably, Princess Augusta of Hesse-Cassel, a distant cousin. They produced George III's first legitimate grandchild. No wonder, Dolly, as he was affectionately called by his doting parents and sisters, was the family favourite. He appears almost domestically dull in comparison with his brothers.

All George III's sons were affected disastrously by the

Royal Marriages Act. They were forced into liaisons with actresses and demi-mondaines and the less satisfactory sprigs of the British aristocracy. Then, after the death of the Prince Regent's daughter, Princess Charlotte, they forced themselves into alliances with the only women who were both suitable and available. Suddenly, the courts of the lesser German principalities and duchies became like a crowded market, full of Hanoverian Princes intent on finding a Protestant bride who was neither excessively ugly nor totally destitute. It was a ludicrous sight, and a pathetic situation for the Princes to find themselves in.

But at least they had the opportunity to maintain mistresses and to seek out wives. The daughters of George and Charlotte had no such chances. They were always intensely overprotected. The Queen had supervised their education with considerable diligence, and they threatened to become bluestockings. Kew, Windsor, London, and later Weymouth, were their geographical limits. Much later, in 1811, Princess Sophia wrote to the Prince of Wales, referring to herself and three of her sisters as "four old cats." "I wonder," she said, "you do not vote for putting us in a sack and drowning us in *The Thames*." But it had always been so. Windsor, in particular, which they christened "the Nunnery," was like a prison, from which the girls could only issue forth on their very best behaviour.

And yet, Princess Augusta and Princess Elizabeth managed to conduct clandestine love affairs; Princess Sophia and Princess Amelia followed their example; Princess Mary even succeeded in marrying her highly unsuitable cousin, William, Duke of Gloucester, known to everyone as "Silly Billy." But it was all romantic nonsense, all unsatisfying Dead Sea Fruit. George III, devoted to his daughters, could not bring himself to arrange marriages which would take them over the Channel to distant German courts. With the sole exception of Princess Charlotte, the Princess Royal, they were shackled to their parents until it was almost too late—or more often far too late.

Not that Charlotte's path to matrimony was covered with primroses. She was determined to marry but she was approaching thirty. Her doctors were alarmed at her nervous state of mind:

Convinced that she now has no chance of ever altering her condition; afraid of receiving any impressions of tenderness or affection; reserved and studious; tenderly loving her brothers and feeling strongly every unpleasant circumstance attending them, she is fallen into a kind of quiet desperate state, without hope and open to every fear; or in other words what is commonly called broken-hearted.

Where was the Prince Charming who would carry her off?

He was found in the unlikely person of Prince Frederick of Württemberg. On the face of it, he was not wholly satisfactory. He was fat and he was forty. He also possessed three children by his former wife, Augusta of Brunswick, a niece of George III, who had disappeared in mysterious circumstances and was officially said to have died in a Russian prison of a "putrid fever." The King was not eager to give his permission to the betrothal, and matters were further delayed by Princess Charlotte turning bright yellow with jaundice. Finally, though, everything was set for May 1797. The Prince of Württemberg cut a less than dashing figure. His corpulence was extreme—Gillray enjoyed himself with some scurrilous cartoons and the British public christened Frederick the "Great Bellygerent"—and his appearance in a wedding costume of "silk shot with gold and silver richly embroidered" and bedecked with foreign orders must have been prominent, to put it kindly.

Sir Gilbert Elliot was present at the Chapel Royal, and wrote to his wife. The main impression which he derived was that everyone, except the bridegroom, burst into tears. The King cried, the bride cried, her sisters cried; wailing and lamentation continued throughout the three-hour service. Only the bridegroom restrained himself. Perhaps his corsets were too tightly laced, though Elliot thought that "like all affairs of State" the Duke's belly had been a little exaggerated, while admitting that it was "very great." Eventually the happy pair departed on their honeymoon, and Charlotte prepared to join her husband in the exhausting game of choosing the right side during Napoleon's German campaigns.

Charlotte's marriage, as it was to turn out, was the single reasonably straightforward ceremony which George III's daughters were to witness. Princess Elizabeth was optimistic, as can be seen from a letter which she wrote at the time to the Prince of Wales:

I trust that the Princess Royal's lot being determined upon it may open the way for others, for times are much changed and every young woman who has been brought up as we have through the goodness of mama must look forward to settlement, which, was I to say I did not, your own good sense must tell you is false.

Elizabeth continued to place her faith in her parents and their presumed willingness to arrange a suitable match for her. She was to wait until 1818, when she was forty-seven. Once, she had nurtured hopes of marriage to Louis-Philippe d'Orléans, in spite of the fact that he was a Catholic, the son of a regicide, and himself a revolutionary; but this had come to nothing when he departed to wed the daughter of the King of the Two Sicilies.

Now, suddenly, there appeared in London yet another German Frederick, the Prince of Hesse-Homburg. It was not the first time that he had featured in marriage negotiations with a daughter of George III. In 1804 he had selected Princess Augusta for his attentions, only to find the King so distrait that he did not even bother to acknowledge his letter of intent. Frederick was two years older than Elizabeth and had never married. He did not find favour with London society. He was nicknamed "Humbug," his luxuriant whiskers were mocked and he was put down as "a vulgar-looking German Corporal"; it was rumoured that he bathed infrequently and smelled of garlic and tobacco. To cap it all, he split his trousers at a royal levée and had to be pushed quickly into a pair of breeches which, curiously, the Duke of York happened to have with him.

But, in spite of the general ribaldry and her mother's strong disapproval, Elizabeth was utterly charmed by her suitor, and determined that the marriage should go ahead. And so it did. Elizabeth wore a silver tissue wedding-dress, Frederick was in the uniform of an Austrian general. When they left for Royal Lodge and their honeymoon, the Prince was sick, and was forced to sit outside. It was all somewhat farcical, and Elizabeth began to have slight qualms about leaving England. But the marriage was a huge success, and Frederick and Elizabeth lived in complete amity and affection until his death in 1829.

Between the marriages of the Princess Royal and Princess Elizabeth, the Princesses Augusta, Sophia and Amelia had all fallen in love, in each case with a member of the royal household. It was inevitable. They had seen their sister marry, and were more realistic, or pessimistic, than Elizabeth. Princess Augusta was, perhaps, the luckiest of the three. Her choice was Sir Brent Spencer, who was both handsome and personable, a dashing soldier who reached the rank of major-general as Arthur Wellesley's second-in-command in the Peninsula. The romance continued for ten years, and Augusta eventually sought the Prince of Wales's permission to marry. Although there is no real evidence, it is generally thought likely that permission was granted.

Princess Sophia was less discreet. General Garth, like Spencer, was a soldier and a courtier, but he was also thirty-three years older than the princess, and far from handsome. Princess Mary referred to him disparagingly as "the Purple Light of Love," because of a large birthmark, and Charles Greville called him "a hideous old Devil." But Garth was available, that was all that mattered. And, at the age of twenty-three, Princess Sophia gave birth, at Weymouth, to a son, whose father was certainly General Garth. There were rumours that the real father was Ernest, Duke of Cumberland, and that the General had gallantly stepped in to avert a mammoth scandal, but this story has no validity since Cumberland was abroad at the time of conception.

Garth was nothing if not a gentleman, and appears to have retained the approval of the Royal Family. He lived on until 1829, dying at the age of eighty-five. The son of the liaison, Captain Thomas Garth, whom Greville dubbed "an idiot as well as a scoundrel," made an attempt to blackmail his royal relations, failed, and departed abroad. He was not heard of again. Princess Sophia was left with nothing but memories, facing the world with dignity and increasingly given to chest cramps, which may well have been psychosomatic, an attempt to win sympathy.

Princess Amelia was the most pathetic of all the sisters, for not only was she hopelessly in love, she was also dying of consumption. Like Augusta and Sophia, she wished to marry a middle-aged general and court equerry, in this case Sir Charles Fitz Roy, who was descended from one of Charles II's bastards and could therefore be claimed as a very distant cousin. The relationship was almost certainly unconsummated, but it was none the less passionate. Princess Amelia, perhaps sensing that time was running out, poured out all her pent-up feelings in a letter to Fitz Roy in 1807:

O, Good God, why not be together? I pine after my dear Charles more and more every instant . . . Your dear letter!—O what a treasure! I shall keep it, and read it over and over every day . . . I really must marry you, though inwardly united, and in reality that is much more than the ceremony, yet that ceremony would be a protection. O my precious darling, how often do I say—would to God my own husband and best friend and guardian was here to protect me.

Some thought that they were married, the Prince of Wales was certain of it, and Amelia herself constantly referred to Fitz Roy as "my beloved husband Charles," but it was probably wishful thinking. The Princess's closest friend, Mrs. Villiers, had no doubt at all that no marriage ceremony had ever taken place. Amelia may have obtained the Prince of Wales's permission to marry as soon as he was made Regent during their father's illness, but she never won over her mother, who deplored the whole business. She was in any case too ill for it to matter. In the autumn of 1810, she composed her last will and testament, and included in it a last outpouring of her feelings for Fitz Roy: "I live but for you. I love you with the purest affection, the greatest gratitude: I owe you everything."

She died on November 2, and the news of her death was brought to Fitz Roy by Princess Mary. The Prince of Wales and the Duke of Cambridge were the executors of their dead sister's will, and they persuaded the chief legatee to surrender his claims. Poor Charles Fitz Roy was a distressing reminder of Princess Amelia's infatuation, and if that could not be forgotten, at least he could.

Five and a half years later, it was Princess Mary who was allowed to marry. No one thought much of the Duke of Gloucester—"Silly Billy," "the Cheese," or "Slice," as he was variously nicknamed—but Mary would brook no interference, and she was proved correct to do so. They settled at Bagshot Park, and Mary wrote to her eldest brother: "The more I see of the Duke, the more I am convinced of his honourable character and excellent heart." Eccentric he may have been, and he was rumoured to treat his wife in a tyrannical way, refusing to allow her to travel on a Sunday, but Mary remained, at least outwardly, devoted to him. She nursed him with the greatest care when he was dying in 1834, and she mourned him sincerely. She was to live on for a further twenty-three years. Queen Victoria was fond of her and referred to her as "dear Aunt Gloucester." When she was over eighty, Princess Mary sent a telescope as a present to the future Edward VII. She died on April 30, 1857. The last link with the days of George III had been severed.

The children of George III and Queen Charlotte, whatever their failings, were an extraordinary collection of human beings. Almost without exception, they were deeply devoted one to the other, and always ready to lavish sympathy and understanding when, as so often happened, these were needed. Their characters were not dull, nor were they sanctimonious: perhaps it would have been the height of hypocrisy if they had been. But, ultimately, the impression remains that they are more to be pitied than reviled.

VIII

The Table and the Ring

Whereas I, William Willis, commonly known as the *fighting* Quaker, have fought Mr. Smallwood about twelve months since, and held him the tightest to it, and bruised and battered him more than any one he ever encountered, though I had the ill-fortune to be beat by an accidental fall; the said Smallwood, flushed with the success blind fortune then gave him, and the weak attempts of a few vain Irishmen and boys, that have of late fought him for a minute or two, makes him think himself unconquerable; to convince him of the falsity of which, I invite him to fight me for one hundred pounds . . . when I doubt not but I shall prove the truth of what I have asserted, by pegs, darts, hard blows, falls and cross-buttocks.

Daily Advertiser, April 26, 1742

George Harley Drummond, of the famous banking-house . . . only played once in his whole life at White's Club at whist, on which occasion he lost £20,000 to Brummell. This even caused him to retire from the banking-house of which he was a partner.

The Reminiscences of Captain Gronow

A society that is bored almost invariably finds stimulation from danger; the only question is whether that danger is shared or merely observed. In the dying fall of the Roman Empire, ever more bloodthirsty gladiatorial contests had to be produced for jaded patrician and plebeian appetites; the second half of the twentieth century prefers to experiment with lethal drugs and equally lethal speed. The England of the eighteenth and early nineteenth century was even more indiscriminate, combining a love of pugilistic battles with a craze for fast and reckless driving and riding. And over all hung the spirit of the gaming tables, of wagers which could ruin a man overnight, dissipate a vast family fortune, or elevate a fishmonger to a position where he could dictate to the aristocracy and the *ton*.

Andrew Steinmetz, who besides being a Middle Temple barrister and a musketry instructor in the militia turned his pen to such ill-assorted subjects as the Jesuits, the history of duelling, and Japan, fixed upon 1777 as the year when the passion for gambling began to dominate society, though he blamed its more outrageous manifestations on that inevitable scapegoat, the French Revolution. With superb chauvinism, he denounced the evil influence exercised from beyond the Channel:

Then came upon the nation the muddy flood of French emigrants—a set of men, speaking generally, whose vices contaminated the very atmosphere. Before the advent of these worthies the number of gambling houses in the metropolis, exclusive of those so long established by subscription, was not more than half-a-dozen; but by the year 1820 they had increased to nearly fifty. Besides *Faro* and *Hazard*, the foreign games of *Macao, Roulette, Rouge et Noir*, etc., were introduced, and there was a graduated accommodation for all ranks, from the Peer of the Realm to the Highwayman, the Burglar, and the Pick-pocket.

Steinmetz lists eight established clubs (although the Travellers' sounds distinctly mild in atmosphere, Rule 10 of the club directing that "no dice and no game of hazard be allowed in the rooms of the club, nor any higher stake than guinea points, and that no cards be introduced before dinner"): Almack's, the Cocoa-Tree, Graham's, Brooks's, White's, Wattier's, Crockford's and the Travellers', the last chiefly memorable for the fact that Talleyrand played whist there, badly.

Each club had its own distinctive peculiarities. Steinmetz describes the atmosphere at Almack's:

The gamesters began by pulling off their embroidered clothes, and putting on frieze great coats, or turned their coats inside out for luck! They put on pieces of leather (such as are worn by footmen when they clean knives) to save their laced ruffles; and to guard their eyes from the light, and to keep their hair in order, wore high-crowned straw hats with broad brims adorned with flowers and ribbons; they also wore masks to conceal their emotions when they played at *quinze*. Each gamester had a small neat stand by him, to hold his tea, or a wooden bowl with an edge of ormolu, to hold the rouleaus or guineas.

Stakes were high, as were expectations: on March 21, 1772, it was noted, "Mr. Thynne having won only 12,000 guineas during the last two months, retired in disgust." By 1814, however, the character of Almack's had quite altered. Dancing was now the thing, and it was the patronesses who held sway, laying down the strictest rules as to dress and deportment, and even turning away the Duke of Wellington from the club's doors because he was wearing trousers instead of knee-breeches. Princess Esterhazy, a *"bon enfant,"* as Captain Gronow thought her, Lady Castlereagh, Countess Lieven, "haughty and exclusive," and the other dragons would not have accorded well with the straw-hatted and flower-bedecked gamblers of earlier decades.

The stakes at the Cocoa-Tree were certainly no lower than those at Almack's. Horace Walpole wrote to his friend, Sir Horace Mann, in 1780:

Within this week there has been a cast at Hazard at the Cocoa-Tree (in St James's Street) the difference of which amounted to one hundred and fourscore thousand pounds! Mr. O'Birne, an Irish gamester, had won one hundred thousand pounds of a young Mr. Harvey of Chigwell, just started into an estate by his elder brother's death. O'Birne said,—"You can never pay me." "I can," said the youth, "my estate will sell for the debt." "No," said O'Birne, "I will win ten thousand,—you shall throw for the odd ninety." They did, and Harvey won!

Brooks's and White's were both notorious for the eccentricities of their members, though White's, perhaps because it was even more exclusive, provided the town with better gossip. Steinmetz gives a vivid description of the members' desire to wager on literally anything,

on births, deaths, and marriages; the length of a life; the duration of a ministry; a placeman's prospect of a coronet; the last scandal at Ranelagh or Madame Cornely's, or the shock of an earthquake. A man dropped down at the door of White's. He was carried into the house. Was he dead or not? The odds were immediately given and taken for and against. It was proposed to bleed him. Those who had taken the odds that the man was dead protested that the use of a lancet would affect the fairness of the bet.

Horace Walpole tut-tutted over a scandal back in 1744:

One of the youths at White's has committed a murder, and intends to repeat it. He betted £1,500 that a man could live twelve hours under water; hired a desperate fellow, sunk him in a ship, by way of experiment, and both ship and man have not appeared since. Another man and ship are to be tried for their lives instead of Mr. Blake, the assassin.

They did indeed bet on everything and anything: on which of two flies would reach the top of a window-pane, or which of two raindrops would reach the bottom; on whether Beau Nash would outlive the playwright Cibber; on whether a tremor had been caused by an earthquake or by an explosion at some powder-mills. Those who were prepared to ration their alcoholic intake could live comfortably, even extravagantly, off their winnings. Gronow gives one example:

General Scott, the father-in-law of George Canning and the
Duke of Portland, was known to have won at White's £200,000,
thanks to his notorious sobriety and knowledge of the game of
whist. The general possessed a great advantage over his companions by avoiding those indulgences at the table which used to
muddle other men's brains. He confined himself to dining off
something like a boiled chicken, with toast-and-water.

General Scott might have found the cuisine of Wattier's
Club less easy to resist. This establishment was founded in the
most capricious way. Gronow tells the story:

Upon one occasion, some gentlemen of both White's and
Brooks's had the honour to dine with the Prince Regent, and
during the conversation the prince inquired what sort of dinners
they got at their clubs, upon which Sir Thomas Stepney, one of
the guests, observed that their dinners were always the same, "the
eternal joints, or beef-steaks, the boiled fowl with oyster sauce,
and an apple-tart—this is what we have, sir, at our clubs, and
very monotonous fare it is." The prince, without further remark,
rang the bell for his cook, Wattier, and, in the presence of those
who dined at the royal table, asked him whether he would take a
house and organize a dinner club. Wattier assented, and named
Madison, the prince's page, manager, and Labourie, the cook,
from the royal kitchen. The club flourished only a few years,
owing to the high play that was carried on there . . . The dinners were exquisite; the best Parisian cooks could not beat
Labourie.

"But, in the reign of George IV," continues Gronow, "a
new star rose upon the horizon in the person of Mr. William
Crockford, and the old-fashioned games of faro, macao, and
lansquenet gave place to the all-devouring thirst for the game
of hazard." Crockford, in many ways, epitomises his age.
Born probably in 1775, in his father's fish-shop by Temple
Bar, in one of the most notorious slums of the day, Crockford
was determined to rise in society. He had no obvious attributes, neither breeding, nor money, nor certainly good looks,
as can be seen from Rowlandson's accurate drawing of him.

Instead, he had a way with women, who responded to his down-to-earth sexual appetites, and he possessed the will to succeed. Gronow describes his rise to affluence:

Crockey, when still a young man, had relinquished the peaceful trade of a fishmonger for a share in a "hell," where, with his partner Gye, he managed to win, after a sitting of twenty-four hours, the enormous sum of £100,000 from Lords Thanet and Granville, Mr. Ball Hughes, and two other gentlemen whose names I do not now remember. With this capital added to his former gains, he built the well-known palace in St. James's Street, where a club was established and play organized on a scale of magnificence and liberality hitherto unknown in Europe.

Crockford's opened its doors in 1827. The *Edinburgh Review* was positively lyrical:

It rose like a creation of Aladdin's lamp; and the genii themselves could hardly have surpassed the beauty of the internal decorations, or furnished a more accomplished *maître d'hôtel* than Ude. To make the company as select as possible, the establishment was regularly organized as a club, and the election of members vested in a committee. Crockford's became the rage, and the votaries of fashion, whether they like play or not, hastened to enrol themselves. The Duke of Wellington was an original member, though (unlike Blucher, who repeatedly lost everything he had at play) the great captain was never known to play deep at any game but war or politics. Card-tables were regularly placed, and whist was played occasionally; but the aim, end, and final cause of the whole was the hazard bank, at which the proprietor took his nightly stand, prepared for all comers.

And the proprietor prospered. According to *The Times*, Lords Rivers, Sefton and Chesterfield were thought to have lost £100,000 each, and, as Gronow remarked, "one may safely say, without exaggeration, that Crockford won the whole of the ready money of the then existing generation."

Everyone belonged to Crockford's during its short but spectacular existence. Talleyrand and Pozzo di Borgo were

only two among a host of foreign diplomats and statesmen
who automatically joined. Bulwer Lytton and Disraeli,
Croker and Alvanley, soldiers, corinthians, wits and dandies,
all were content to lose their money and sample Monsieur
Ude's cuisine. And Crockford himself, ugly, coarse, bloated,
looked on:

The old fishmonger himself, seated snug and sly at his desk in the
corner of the room, watchful as the dragon that guarded the
golden apples of the Hesperides, would only give credit to sure
and approved signatures. Who that ever entered that dangerous
little room can ever forget the large green table with the
croupiers, Page, Darking, and Bacon, with their suave manners,
sleek appearance, stiff white neck-cloths, and the almost miracu-
lous quickness and dexterity with which they swept away the
money of the unfortunate punters when the fatal cry of "Deuce
ace," "Aces," or "Sixes out," was heard in answer to the caster's
bold cry of "Seven," or "Nine," or "Five's the main."

It was a heady atmosphere, the constant threat of ruin
looming out of the comforting but not over-ostentatious luxury of blue and crimson velvet, chandeliers and Ionic columns; but, as Gronow pointed out, "the brightest medal has
its reverse, and after all the wit and gaiety and excitement of
the night, how disagreeable the waking up, and how very unpleasant the sight of the little card with its numerous figures
marked down on the debtor side in the fine bold hand of Mr.
Crockford." The former fishmonger was estimated to be a
millionaire, and to be owed half as much again. His clients'
debts sometimes ran so high that he was obliged to cancel
them and insist, in the future, on payment in cash.

Like a great bubble, buoyed up to the point of hypertension, it could not last. In 1840, Crockford decided to retire. London was outraged and shocked. Disraeli wrote to his
sister:

'Tis a thunderbolt, and nothing else is talked of . . . Some
members are twelve years in arrear of subscriptions. One man

owes £700 to the coffee-room; all must now be booked up. The consternation is general. Moors that were hired are given up, and yachts destined to the Mediterranean must now lie in harbour.

The great palace was now less than a shadow of its former self. Gronow penned a sad epitaph:

Alas, poor Crockey's, shorn of its former glory, has become a sort of refuge for the destitute, a cheap dining-house. How are the mighty fallen! Irish buckeens, spring captains, "welshers" from Newmarket, and suspicious-looking foreigners, may be seen swaggering after dinner through the marble halls and up that gorgeous staircase where once the chivalry of England loved to congregate; and those who remember Crockford's in all its glory, cast, as they pass, a look of unavailing regret at its dingy walls, with many a sigh to the memory of the pleasant days they passed there, and the gay companions and noble gentlemen who have long since gone to their last home.

Or as the *Edinburgh Review* put it rather more pithily: "He retired in 1840, much as an Indian chief retires from a hunting country when there is not game enough left for his tribe, and the club tottered to its fall."

Crockford himself was surrounded by the aura of speculation for the rest of his life. Anything from somewhat shady dealings on the Turf to the promise of a mysterious gold-mine in Scotland attracted him. From his vast and elaborate house in Carlton House Terrace, he continued to dip a finger in any pie. He died in 1844, shattered by the result of the Derby, in which his much-fancied horse, Ratan, had come in a poor seventh. The horse had been nobbled, and the ensuing uproar was too much for Crockford. The irony was that, for once, "the old fishmonger" was almost certainly guiltless. His club closed on January 1, 1846, the premises being taken first by the Military, Naval and County Service, briefly by a second-rate dining establishment called the Wellington, and then by the Devonshire Club. William Crockford's memory was resurrected when a new gambling club bearing his name was opened in London in 1928. Six years later it moved, ironically, to 16 Carlton House Terrace.

One of Crockford's main antagonists, who haunted him until his dying day, was a man called John Gully. Their battles of wits were always conducted on the Turf, but Gully had first come into public prominence as a boxer, commencing his career against the champion, Henry Pearce, or the "Game Chicken" as he was dubbed.

The world of the prize fight was, in many ways, a microcosm of the eighteenth and early nineteenth centuries. All the innate need for violence was satisfied by the slogging matches, which were so often what the boxing contests were: the deep feeling of unrest increasingly prevalent throughout the working classes could find some outlet in the atmosphere of the crowds, the sight of blood, and the smell of fear and danger. And, at the other end of the scale, the Fancy could enjoy themselves by mixing with their social inferiors, experiencing a *frisson* of pleasure when rubbing shoulders with the rough and the criminal; act as patrons to the likelier fighters, and once again win or lose extravagant sums of money by betting on their favourites.

At its best and purest, boxing was no doubt an art, and Pierce Egan, the doyen of the sporting commentators and author of the classic *Boxiana*, was lyrical in its support:

Prejudice does much in favour of our native soil; but upon a dispassionate review of those countries where pugilism is unknown, we find that upon the most trifling misunderstanding, the life of the individual is in danger. In Holland the long knife decides too frequently; scarcely any person in Italy is without the stiletto; and France and Germany are not particular in using stones, sticks, etc. to gratify revenge; but in England, the fist only is used, where malice is not suffered to engender and poison the composition and induce the inhabitants to the commission of deeds which their souls abhor and shudder at, but an immediate appeal of boxing, the by-standers make a ring, and where no unfair advantage is suffered to be taken of each other. The fight done, the hand is given in token of peace; resentment vanishes; and the cause generally buried in oblivion.

At its worst boxing appealed to the kind of man who enjoyed watching a public hanging. It could be crooked, almost invariably brutal and brutalising, and the veneer of respectability bestowed by the patronage of the aristocracy was never more than skin-deep. What, though, cannot be denied is that the world of the prize fight had a colour and excitement, however spurious, which was unique.

James Figg was the first champion, and the man who established boxing as something approaching a respectable sport. He opened an academy, Figg's Amphitheatre, where expertise with the sword, the cudgel and the fists was taught, and as Pierce Egan recorded it was "patronised by the noble and the great, and not disturbed but tolerated by the magistrates." Figg died in 1740, or as Egan, ever ready with a suitable metaphor, put it, "Death gave him his knockdown blow," and Jack Broughton became the new star. Egan thought well of him, though he never saw him fight, being born twenty-four years after Broughton's last contest:

His form was athletic and commanding; there was an importance about it which denoted uncommon strength, and which every spectator felt impressed when they beheld him. Six feet, wanting an inch, in height; and fourteen stone, or thereabouts, in weight . . . He was intelligent, communicative, and not destitute of wit.

Broughton attempted to lay down rules, and these are worth quoting in full, since they formed the basis for the conduct of prize fights for the rest of the century, allowing for minor variations:

1. That a square of a yard be chalked in the middle of the stage; and every fresh set-to after a fall, or being parted from the rails, each second is to bring his man to the side of the square, and place him opposite to the other, and till they are fairly set-to at the lines, it shall not be lawful for one to strike the other.

2. That in order to prevent any disputes, the time a man lies after a fall, if the second does not bring his man to the side of the square within the space of half a minute, he shall be deemed a beaten man.

3. That in every main battle, no person whatever shall be on the stage except the principals and their seconds; the same rule to be observed in by-battles, except that in the latter, Mr. Broughton is allowed to be upon the stage to keep decorum, and to assist gentlemen in getting to their places; provided that he does not interfere in the battle and whoever pretends to infringe these rules to be turned immediately out of the house. Every body is to quit the stage as soon as the champions are stripped, or before they set-to.

4. That no champion shall be deemed beaten, unless he fails coming up to the line in the limited time; or that his own second declares him beaten. No second is to be allowed to ask his man's adversary any questions or advise him to give out.

5. That in by-battles, the winning man to have two thirds of the money given, which shall be publicly divided on the stage, notwithstanding any private agreements to the contrary.

6. That to prevent disputes, in every main battle, the principals shall, on coming on the stage, choose from among the gentlemen present, two umpires, who shall absolutely decide all disputes that may arise about the battle; and if the two umpires cannot agree, the said umpires to choose a third, who is to determine it.

7. That no person to hit his adversary when he is down, or seize him by the ham, the breeches, or any part below the waist; a man on his knees to be reckoned down.

Broughton's downfall came in 1750, when a butcher called Slack disposed of him in a mere fourteen minutes, much to the amazement of the crowd and the personal chagrin of the Duke of Cumberland who lost a couple of thousand pounds. Egan considered that there was a moral to the story: "Profit by his loss, be not too confident, and remember that it was occasioned by one fatal error, neglect of training!!" The eclipse of the champion appears to have had a disastrous effect on boxing as a whole. Slack reigned for a while, also under Cumberland's patronage, but it was not until the 1780s that a real revival took place, and boxing entered a golden age. The next forty years saw a series of epic struggles, and the rise and fall of boxers who were household names: Tom Cribb, Daniel Mendoza, Jem Belcher, John Jackson, Henry Pearce and Tom Hickman.

A whole new language of boxing began to emerge. Claret was tapped and corks drawn, the black-letter gentry (journalists) scribbled away, and the boniface did good business with Mr. Lushington (publican and drunkard respectively). Cyprians and rampers (prostitutes and footpads) abounded, and Johnny Raws were ripe for gammoning. Nib sprigs (gentlemen) and prigs (thieves) mixed, and everyone kept a weather eye open for the scouts, or constables. A great deal of daffy, or gin, was consumed, and a great many corinthians were cut up (the pleasant euphemism for bankrupted). Needless to say, the boxers had their curious nicknames. Hickman was the Gas-Light Man, Molineaux was the Moor, Henry Pearce the Game Chicken, and John Jackson the Commander-in-Chief.

Promoters of the game were always in search of likely looking contenders, and talent scouts often came up with a complete unknown who could be transformed into a potential champion. Sometimes, though, appearances were deceptive. There was a particular vogue for black boxers, because of the great success of Molineaux. Tom Oliver, an inveterate optimist, provided one anecdote which caused much merriment. Egan tells the story with consummate relish and raciness:

In one of Oliver's peregrinations through the streets of London, he met with a fine slashing Yankee Black: Tom was very much pleased with his form, and flattered himself a second Molineaux was at hand. Without hesitation Tom Oliver entered into conversation with him on the subject; told the man of colour, if he would attend to his instructions, he might soon make a little fortune, and invited him, as usual, home to dinner. "Tanky, massa," replied the sable hero, "me like de chink; very goot for poor Blacky—me do every ting you biddy me." Tom in a great hurry got home, ordered his affectionate rib to produce the rump steaks for his guest without loss of time: and the grub and the bub were soon afterwards on the table, to furnish the victualling office of the hungry overjoyed Black. "If they can grub well," said Oliver, "I am satisfied it is a good point towards milling well; but if a cove can't pick, I would not give much for him as a fighting man."

Blacky punished the steaks, swallowed all the potatoes, and took the lining out of a quart of porter, like winking. "Well done," cries Tom, "By heavens! you are a fine grubber!" The Black blushed at the remark, and unfortunately giving a glance at Oliver's face, the latter, in an instant, recollected he had seen his black mug before, at his friendly board; and starting up not exactly after the elegant manner of Hamlet, alarmed at the appearance of his father's ghost, but placing himself in a fighting attitude, exclaimed, in an angry tone of voice, "Why blow my dickey, you are the same impostor that devoured my beef-steaks and other comforts six months ago; and when I gave you only a gentle tap in your guts you roared out ten thousand murders. Bolt! Brush! Begone! And never let me see your ugly black mug any more; or else I will have my beef-steaks out of your hide." The black, scarcely knowing how to make his exit with anything like safety to his person, cried out, "Me go directly, Massa Oliver, but you wrong to say only gentle tap! No! No! More like de kick of de great cart horse! My belly never been well since—it growl all day—growl all night—growl ever since! Me go, Massa—I am gone. Me always say, I do as you biddy me."

There was a comic side to prize fighting, but usually the atmosphere was all too serious and deadly. The actual contests could be over within a few minutes—Jem Belcher disposed of Gamble in five rounds, after two blows, "one in the stomach that nearly deprived him of breath, and the other on the kidneys which instantly swelled up as big as a twopenny loaf"—or they could drag on endlessly. The epic struggle between Henry Pearce and John Gulley went to fifty-nine rounds and lasted an hour and ten minutes, an astounding record for those days; and Cribb only disposed of Molineaux in the thirty-ninth round. But one of the greatest and most memorable contests was that between Hickman, the Gas-Light Man, and Neat, on Hungerford Downs on December 11, 1821. Pierce Egan sets the scene:

It was a delightfully fine morning, the sun adding splendour to the scene, giving the whole a most picturesque appearance . . . A charming country on both sides of the road; the town of Hungerford at a distance, with the spire of the church; the ring on the Downs, surrounded with waggons and coaches, marquees, etc., rising proudly like an amphitheatre, formed so pleasing a feature, as to render description no easy task. The spot was selected for this combat under the judicious management of Mr. Jackson, and the ring was so well arranged, that 25,000 persons who were present, had all an excellent sight of the battle! . . . At a few minutes after one, Neat, arm-in-arm with his backer and Belcher, appeared in the outer space, and threw up his hat; but the sun being in his eyes, it did not reach its intended destination, when Belcher picked it up, and threw it into the ring; and shortly afterwards, the Gas, in a white topper, supported by his backer and Shelton, repeated the token of defiance, and entered the ring sucking an orange . . . The odds had completely changed on the preceding evening; and, on the ground, Neat was backed 5 to 4, besides numerous even bets. Upwards of £150,000, it is calculated, had transferred clies [pockets] on this event. The Gas weighed twelve stone, and Neat nearly fourteen. The colours, deep blue for Gas, and the yellow-man for Neat, were tied to the stakes.

Hickman started well enough, but received a tremendous right to the head in the fourth round, and Neat finished the sixth round "by grassing him with a belly pincher that would have floored an ox." By the tenth, Hickman was staggering, and he was knocked down in the thirteenth. But he held on, and by the sixteenth was little better than a swaying, battered punch-bag. Egan describes the eighteenth and final round:

On the Gas appearing at the mark, instead of putting up his arms to fight, he endeavoured to button the flap of his drawers in a confused state; but Neat scorned to take advantage of his defenceless, pitiable situation, and, with the utmost coolness, waited for him to commence the round. The Gas, as his last effort, endeavoured to show fight, but was hit down, which put an end to the battle by his proving insensible to the call of time. The above contest occupied twenty-three and a half minutes. Neat jumped up as a token of victory, amidst the proud and loud shots which pronounced him the conqueror. He immediately went and shook the hand of his brave but fallen opponent, before he left the ring. A medical man bled Hickman on the spot, without delay, and every humane attention was paid to him by his backer and his seconds. He remained for a short time in the ring, in a complete state of stupor, and was carried to a carriage on the shoulders of several men, and conveyed, with the utmost expedition, to the Castle Inn, Speen-hill, near Newbury, and immediately put to bed.

The fight between Hickman and Neat marked the end of the golden age of boxing. Hickman himself died as violently as he had lived, in a coach accident when he was clearly drunk. But he received a showy funeral, and John Jackson organised a benefit for the widow and children. Egan penned a brief and not entirely complimentary obituary:

When perfectly sober, Hickman was a quiet, well-behaved and really a good-natured fellow, but at times, when overcome with liquor, he was positively frightful, nay—mad . . . Like Hooper, the tin-man, Hickman had been spoiled by his patron, who made him his companion. That Hickman was angry about losing his fame there is not the least doubt; and he must have felt it severely, after boasting at the Fives Courts, that "the Gas should never go out!" and, in his fits of intemperance and irritation, he often asserted that he had received more money for losing than Neat did by winning the battle.

The moral is clear: remain sober and, above all, know your place.

Only Jackson, the Commander-in-Chief, appeared to be on a higher plane, somehow above criticism, as a vivid description of him in 1784 indicates:

He had on a scarlet coat, worked in gold at the button-holes, ruffles, and frill of fine lace, a small white stock, no collar (they were not then invented), a looped hat with a broad black band, buff knee-breeches, and long silk strings, striped white silk stockings, pumps, and paste buckles; his waistcoat was pale blue satin, sprigged with white. It was impossible to look on his fine ample chest, his noble shoulders, his waist, (if anything too small), his large, but not too large hips (the fulcrum of the human form, whether male or female), his limbs, his balustrade calf and beautifully turned but not over delicate ankle, his firm foot, and peculiarly small hand, without thinking that nature had sent him on earth as a model. On he went at a good five miles and a half an hour, the envy of all men, and the admiration of all women.

At the coronation of George IV, Jackson donned the uniform of a royal page in his capacity as leader of a troop of pugilists posted to keep order in the crowd; the following year the Duke of Clarence was among those who contributed towards a plate service to be presented to the much-admired boxer. Jackson was a figure of undeniable attraction. Even his mausoleum—he died in 1845—was out of the ordinary. Mr. Thomas Butler was commissioned to produce something suitable for erection in Brompton Cemetery, and he excelled himself. The most striking section showed a totally naked gladiator with a mournful aspect and a strategically-placed laurel wreath below the belt, and, above him, a somewhat dyspeptic lion looking equally sorrowful. It was a very grand finale.

By then, though, the great days were over. The influence of the Pugilistic Club—whose distinguished members wore blue coats and yellow kerseymere waistcoats, with "P.C." engraved on the buttons—the Fair Play Club and the other institutions formed to keep the essence of pugilism pure had waned. Pierce Egan looked back in nostalgia:

Within the last twenty-five years the morality in the prize ring has been very great indeed; the renowned Jem Belcher, the pride of Bristol, and the admiration of the London ring; the out-and-out game chicken, Henry Pearce, a boxer of rare pretensions, and never defeated; and the confident, gay, anglo-Irish boy, Jack Power, that could "hit and get away" from every body, except the grand finisher of the human race! Bob Gregson, the Poet Laureate to the prize ring, was likewise compelled to yield to his devouring grip in the midst of a sonnet; the *nonpareil*, Jack Randall, could get out of trouble like magic, but, with all his science, he could not escape from the paralizing corner of the "gristly foe"; and the hardy Welshman, Ned Turner, who never turned his back upon danger, was floored to rise no more! Old Dutch Sam, the phenomenon, who had astonished every body with his tactics, was ultimately astonished, surprised and captured, before he was prepared for the attack of the grim general . . . Tom Tring, one of the finest made men of his time, porter to the late King George IV, when Prince of Wales, and who challenged all England for £1,000 aside, was, after all his boasting, defeated in a second by the skeleton boxer; the ferocious, determined, neck-or-nothing Gas-light Man, Tom Hickman, received his *quietus* in an instant; and the muscular, hardy, strong White-headed Rob, was forcibly ejected from his prime "lush crib" before he could return a blow. The "lively kid," Stockman, proved saucy and desperate to the last moment of his existence, and even struggled with Death to obtain the victory. "He's coming, Jem," said he to his brother, "it's all up!" And again, as if trying to stop him in attitude, shouting, "D-n his eyes, he's coming!" fell backwards, and gave up the ghost.

Egan, like all sports commentators, thought he was looking back to a time of giants, of real champions. He was able to eliminate from his memory the rigged fights, the unscientific brutality, the awful condescension of the Fancy, the lawlessness and the drunkenness, the whores and pimps and pickpockets, the crowds baying for blood, and the atmosphere of sweat and desperation. Instead, he remembered the colour and excitement, the famous contests and the cream of the fighters, the vast crowds streaming on to the field, the fine coaches and curricles, the instances of humanity and nobility. The world of *Boxiana* was, of course, a mixture of the two.

The aristocracy and squirearchy of the latter half of the eighteenth and first quarter of the nineteenth centuries had a passion for sports and games and outdoor pursuits of any description. It was the heyday of coaching, with foul-mouthed Sir John Lade on the Brighton Road, the whips of the Four in Hand Club, and striped-waistcoated "tigers" up behind on vehicles of skeletal construction and alarming speed. It was an age when everyone rode to hounds or shot or played the new game of cricket. But, above all, it was the age of the gambler. Boxing was, perhaps, the opiate of the masses, but gambling was a fever which held the entire nation in thrall.

IX

The King's Malady

The King was prevailed upon not to go to chapel this
morning. I met him in the passage from the Queen's
room; he stopped me, and conversed upon his health near
half-an-hour, still with that extreme quickness of speech
and manner that belongs to fever; and he hardly sleeps,
he tells me, one minute all night; indeed, if he recovers
not his rest, a most delirious fever seems to threaten him.
He is all agitation, all emotion, yet all benevolence and
goodness, even to a degree that makes it touching to hear
him speak. He assures everybody of his health; he seems
only fearful to give uneasiness to others, yet certainly he
is better than last night. Nobody speaks of his illness, nor
what they think of it.

Fanny Burney, October 26, 1788

Nine days before Fanny Burney's graphic and moving diary
entry, George III suffered a bilious attack during the night
and, at 7:25 in the morning, sent for his physician, Sir George

Baker, with a particular request for one of the opium pills which always eased his pain. Sir George recorded the event and the King's symptoms:

I found his Majesty sitting up in his bed, his body being bent forward. He complained of a very acute pain in the pit of the stomach shooting to the back & sides, and making respiration difficult & uneasy. This pain continued all the day, though in a less degree of acuteness towards the evening; but it did not cease entirely until the bowels had been emptied. It was observable that, during the extreme severity of pain the pulse was only at sixty strokes in a minute, and that the pulse became quicker in proportion as the pain abated. At night it was at ninety.

Sir George Baker was not unduly perturbed. The King complained of a rash, but his physician could only discern faint traces. George's further complaint of rheumatism and cramp in the leg muscles was hardly surprising. The previous day, as Sir George discovered, his royal patient had risen early, "walked on the grass several hours, and without having changed his stockings which were very wet, went to St. James's." Worse still, he had devoured four large pears at supper. Sir George prescribed the invariable mixture of castor oil and senna, and then, in order to counteract the considerable pain caused to the King by these purgatives, laudanum, which had the undesired effect of closing the bowels. But Sir George knew no better approach, and alternated the purgative doses with laudanum three times during the subsequent twenty-four hours.

It was not the King's first serious illness. In 1762, he had been in acute discomfort from January until the end of March, and again in May and July, suffering from fever, coughing, a rapid pulse, insomnia and loss of weight. The royal physicians diagnosed consumption, and applied the currently accepted and useless remedies. Horace Walpole wrote to his friend Sir Horace Mann:

The King had one of the last of these strange and universally epidemic colds, which however have seldom been faithful: he had a violent cough and oppression on his breast, which he concealed, just as I had; but my life was of no consequence, and having no physicians in ordinary, I was cured in four nights by James's powders, without bleeding. The King was blooded seven times and had three blisters.

In addition to the bleeding, the doctors prescribed asses' milk, considered to be a sovereign remedy for consumption, gout, scurvy, nervous disorders, and even "the Decays of Old Age," and hoped for a westerly wind so that the King could take some air.

In 1765, George suffered a recurrence of the illness. Grenville recorded that Sir William Duncan, the royal physician, had come to inform him that "the King, who had a violent cold, had passed a restless night, and complained of stitches in his breast." Blooding again seemed to be the only answer, but it certainly had no lasting effect. One day, the King was better, cheerful and good-humoured; then there was a relapse; then he recovered his old animation. But, gradually, the illness subsided and except for a brief recurrence in February 1766 the King appeared to have made a total recovery.

It was not until June 1788 that a further attack is recorded. The King himself wrote to William Pitt,

A pretty smart bilious attack prevents my coming this day to town. I am certainly better than yesterday, and if it goes on mending this day, I shall hope to see Mr. Pitt in town tomorrow. Sir George Baker approves of what I have done, and I trust his advice will remove the remains of this complaint. On returning from the review [of the Foot Guards] I was forced to take to my bed, as the only tolerable posture I could find. To be sure I am what one calls a cup too low, but when thoroughly cleared I hope to feel equal to any business that may occur.

The Queen thought that the King's attack had been brought on by the dry, hot weather. Others thought they discerned the symptoms of gout, but the memoirist Sir Nathaniel Wraxall dismissed such a notion, at the same time shedding an interesting light on the King's eating habits:

Probably, the humour might have exhausted its force in the extremities, in the shape of gout, if his majesty had eat and drunk like almost any other gentleman. But his natural disposition to temperance . . . impelled him to adopt the habits of an ascetic. The most simple food, taken in very moderate quantity, constituted his repasts. Yet his German origin shewed itself in his predilections: for sour crout was one of his favourite dishes . . . His ordinary beverage at table was only composed of a sort of lemonade, which he dignified with the name of *cup;* though a monk of La Trappe might have drunk it without any infraction of his monastic vow.

No one at this time made any reference to madness or a nervous disease.

Sir George Baker decided that the King should take the waters at Cheltenham, and he agreed with delight. He was happy to leave London during July, and was prepared to remain at Cheltenham until the Three Choirs Festival at the beginning of August. Lord Fauconberg, one of the Lords of the Bedchamber, offered his house, Bays Hill Lodge, and the royal party set out in a high good humour. Cheltenham proved an instant success. Nathaniel Wraxall describes the country gentleman's existence which the King led:

He visited the spring at so early an hour, that few of his subjects were found there to meet him. Constantly on horseback, when the weather permitted, from eleven to three, he sat down at four to dinner; strolled out like a citizen with his wife and daughters, on the public walk soon after seven; and by eleven at night, everything was as completely hushed at Bays Hill Lodge as in a farmhouse.

The King was assiduous in following the regime laid down by his physician. He wrote, in the third person, to Sir George Baker:

The King took the Rhubarb Pills the Night He came and having omitted to bring a Saline Draught with Soluble Tartar, added a glass of the Cheltenham Waters, these had no effect on Sunday; as no heat appeared He began the Waters on Monday Morning

at Six . . . The Waters certainly agree they only give good
Spirits and Appetite; the Diet has been regularly Mutton and Potatoes.

Sir George wrote back with a word of admonition:

The influence of St. Swithin in the weather is now interrupted,
and in consequence your Majesty will be more at liberty to ex-
tend your airings and pursue your favourite system of exercise.
On this occasion may I be allowed to give your Majesty a caution? During the use of Cheltenham-water (which in part is
chalybeate) strong exercise ought to be avoided, for whatever
brings fatigue will at the same time heat the constitution, so that
the water will become rather injurious than salutary.

The King chose to ignore the advice, but replied with further
medical details:

The King cannot sufficiently express the benefit he finds from
this Salutary Spring. He has never been in the least heated, He
finds a Pint and half the proper quantity to give him two open-
ings, these only clear him without any sinking on the contrary
He finds himself in better Spirits and has never been obliged to
take the Rhubarb Pills.

Everyone seems to have enjoyed themselves. George had
never before experienced such freedom, and he made the
most of it, stopping to talk to passers-by, sinking a well in the
garden, going to the theatre to see Mrs. Jordan (later to become the Duke of Clarence's mistress), and attending a performance of *Messiah*. The waters of Cheltenham coupled
with the absence from London had worked wonders on the
royal constitution. The King and his party left for Windsor
on August 16.

The beneficial effect of Cheltenham proved all too short-
lived. Philip Withers, one of the King's pages, later recorded
a particularly disturbing occurrence in Windsor Great Park
(the subtitle to his work, "Variety of Entertaining Anecdotes," may indicate a degree of sensation-seeking). The
King was out driving with the Queen, when he suddenly

pulled the horses up, descended from the carriage, and approached an oak tree:

At the distance of a few yards he uncovered and advanced, with the utmost respect, and then, seizing one of the lower branches, he shook it with the most apparent cordiality and regard, just as a man shakes his friend by the hand. The Queen turned pale with astonishment, the reins dropped from her hands . . . At last Her Majesty became attentive to her situation, and, as the reins were happily within reach, they were recovered, and the Queen commanded me to dismount and to go and intimate, in a soothing voice and suppliant terms, that Her Majesty wished for his company. On my approach, I perceived the King was in earnest conversation, for His Majesty anticipated the answer from his royal friend, and then made a reply. It was the King of Prussia with whom His Majesty enjoyed this rural interview: continental politics were the subject. What I heard it would be unpardonable to divulge. I cannot, however, withhold a remark that must fill every loyal bosom with pleasure; His Majesty, though under a momentary dereliction of reason, evinced the most cordial attachment to freedom and the Protestant faith.

The King's doctors were beginning to panic, on the realisation that they had no expertise with which to treat the alarming symptoms. Sir George Baker noted on October 29:

I found His Majesty at his concert, not seeming to attend the music, but talking incessantly. His pulse was 84. He now complained that he was of late become near-sighted; that his vision was confused, and that whenever he attempted to read a mist floated before his eyes, & intercepted the objects. He likewise mentioned to me, as a cause of great distress, that having in the morning selected a certain prayer, he was found himself repeating a prayer which he had not proposed to make use of.

Baker decided to call in Dr. William Heberden, but even this distinguished physician was clearly baffled.

One of the worst days was November 5. Fanny Burney sensed the atmosphere of impending doom which enveloped Windsor:

Above   The children of George III at Windsor, by Benjamin West

Below   The Princess Charlotte, Augusta and Elizabeth, by Thomas Gainsborough

Above, *left*   William, Duke of Clarence, later William IV, by Sir Martin Archer-Shee   *Above*, *right*   Augustus, Duke of Sussex, by Guy Head   *Below*, *left*   Edward, Duke of Kent, by Henry Edridge *Below*, *right*   Ernest, Duke of Cumberland, by Thomas Rowlandson

Above George, Prince of Wales, by John Hoppner

Left Beau Brummell, by John Cooke

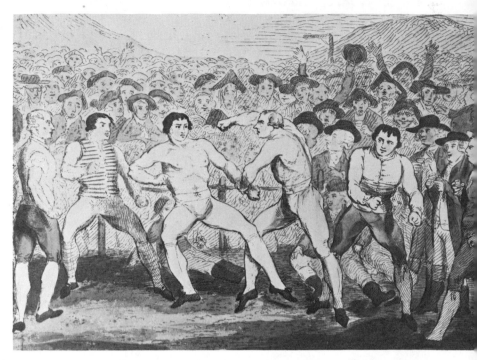

Fewterel and Jackson, 1788, by James Gillray

Cribb and Molineaux, 1811, by Thomas Rowlandson

Above The Great Subscription Room at Brook's, by Thomas Rowlandson and Augustus Pugin

Below Crockford's Club, by Thomas Shepherd

Left A Dandy, by James Gillray

Below "Characters in High Life," 1795, by H. Humphrey

George IV in Highland dress, by Sir David Wilkie

Above The Music Room at the Brighton Pavilion, by Augustus Pugin

Below The West Front of the Brighton Pavilion, by Humphrey Repton

At noon the King went out in his chaise, with the Princess Royal, for an airing. I looked from my window to see him; he was all smiling benignity, but gave so many orders to the postillions, and got in and out of the carriage twice, with such agitation, that again my fear of a great fever hanging over him grew more and more powerful. Alas! how little did I imagine I should see him no more for so long—so black a period!

The Queen was distraught, and the arrival of the Prince of Wales did not help:

The King, at dinner, had broken forth into positive delirium, which long had been menacing all who saw him most closely; and the Queen was so overpowered as to fall into violent hysteries. All the Princesses were in misery, and the Prince of Wales had burst into tears.

The Prince of Wales, lachrymose at the best of times, had better reason than ever before. The King, according to his son's no doubt somewhat biased evidence, had suddenly leaped upon him, seized him by the collar, and hurled him against the wall. Hungary water had to be applied to the Prince's temples, though it is not recorded how the King was soothed.

Fanny Burney waited in an agony of trepidation:

Two long hours I waited—alone, in silence, in ignorance, in dread! I thought they would never be over; at twelve o'clock I seemed to have spent two whole days in waiting. I then opened my door, to listen, in the passage, if anything seemed stirring. Not a sound could I hear. My apartment seemed wholly separated from life and motion. Whoever was in the house kept at the other end, and not even a servant crossed the stairs or passage by my rooms.

Finally, a page appeared to summon her to the Queen's presence. Miss Burney was appalled by what she saw:

My poor royal Mistress! never can I forget her countenance—pale, ghastly pale she looked; she was seated to be undressed, and attended by Lady Elizabeth Waldegrave and Miss Goldsworthy; her whole frame was disordered, yet she was still and quiet. These two ladies assisted me to undress her, or rather I assisted them, for they were firmer, from being longer present: my shaking hands and blinded eyes could scarce be of any use. I gave her some camphor julep, which had been ordered her by Sir George Baker. "How cold I am!" she cried, and put her hand on mine; marble it felt! and went to my heart's core!

Fanny Burney barely slept that night, and was up at six o'clock. When she saw the Queen, she burst into tears. Charlotte

looked like death—colourless and wan; but nature is infectious; the tears gushed from her own eyes, and a perfect agony of weeping ensued, which, once begun, she could not stop; she did not, indeed, try; for when it subsided, and she wiped her eyes, she said, "I thank you, Miss Burney—you have made me cry—it is a great relief to me—I have not been able to cry before, all this night long."

It had been a terrible night. The King had been convinced that his wife had been spirited away, and had appeared in her room, candle in hand, to reassure himself. The shock to her had been considerable.

They could all hear the King talking away incoherently in the next room, and the physicians attempting to calm him. Once, he burst out:

I am nervous; I am not ill, but I am nervous: if you would know what is the matter with me, I am nervous. But I love you both very well; if you would tell me truth: I love Dr. Heberden best, for he has not told me a lie: Sir George has told me a lie—a white lie, he says, but I hate a white lie! If you will tell me a lie, let it be a black lie!"

Sir George Baker was now at his wits' end, far from well himself, and has sent for yet another colleague, Dr. Richard Warren, the Prince of Wales's physician.

This was an ill-considered move. Warren was a society

doctor—there was a current joke that when he inspected his own tongue every morning, he automatically transferred a guinea from one pocket to another—but, much worse, the King had a particular aversion for him, mainly because he sensed, quite rightly, that Warren was determined to help the Prince of Wales's ambitions, and co-incidentally his own, whenever possible. Lady Harcourt voiced a general opinion:

From this fatal step many of the evils that followed resulted; and I have ever been of opinion that Sir George Baker's natural timidity, increased by the danger he saw coming on, made him act as he did, that some other of the faculty might be sent for to share with him the responsibility of the situation. Warren was a man of very different character; he was at that time considered, at least by the fashionable world, as being at the head of his profession . . . His being sent for to Windsor gave dissatisfaction to many of the King's most attached friends, and his Majesty said to him, the first time he went into his room, "You may come here as an acquaintance, but not as *my* physician; no man can serve two masters; you are the Prince of Wales's physician, you cannot be mine." Similar marks of dislike were shewn him by the King throughout the whole course of his illness.

Warren left Lower Lodge, without even speaking to the Queen, and went at once to the Prince of Wales at the Castle. According to Lady Harcourt, "He immediately announced the King's life to be in the utmost danger, and declared that the seizure upon the brain was so violent, that, if he did live, there was little reason to hope that his intellects would be restored." Sir George Baker's control over the King had ceased. The shift in power had commenced. Fanny Burney commented:

From this time, as the poor King grew worse, general hope seemed universally to abate; and the Prince of Wales now took the government of the house into his own hands. Nothing was done but by his orders, and he was applied to in every difficulty. The Queen interfered not in anything; she lived entirely in her two new rooms, and spent the whole day in patient sorrow and retirement with her daughters.

William Wyndham Grenville, who was to be appointed First Lord of the Treasury on Pitt's death, noted the constitutional problems:

In the event which Sir George Baker's note [a report to Pitt on November 8] gives reason to apprehend, there will be the greatest embarrassment as to the mode in which it is possible to proceed to any appointment of a Regent. The Parliament is now prorogued only until 23rd instant [in fact, the 20th], and must meet at that time, because no person but the King has authority to prorogue it further . . . Parliament cannot proceed to business without the session being opened by the King, or by some Commission authorised by him. No Regent can be appointed or authorised to exercise acts of royal authority but by Act of Parliament; nor can any such Act be valid and binding in law without the King's consent . . . It is a heavy calamity that is inflicted upon us in any case except that of his perfect recovery; but in the event which there seems most ground to fear, it may give rise to serious and difficult questions, such as cannot even be discussed without shaking the security and tranquillity of the country.

The Prince of Wales summoned William Pitt to Windsor. The doctors were pessimistic: the King might die, but failing that eventuality permanent insanity was the best that could be hoped for.

During November, the King's condition lurched hither and thither. On November 12, the royal equerry Robert Fulke Greville witnessed an especially violent outburst:

At length this Extreme agitation, continued through the two last hours, caused a Violent perspiration—He called to have the Windows opened, and complained of burning . . . About 3 o'Clock this day He became more violent & his talking was hurried & agitated to a great degree, & in consequence He put Himself in a violent perspiration. At this time his pulse rose to 130 . . . but at five o'Clock this Evening H.M. became exceedingly turbulent, &

made strong efforts to get out of bed—His exertions with great agitation of Words, continued about an hour.

The King's feelings for Dr. Warren had not changed. Greville noted that, on one occasion, he refused to have his pulse felt, pushed the doctor away and, after being restrained, "retired from Dr. Warren pale with Anger, & foaming with rage."

The physicians were divided among themselves, joining together to issue bulletins, but contradicting one another in private. Sir Lucas Pepys, the latest recruit, assured Fanny Burney that the King would certainly recover, though not immediately, while Warren continued to give thoroughly gloomy prognostications, which delighted the Prince of Wales and the Whigs. They were now using a strait-waistcoat to control the King, and Greville wrote sadly to his brother on November 24, "He has appeared several times to have that sort of consciousness of his situation which lunatics are observed to possess, and to use the same sort of methods for concealing it." Sir Gilbert Elliot, a fervent Whig, was convinced of the King's madness:

The physicians talk of fever, but I am inclined to believe he has never yet had any fever, in the common acceptance of that word, and that they avail themselves of some occasional quickness of pulse to avoid the true name of his disorder, and also to avoid the declaration of a circumstance which would make his case much more hopeless—I mean that of delirium without fever.

There were now seven physicians in attendance on the King. They decided that he should leave Windsor for Kew, conceivably for their own convenience as the frequent journeyings to Windsor had removed them from their other patients, but also because Kew was more private and the King would not be seen by casual passers-by who might exaggerate his condition. The King opposed the move with great vehemence, but finally he was persuaded, or coerced.

The royal party was established in the Queen's Lodge at

Kew on Sunday, November 30. The move had been precipitate, so much so that few preparations had been made to welcome the King and Queen. The weather was cold, and the house was not suitable for the winter. Fanny Burney noted:

Here, in all its dread colours, dark as its darkest prognostics, began the Kew campaign . . . I waited very long in the cold dark passages below, before I could find any one of whom to ask intelligence. The parlours were without fires, and washing. I gave directions afterwards to have a fire in one of them by seven o'clock every morning. At length I procured the speech of one of the pages, and heard that the night had been the most violently bad of any yet passed!—and no wonder!

On December 5, she heard some encouraging news, "that Dr. Willis, a physician of Lincoln, of peculiar skill and practice in intellectual maladies, had been sent for by express."

Dr. Francis Willis was a clergyman, the Rector of St. John's, Wapping, but he had also established a reputation for treating the insane at a private asylum he ran in Lincolnshire. Society sneered at him. Lord Sheffield wrote: "He is considered by some as not much better than a mountebank, and not far different from some of those that are confined in his house." He shocked Greville deeply by his descriptions of his methods. He considered his patients like "horses in a manège," to be broken in, and believed implicitly in the use of the strait-waistcoat. His son, Dr. John Willis, and three keepers were to assist him. Fanny Burney, on the other hand, greatly approved of the newly arrived doctor: "These Willises are most incomparable people. They take a pleasure, that brightens every particle of their countenances, in communicating what is good, and they soften all that is bad with the most sedulous kindness." It is open to doubt whether treatment, which consisted in the main of doses of tartar emetic and digitalis, the application of blisters, and recourse to the strait-waistcoat as a method of control and of punishment for the least infraction of the Willises' regulations, can really be equated with "sedulous kindness."

But whatever methods Dr. Willis used, and leaving aside the question of whether they were in the slightest way efficacious, the King began to get better. The Whig supporters of the Prince of Wales despaired of forcing the Regency Bill through the House of Commons while the King could still be considered insane, and Willis continued to give optimistic reports to William Pitt. Fanny Burney caught her first glance of the King for many months on February 1. Terrified of suddenly coming across him in the gardens at Kew, she had expressly consulted Dr. John Willis and been told that she had nothing to fear as the King would be taking exercise that day at Richmond.

Taking, therefore, the time I had most at command, I strolled into the gardens. I had proceeded, in my quick way, nearly half the round, when I suddenly perceived, through some trees, two or three figures. Relying on the instructions of Dr. John, I concluded them to be workmen and gardeners; yet tried to look sharp, and in so doing, as they were less shaded, I thought I saw the person of His Majesty! Alarmed past all possible expression, I waited not to know more, but turning back, ran off with all my might. But what was my terror to hear myself pursued!—to hear the voice of the King himself loudly and hoarsely calling after me, "Miss Burney! Miss Burney!"

Miss Burney, however, did not stop, but careered on like a myopic rabbit, "in search of some short passage, for the garden is full of little labyrinths, by which I might escape." But the King continued his pursuit, and he in turn was followed by the Willises, urging him not to overheat himself. Miss Burney takes up the story:

Heavens, how I ran! I do not think I should have felt the hot lava from Vesuvius—at least not the hot cinders—had I so run during its eruption. My feet were not sensible that they even touched the ground . . . On I flew; and such was my speed, so almost incredible to relate or recollect, that I fairly believe no one of the whole party could have overtaken me, if these words, from one of the attendants, had not reached me, "Dr. Willis begs you to stop!" "I cannot! I cannot!" I answered, still flying on, when he called out, "You must, ma'am; it hurts the King to run."

She stopped. And when the King reached her, he asked her the most unnervingly natural question: "Why did you run away?" It was quite unanswerable, but fortunately the King seemed so overjoyed to see her that he did not wait for a response but kissed her on the cheek instead: "What a conversation followed! When he saw me fearless, he grew more and more alive, and made me walk close by his side, away from the attendants, and even the Willises themselves, who, to indulge him, retreated." The King had had no opportunity for ordinary conversation for months past, and now he made up for the vacuum in his life. He spoke about his health and about the shortcomings of his pages; about Dr. Burney and Handel—"then he ran over most of his oratorios, attempting to sing the subjects of several airs and choruses, but so dreadfully hoarse that the sound was terrible"; about Fanny's old friend Mrs. Delany, the Duke of Beaufort and other mutual acquaintances. Finally, he said very deliberately, "I shall be much better served; and when once I get away, I shall rule with a rod of iron!"

In spite of certain eccentric characteristics, the King was undoubtedly recovering, as Fanny Burney's diary entries bear witness. Even a modicum of wit entered into some of his conversations. One day he stopped to talk to Eaton, his botanic gardener, in the Exotic Garden. According to Greville, "the King overheard his promise to make up a Basket of Exotic Flowers for the Doctor some of these days; and on hearing this, he added, 'Get another basket, Eaton, at the same time, and pack up the Doctor in it, and send him off at the same time.'" He also commissioned Vulliamy the watchmaker to design a gold watch to be presented to Willis when he left Kew.

The Whig Opposition became increasingly nervous. Sir Gilbert Elliot wrote on February 12: "The King has been really considerably better the last two days. Sir G. Baker . . .

says that he conversed rationally and coherently, with a great deal of recollection, for twenty-five minutes." Even Dr. Warren had to admit that the King appeared to be cured. And on February 19, the Lord Chancellor, Lord Thurlow, said in the House of Lords, where the Regency Bill was about to be read for the third time, that "the intelligence from Kew was that day so favourable every noble lord would agree with him in acknowledging that it would be indecent to proceed farther with the bill when it might become wholly unnecessary," and promptly moved the adjournment of the House.

The King was now receiving visitors, in particular representatives of the government. On February 23, the Prince of Wales and the Duke of York went to Kew, arriving two and a half hours late. Their father behaved impeccably, as if nothing untoward had occurred but he had merely been resting from the rigours of court life. He himself wrote to the Lord Chancellor: "Care was taken that the conversation should be cordial but without running into particulars. They seemed perfectly satisfied." Satisfied they may have been, disappointed they undoubtedly were.

Pitt saw the King on February 24 and told Greville that

there was not the smallest trace or appearance of any disorder . . . He spoke of his disorder as of a thing past, and which had left no other impression on his mind than that of gratitude for his recovery, and a sense of what he owed to those who had stood by him.

Two days later, a bulletin, signed by Sir George Baker, Sir Lucas Pepys and Dr. Willis, was quite uncompromising: "There appears this morning to be an entire cessation of His Majesty's illness." No more bulletins were issued, by the King's order.

The crisis was over, or appeared to be so. The Regency Bill was shelved, the physicians and keepers began to depart, the King himself dismissed some of the pages who, in his opinion, had been too familiar or too prone to passing details of the royal illness to interested ears at Carlton House. On

March 14, he returned to Windsor. Fanny Burney, as usual, described the affecting scene:

This morning we returned to Windsor, with what different sensations from those with which we left it! All illness over, all fears removed, all sorrows lightened! The King was so well as to go on horseback . . . All Windsor came out to meet the King. It was a joy amounting to ecstasy; I could not keep my eyes dry all day long. A scene so reversed! sadness so sweetly exchanged for thankfulness and delight!

The Willises took their leave, with instructions that the King should continue "taking the Bark twice a day and about twice a week to take 3 quarters of a grain at a time of Tartar Emetic and also to use the warm bath, and foot bath occasionally."

The physicians had no hesitation in reserving the chief glory for themselves. Dr. Willis had a special medal struck, with his head on one side, and the words "Britons rejoice, your King's restored" on the obverse, and was disagreeably surprised when Parliament voted him what he considered a meagre pension of £1,000 a year for twenty-one years (he was seventy-three at the time). His son perhaps did better, with £650 a year for life. The other physicians presented their accounts and were paid on the basis of ten guineas for each visit to Kew, and thirty guineas for each visit to Windsor. Nor surprisingly, Sir George Baker profited mightily, netting £1,380 for his insignificant efforts.

The medical profession in general made much out of the King's illness. All manner of doctors took up their pens to castigate the royal physicians and to say what they would have done. Dr. Robert Jones had some thoughts on the King's convalescence. He should "be indulged in every rational propensity which is agreeable to his mind. His illustrious consort and family ought to have access to him at all times. He should never be contradicted, nor thwarted in any thing that he can request, either in food or drink." "Animal food," wine though not to excess, and soft music would be efficacious, fresh air would not. The Reverend Joseph Townsend claimed that the King had suffered from mania melancholica, and Dr. William Pargeter dilated on the definition of madness. Even the highly eccentric Dr. James Graham, who called himself "Conqueror, under God, of Diseases," and who lived on a diet of vegetables, milk, honey and water, composed a number of lengthy tracts upon the subject and managed to press one on the King while the latter was convalescing at Windsor. It is doubtful whether he read it. The private madhouses, too, began to do a roaring trade.

Although the King had mild recurrences of his illness, in particular, in 1795, it was not until after the turn of the century that a second major crisis involved the whole nation in discussions about lunacy, the medical profession, and the prospect of the Prince of Wales as Regent. In February 1801, he told one of his equerries, General Garth, that he had not slept the previous night, and that he was "bilious and unwell," ominous symptoms indeed. Again the King's attack was blamed on the cold. He suffered, as before, from cramp, constipation, insomnia, a fast pulse, nausea and a feverish sweating. Dr. Thomas Gisborne, who had been in attendance during the later phase of the 1788–89 illness, prescribed that well-known stand-by which had done so much for Horace Walpole, James's Powders.

By a curious coincidence, Dr. Willis's son Thomas called on the King at the Queen's House on February 16, but diagnosed nothing more serious than a heavy cold. But three days later, Pitt was in no doubt that "His Majesty's mind was not in a proper state." Once again, his condition seemed to change day by day. Lord Eldon, the new Lord Chancellor, found him entirely lucid and rational, but Willis, paying a second call, on February 21, noticed "strong marks of fever and irritation," a general restlessness. The King was obviously disturbed and said as much: "I do feel myself very ill, I am much weaker than I was, and I have prayed to God all night that I might die, or that he would spare my reason . . . if it should be otherwise, for God's sake keep from me your father and a regency." It is easy enough to imagine the acute mental agony which must have beset the King as soon as he perceived symptoms similar to those at the outset of his first illness. Although Thomas Willis's father had always maintained that lunacy was curable, he had made no secret of his opinion that George III was mad. The King had graphic memories of the emetics and purges, the blistering and, worst of all, the strait-waistcoat which had been so savagely used at Kew. Now it seemed that the whole appalling nightmare was about to be relived, with no prospect of a second cure.

Thomas Willis tried to calm him, but the signs became increasingly obvious. By night, the King was hopelessly confused, and Dr. John Willis was summoned; he was joined by yet another brother, Dr. Robert Darling Willis, on the Monday.

The Prince of Wales moved with great alacrity, sounding out the new Prime Minister, Henry Addington, about the prospect of a Regency. Addington, however, referred him to Pitt, who took a strong line, demanding that there should be no repetition of the Opposition's scandalous manoeuvrings in the 1788/89 crisis. The Prince of Wales was silenced, and the political atmosphere softened.

At first, the King seemed in danger of collapse. Thomas Willis recorded the facts in his diary:

Soon after this his Majesty put on such an appearance of being exhausted, that his life was despaired of. His pulse too had rapidly increased so that Dr. John thought it absolutely necessary to inform the Duke of York immediately of his fears and also Mr. Addington. And Mr. Addington sent immediately for the Prince of Wales. They all met together about three o'clock at the Queen's House and the result of the meeting was, that Drs. Gisborne and Reynolds, Drs. John and Robert W. perceiving the exhausted state of the King, they gave Him a strong dose of Musk, which had the effect of composing him to sleep for an hour and a half which he had not had for, I think, nearly 48 hours.

Slowly, the extreme danger of the first days passed. Addington took a strong personal interest in the case, perhaps because his own father had been a doctor, and at one point suggested the old country remedy for insomnia of a pillow stuffed with warm hops (the King slept for more than eight hours). By March 7, optimism had crept into the daily bulletin, and the final report on the 11th stated: "His Majesty is perfectly free from fever, but it may require some time, as is always necessary after so severe an illness, to complete recovery." The Prince of Wales and the Duke of Kent visited the King, and on March 14 Pitt came to deliver up his seals of office.

All this time, the Willises increased their power over the royal household. Addington consulted them on everything, and the Queen appeared to have complete faith in them, until John Willis went too far by applying blisters to the King's legs in order to keep him away from a drawing-room. Thomas Willis, who seems to have been the prime mover, whispered in everyone's ear: in the Duke of York's about the Duke of Kent, in Addington's, even in the King's about William Pitt. The King was unimpressed and, on March 30, abused the Willises roundly, reminded them that he was master in his own house, refused to take any further medicines, and told them to leave. They held on with considerable obstinacy, making a further attempt to browbeat the King, but finally they admitted defeat and left the Queen's House on April 14. Five days later, the Prince of Wales saw the King, and recorded the scene: "The King began with the happiness he felt at being able the same day to embrace his son and dismiss Dr. Willis's keepers; that being the first day since his illness that any one of his own servants had been permitted to attend him."

The Willises made one dramatic and final throw. Egged on by Princess Elizabeth, they attempted to kidnap him at Kew.

It was an extraordinary plot, and one which seemed to have failed when the King eluded them. But, apparently quite undaunted, they went to find him at the Prince of Wales's house. Thomas Willis himself, without a trace of guilt, recorded in his diary:

On the King getting sight of me he seemed surprized and would have hastily passed and escaped out of the room but I prevented him . . . I spoke to him at once of his situation and the necessity there was that he should be immediately under control again. His Majesty sat down, turning very pale and . . . looking very sternly at me exclaimed, "Sir, I will never forgive you whilst I live."

But the King could not escape, and he was conducted with less than fit ceremony to the Duke of Sussex's apartment in Kew House and kept a prisoner there until May 19. The Queen appeared to give her approval to the whole extraordinary episode by lending a house on Kew Green to the ambitious Willises.

For nearly a month, there was complete stalemate. The Prince of Wales attempted to wrest his father's person from the Willises so that he could enforce a Regency. Addington did nothing. The Queen did nothing. The Willises administered emetics. The King himself sensibly gave no appearance of anger, but bided his time. On May 19, he acted. Lord Eldon had visited him and he was entirely unequivocal that

he had taken a solemn determination, that unless he was that day allowed to go over to the house where the Queen and his family were, no earthly consideration should induce him to sign his name to any paper or to do one act of government whatever. This resolution he confirmed, with the strongest declaration, that he would abide by, as a gentleman and as a King.

George III simply left the house and walked the few hundred yards to the Queen's apartments.

It was the end for the Willises, although they seemed unmoved and not in the slightest degree nervous. The Lord

Chancellor recommended that Dr. Robert Willis should accompany the King to Weymouth to attend him during his convalescence, to which suggestion the latter reacted strongly and predictably. On June 29, the royal party left Kew, the Willis clan standing among the crowds on Kew Green. Two years later, the sum of £10,000 was shared out amongst them, although the King was never aware of this, as he would certainly have vetoed it. George himself enjoyed his stay at Weymouth, as always, but he did not seem to recover as rapidly as in the old days. For three years, however, there was no crisis.

Then, in February 1804, the King began to experience all the old symptoms: rheumatism, fever, swelling, nausea. Addington immediately consulted the Willises and gave them extraordinary powers, which were never exercised. The Duke of Kent and the Duke of Cumberland refused them access to their father, who also advised against the Willises. Instead, Dr. Simmons, from St. Luke's Hospital for Lunaticks, was put in charge of the case. His method of treatment differed hardly at all from that exercised by the Willises, but mercifully the King was already on the mend.

By now, though, he had become a political pawn. The Whig Opposition realised the importance of the Prince of Wales and began to press for a Regency. But six years were to pass before this could be realised. By then, the King's failing eyesight had made it necessary for him to have a private secretary to act as his reader and writer, and his rapid ageing had shocked all who saw him. On October 25, 1810, he celebrated the fiftieth anniversary of his accession to the throne, and within twenty-four hours he was stricken down yet again.

Spencer Perceval, the Prime Minister, reported that "his conversation was prodigiously hurried, and . . . extremely diffuse, explicit and indiscreet"; Canning, more succinctly and cruelly, said that "he was just as mad as ever he was in his life." Simmons was called in again, but departed almost as rapidly, having been refused the overall control which he demanded. Other doctors were summoned, and in November, Dr. Robert Darling Willis put in an appearance. All the physicians were questioned by the Privy Council, and a Regency Bill was drafted.

It is interesting at this stage to note Dr. Willis's sworn statement, before the Privy Council:

I consider the King's derangement more nearly allied to delirium than insanity . . . In delirium, the mind is actively employed upon past impressions, upon objects and former scenes which rapidly pass in succession before the mind, resembling . . . a person talking in his sleep. There is also a considerable disturbance in the general constitution; great restlessness, want of sleep, and total unconsciousness of surrounding objects. In insanity there may be little or no disturbance, apparently, in the general constitution; the mind is occupied upon some fixed assumed idea, to the truth of which, it will pertinaciously adhere, in opposition to the plainest evidence of its falsity; and the individual is acting, always, upon that false impression. In insanity, also, the mind is awake to objects which are present. Taking insanity, therefore, and delirium, as two points, I would place derangement of mind somewhere between them. His Majesty's illness, uniformly, partakes more of the delirium than of the insanity.

All the doctors seem to have opted against a diagnosis of madness, but the Regency Bill progressed virtually unhindered. It received its third reading on the last day of January 1811, and on February 6 the Prince of Wales took the oath of office as Regent. To all intents and purposes, George III's reign had come to an end.

The last decade of the King's life was pitiful. His attacks came and went, the physicians' treatment remained much the same. The Queen's Council questioned them periodically, but only the most humane, Dr. Heberden, attempted to alleviate his royal master's mental agony:

It is now more than six months, that His Majesty has been indisposed: and it is become of great moment that His Majesty's mind should, if possible, be roused from its disordered actions, and not suffered to degenerate into a state of habitual error . . . The very same restraint, which at one time was calculated to allay irritation, becomes at another a cause of increasing it.

But Heberden's words were to no avail. The barbarous, well-meaning treatment continued, and the Willises once more held sway. In 1812 the Regency was made permanent, and the King was completely isolated from the outside world. It was almost as if he had ceased to live, occasionally visited, or mentioned in gossip, but no more than a wraith, haunting Windsor. By 1817, he was going deaf; the following year, he could not walk. His only amusement was playing the harpsichord, for he retained his passion for music until the end. He was quite oblivious of the marriage and death of his grand-daughter, Princess Charlotte; of the hasty marriages of his sons, Clarence, Kent and Cambridge; even of the death in November 1818 of the Queen.

Sir Henry Halford saw him in January 1819:

The King appeared forcibly impressed—collected himself—used the manner of a solemn, enthusiastic, silent, appeal by lifting up his eyes and his hands—but returned no answer—and precluded all further address by striking rapidly the keys of his harpsichord.

In November of the same year, the Duke of York found him much the same: "He was amusing himself with playing upon the harpsichord and singing with as strong and firm a voice as ever I heard him." But he was looking very old and thin: "The frame is so much weaker that we can no longer look forward . . . to his being preserved to us for any length of time."

And so it was. The final violent outburst coincided with Christmas 1819. He lingered on into the new year, but even his extraordinary strength could not last indefinitely. George III died at 8:32 on the evening of January 29, 1820. He was eighty-one years old; his successor, Prince Regent and Prince of Wales, was almost sixty.

Madness is a convenient shorthand diagnosis; it covers a multitude of sins. Certainly, many of George III's contemporaries, and indeed those who were born after his death, thought that he was mad. The early nineteenth century was a period of political disorder and general discontent, and much of this could be blamed on the weak conduct of the country under George III. And so, he could be held responsible for any social ill or political disaster, from the appalling poverty among the working classes to the loss of the American colonies. One could expect nothing better of a lunatic.

For a century and a half after the death of George III, there was no real attempt to overrule the accepted verdict of his own doctors. Then, in 1969, Ida Macalpine and Richard Hunter published a book entitled *George III and the Mad-Business*, based on two articles which had appeared in the *British Medical Journal* in 1966 and 1968 respectively. They based their diagnosis of the Royal Malady on a concept put forward in the 1930s by Sir Archibald Garrod concerning "inborn errors of metabolism." One such error came to be known as porphyria, because anyone suffering from it was inclined to pass urine of a purple colouring. The symptoms of porphyria included paralysis, delirium, hypertension, and acute pain, all of which were experienced by George III.

Macalpine and Hunter suggest that the King suffered from this rare disease in its most virulent form, and that it would actually have been aggravated by the treatment he received at the hands of the Willises and their minions. They also suggest that porphyria is a hereditary disorder, and that signs of it, in its less violent form, can be seen in a number of George III's ancestors, immediate family, and descendants. In effect, it is *the* Royal Malady.

Persuasive though this diagnosis is, it can, of course, never be proved beyond all shadow of doubt. What is certain is that Goerge III suffered appalling mental and physical pain; and that, not for the first nor the last time, the doctors did not know what they were doing.

Part Four

GEORGE IV
1762–1830; King, 1820–30

The most extraordinary compound of talent, wit, buffoonery, obstinacy and good feeling—in short a medley of the most opposite qualities, with a great preponderance of good—that I ever saw in any character in my life.

The Duke of Wellington

This delightful, blissful, wise, pleasurable, honourable, virtuous, true and immortal Prince was a violator of his word, a libertine over head and ears in debt and disgrace, a despiser of domestic ties, the companion of gamblers and demireps, a man who has just closed half a century without one single claim on the gratitude of his country or the respect of posterity.

Leigh Hunt

I look through all his life and recognise but a bow and a grin. I try to take him to pieces, and find silk stockings, padding, stays, a coat with frogs and a fur collar, a star and blue ribbon, a pocket handkerchief prodigiously scented, one of Truefitt's best nutty-brown wigs reeking with oil, a set of teeth and a huge black stock, under-waistcoats, more under-waistcoats, and then—nothing.

William Makepeace Thackeray

He always had money. When he died they found £10,000 in his boxes and money scattered about everywhere, a great deal of gold. There were above 500 pocketbooks, of different dates, and in every one money—guineas, one pound notes, one, two, or three in each. There never was anything like the quantity of trinkets and trash that they found. He had never given away or parted with anything. There was a prodigious quantity of hair—women's hair—of all colours and lengths, some locks with the powder and pomatum still sticking to them, heaps of women's gloves, *gages d'amour* which he had got at balls, and with the perspiration still marked on the fingers, notes and letters in abundance, but not much that was of any political consequence, and the whole was destroyed.

Charles Greville

He was all heart . . .

Princess Elizabeth, George's sister

X

Royal Geordie

The news has flown frae mouth to mouth,
The North for ance has bang'd the South;
The de'il a Scotsman's die o' drouth,
   Carle, now the King's come!

Chorus:
Carle, now the King's come!
Carle, now the King's come!
Thou shalt dance, and I will sing,
Carle, now the King's come!

                    Sir Walter Scott

The *Royal George* sailed from Greenwich on August 10, 1822. The First Gentleman of Europe was on his travels again. A royal progress to Scotland was inevitable for a number of excellent reasons. The previous year, George IV had visited Ireland and Hanover, and the good citizens of Edinburgh were beginning to display signs of jealousy. Moreover, the King's political advisers considered that, with the final extinction of Jacobite hopes with the death of the Cardinal of

York, the time was ripe for a display of *rapprochement;* no representative of the Hanoverian dynasty had crossed the border since the Duke of Cumberland, and his name hardly evoked the happiest of memories. George himself was less than enthusiastic. He was nervous that the Calvinist streak in his northern subjects might manifest itself to his personal discomfort. He remembered that his ancestor Mary had been roundly denounced as nothing better than a whore, and was disagreeably aware that his own moral standards might be misconstrued; he had only recently exchanged the favours of Lady Hertford for those of Lady Conyngham, surely sufficient grounds for banishment to the stool of repentance. But the politicians reassured him, pointing out that his alternative plan for a visit to the Continent would be far too expensive. So, George dutifully ordered his kilts and, for good measure, some flesh-coloured tights to keep out the cold.

The King's departure from Greenwich aroused the keenest interest. Information stemming from Carlton House about the precise details were somewhat sketchy, and the roads to Greenwich were crammed with coaches and carts and even caravans days in advance of the actual sailing. The local inhabitants had seen nothing like it since Nelson's lying-in-state. There was something for every taste, from the sight of certain ladies ambitiously clad in tartan to the splendours of the city state barges. A contemporary eye-witness describes the scene:

Immediately in front lay the *Royal George* yacht, in every way equipped for sea, and distinguished by her superior size and decorations from all the surrounding vessels. At each end of her were moored the *Comet* and *James Watt* steam-boats, by which she was to be accompanied on her voyage. Again, to the left was ranged an infinite number of pleasure yachts, gayly decorated with appropriate flags and streamers. Beyond these were three large steam-boats, engaged for the day by casual spectators, and filled with well-dressed companies. Beside these there was a vast variety of craft of all descriptions, including pleasure-boats, wherries, ship-boats, funnies, skiffs, filled with parties impatiently awaiting the approaching spectacle, occasionally moving from place to place, and thereby giving a singular and pleasing animation to the whole. Beyond these again were seen the shores of the Isle of Dogs, which exhibited immense clusters of spectators arranged on scaffolds erected for the purpose, and for miles lining the banks of the river. The effect produced by the whole, accompanied as it was by the contemplation of the cause by which it was occasioned, was extremely grand.

Finally, on the Saturday afternoon, the patient spectators, some of them by now distinctly the worse for wear, were rewarded. A capacious caravan, filled with the King's luggage and a number of servants, left Carlton House, and three-quarters of an hour later George, dressed in a blue surtout, white trousers, a forage cap, and Wellington boots, entered his carriage, which was drawn by four matched bays. The cavalcade set out on a somewhat leisurely progress through Whitehall and over Westminster Bridge. At half-past two, the King's Lord Steward, the complaisant Lord Conyngham, arrived at Greenwich, and he was followed by Lords Harrowby, Liverpool and Westmorland, and by the Foreign Secretary, Lord Londonderry:

The shore in every part was lined with spectators. Every house was crammed from top to bottom: the hospital, its grounds and enclosures, were completely filled. The pensioners flanked each side of the path from the western gate to the stairs at which the King was to embark; and parties of the royal marines were stationed through the whole line to preserve order. Mr. Minshull, the magistrate of Bow Street, was at the western gate with a strong body of police.

At last, the King's carriage appeared (he had been delayed by a large contingent of schoolchildren—"Their appearance was very pleasing; and his Majesty appeared gratified with the artless expressions of attachment evinced by his juvenile subjects"), and the royal standard was hoisted on the Hospital. There was a moment's confusion when two of the horses drawing the carriage immediately behind the King's stumbled and fell, throwing the groom, but George was soon safely ensconced in the Governor's house. After a few minutes, he re-emerged and prepared to enter his barge. "At the moment that he descended the steps from the Royal Hospital, he was greeted by the vast multitude ashore and on the river with cheers which were truly astounding. The hats and handkerchiefs of tens of thousands of persons of both sexes were waving in the air."

The *Royal George* was towed by the *Comet* as far as Woolwich, but well before Gravesend the wind was sufficiently strong to allow the hawser to be unslung and the royal yacht to proceed under sail. The King appeared on deck in full naval uniform with cocked hat; the royal descent on Scotland was under way.

The voyage was uneventful. Off Aldeburgh, the *Royal George* was passed by the *Czar*, "having convicts on board, who hoisted her colours, manned her cross-trees and masthead, and cheered his Majesty, the convicts, who had been admitted upon deck by the captain, most cordially joining." The two steam-boats were reconnected to the yacht, and by August 12 the royal squadron was off Scarborough. A gale sprang up that evening and did not die down until North Berwick had been passed. At last, early in the afternoon of August 14, the *Royal George* dropped anchor off Leith. Robert Peel, the Minister deputed to attend the King, went on board, and returned with the news that George had decided to postpone his landing until the following day. The royal yacht was surrounded by boats, and the King, now dressed in blue pantaloons, a military cloak and a cap with an oilskin cover, thoroughly enjoyed himself acknowledging the cheers. But he retained his warmest welcome for a visitor who arrived in Admiral Sir John Beresford's barge. "What!" he cried, "Sir Walter Scott? The man in Scotland I most wish to see! Let him come up." Sir Walter had arrived to present George with a St. Andrew's Cross made of silver set with cairngorms and tiny pearls, and bearing the inscription in Gaelic, "Long Life to the King of Scotland." The King was delighted and toasted Sir Walter in a glass of whisky. Scott was given the glass as a memento, stowed it away in his Windsor uniform, but later broke it. He stayed for dinner on the yacht, and the King's good humour was not even affected by news of Londonderry's suicide.

George IV's arrival off Leith was the culmination of weeks of strenuous preparation by Scotland's literary conscience, "the bard of chivalry and romance." Scott had seized the opportunity with fervour. As soon as the official letter from Lord Melville, the Lord Privy Seal for Scotland, confirming the royal visit, had been received by the Lord Provost of Edinburgh on July 18, Scott did not rest. Banquets were planned, a bonfire was built on Arthur's Seat, carriages were ordered, stands for spectators were constructed, loyal addresses were prepared by public bodies ranging from the General Assembly of the Church of Scotland and the Society in Scotland for propagating Christian Knowledge, to the Corporations of Goldsmiths and Bakers. On August 9, an extraordinary meeting of the Highland Society had been held; the Company of Archers began to drill in full uniform—"a Robin Hood tartan jacket, tartan trews, the Highland hose, the flat blue bonnet, the ruff, Robin Hood belt, and white satin bow-case, worn as a scarf"; the Celtic Society, Walter Scott's pride and joy, which had only been founded two years before, received their colours at his own hands; the regalia of Scotland were moved from Edinburgh Castle to Holyroodhouse; medals were struck; the burghers of Leith planned cannily to convert the log of mahogany on which the King would step when landing in Scotland for the first time into memorial snuff-boxes; and both Leith and Edinburgh were given over to masons and decorators, architects and artisans.

The popular versifiers had a field-day—or, as a kindlier commentator put it: "The muse of Caledonia, ever enthusi-

astic, ever watchful of the national glory, inspired her votaries on the present occasion with strains expressive of the
most wild and animated joy." Sir Walter Scott himself
penned some deplorably bathetic stanzas:

> My trusty Provost, tried and tight,
> Stand forward for the Good Town's right,
> There's waur than you been made a knight—
>   Carle, now the King's come!
>
> But yonder come my canty Celts,
> With dirk and pistol at their belts,
> Thank God, we've still some plaids and kilts—
>   Carle, now the King's come!

But a certain Mr. John Mayne also gave of his best:

> King George the Fourth is coming down
> To see his friends in Embro town,
> To hold his court, and wear the crown
>   O'Scotland's kings, and a' that.
> And a' the chieftains o' the North,
> Lords, leddies, lairds, and men of wirth,
> Are flocking to the frith o'Forth,
>   To welcome him, and a' that.

And the author of "Stanzas for the King's Landing," who
preferred to remain anonymous, became totally carried away
by the Caledonian muse:

> The eagle screams upon Benmore,
>   The wild-deer bounds on Cheviot fell;
> Step boldly, King, on Albyn's shore;
>   Son of her Lords, she greets thee well.
> The voice that hath been silent long,
>   Awakes to harbinger thy path;
> Once more she weaves th'ancestral song,
>   Once more 'tis 'Righ gu-Brath'.

There were other poems, of a more reprehensibly satirical
nature, but only the rude minority guffawed at invitations in
verse "to kneel and kiss Royal Geordie's bum."

While the King prepared to step boldly on Albyn's shore, Edinburgh prepared to enjoy herself. The great bonfire on Arthur's Seat was lit, "and, though dimmed by the rain, its dark red glow, amidst the clouds and darkness that enveloped it, and, seen through which, it appeared at an immeasurable height, had an astonishingly grand effect." But there were further illuminations:

A large crown on the top of the gas-house chimney, illuminated with gas, presented a no less striking appearance to the citizens. The shaft of masonry on which it rested was rendered invisible by the humidity of the atmosphere; so that, when viewed at a distance from the east, the crown looked like a splendid meteor suspended in the firmament.

The rain ceased on the morning of August 15 and, as the same indefatigable commentator noted in a fine flight of fancy,

our revered Monarch, as he ascended the deck, beheld the Scottish capital, with its towers and palaces, basking in the rays of an autumnal sun, and the surrounding country spread out before him in all its loveliness. The firth was covered with innumerable boats and vessels, in their gaudiest apparel; and from many of them arose the strains of the bagpipe, which floated over the waters, and were heard in the distance, wild, yet pensive, like the voice of Scotland's Genius, welcoming her Sovereign to her hospitable shores.

The art of romantic description was then superseded by that of speculation:

What were the emotions of the King when he beheld this glorious scene;—when he contemplated the abodes of his illustrious ancestors;—when he looked around, and saw the distant Grampians,—Dunfermline, where all that was perishable of the great Bruce slumbers in dust,—and scenes innumerable, consecrated in the hearts of the patriot and the scholar! It is not difficult to imagine what were the feelings which the contemplation of such a scene must have conjured up in the generous breast of his Majesty. Certain it is, that he caught the spirit of the country, as if by "soft infection"; for, doffing his ordinary suit, he equipped himself in the Highland garb [Mr. George Hunter, of Princes Street, had furnished two complete outfits in the Royal Stuart tartan, including kilt, coat, hose and bonnet]; and, conscious now that he was "every inch" a Scottish king, appeared most ardently animated.

A sizeable procession had formed up in Queen Street at nine o'clock and set off for Leith two hours later. Members of the Celtic Society and kilted highlanders, heralds and judges, the Lord High Constable the Earl of Erroll, whose robes of office were not ready in time and who was obliged to appear in the uniform of a lieutenant of Lancers, trumpeters and yeomen, White Rod, the Lord-Lieutenant of Midlothian, the Knight Marischal, the Sheriff and, inevitably, Sir Walter Scott: it was a motley but impressive committee of welcome, its numbers shortly swelled by representatives from Leith. Just after noon, the King entered his barge, and a royal salute was fired. George had taken considerable trouble over his clothes (he had changed yet again), and now appeared in the uniform of an admiral, with a thistle and a sprig of heather in his hat, and the St. Andrew's Cross on his breast. An even larger procession, with the King riding in an open landau, set off for Edinburgh, to be met at the city barrier by the Lord Provost, magistrates and town council.

The entire city had turned out for the unique spectacle:

The space of a mile and a half was filled with people in all manner of vehicles, and in every grade of society, from the barefooted lassie to the noble and flaunting dame; from the kilted Highlander to the more haughty and bedizened Southron. Windows, doors, and house-tops were occupied; the branches of the trees became perches for the less elevated, and the ridges of the walls maintained their single files. In the distance, steeples, towers, and turrets, mound and mountain, were put in requisition as a forlorn hope. There was an assembly of the nation.

The King was especially interested in one part of the assembly:

His attention seemed to be particularly drawn to a balcony in
front of the turret-like house which, on the east, flanks the south
side of Picardy Place. This balcony was occupied by a number
of beautiful females . . . The King seemed delighted with the
loyal demonstrations of this fair bevy, to whom he most gra-
ciously bowed.

George was in his element, cheered to the echo, and with fair
women at every turn. He became quite overcome with emotion when he caught his first glimpse of the Castle from Princes Street. "How superb!" he exclaimed. And the sight of
thousands of people thronging the side of Calton Hill moved
him still further.

The carefully planned ceremonial of presentations and re-
views and addresses kept George at Holyrood until half-past
three, when he was at last able to leave for Dalkeith, where he
was to stay as the guest of the young Duke of Buccleuch. In
the evening, the bonfire on Arthur's Seat was re-lit, there was
a fireworks display in George Street, and Leith was lavishly
illuminated, the *chef d'oeuvre* being an extraordinary design
by one of Bewick's pupils for Reid the bookseller's, incorpo-
rating Britannia, a Highland chieftain, a sailor, the royal
yacht and indeed the entire royal squadron, numerous mot-
toes and scrolls, and a portrait of the King with the well-in-
tended but improbable caption, "Fair fa' his honest sonsy
face." The town of Dalkeith also indulged in fireworks, and
on Lord Lothian's estate there was a bonfire requiring 150
cartloads of coal.

August 16 was a day of rest for the tired and over-emo-
tional monarch, who merely received visitors and prepared
for the promised levee at Holyrood. The citizens of Edinburgh had to content themselves with admiring the illuminations. Great ingenuity, intense rivalry and vulgar expenditure had all contributed. The landlord of the Black Bull had
flatteringly chosen the device "Pater patriae"; the Union
Club, less inspired, had selected "Hurra"; Lord Bannatyne's
house revealed George seated, with two seahorses and a fe-

male figure in attendance; the office of the *Weekly Journal* plumped for banner headlines, "Vivat Rex!", "May the King live for ever!", and "'Tis the better for us, boys"; but the ultimate in enterprise was undoubtedly demonstrated by Mr. Gianetti, the perfumer, of George Street—"on one side of his house G.R. and a crown on the other side; a full-length transparency of his Majesty in regimentals, just landed in Scotland, and saying, 'How's a' wi' ye?' Another transparency, a bust of his Majesty crowned with laurel, with emblematical figures, below which, an inscription in French." Who could ask for anything more?

The levee at Holyrood was an exhausting affair, approximately 2,000 people being presented to the King. As the interminable line of dukes, marquesses, earls, viscounts, lords, right honourables, officers of state, judges, honourables, baronets and knights, the French Consul, Members of Parliament, vice- and deputy-lieutenants, magistrates, the clergy, professors, doctors, advocates, generals, lieutenant-generals, major-generals, colonels, lieutenant-colonels, majors, captains, lieutenants, cornets and ensigns, representatives from the naval and military civil department, officers of militia and yeomanry, admirals and captains and lieutenants and ordinary gentlemen, passed in an ever-increasing haze, George must have thought wistfully about the ladies on their balcony. And even then he was forced to preside over a meeting of the Privy Council before he could leave for the comparative peace of Dalkeith. The only light moment had been provided by the portly Sir William Curtis, who appeared in full Highland costume and exchanged somewhat sheepish grins with his monarch, who was similarly and no more persuasively attired.

Sunday was a further day of rest, and much of Monday was given over to a court and closet audience at Holyrood. George had discarded the kilt and looked more comfortable in his fieldmarshal's uniform as he received a series of addresses from the Church of Scotland, the universities, and

the Highland Society. On the Tuesday, the ladies of Edinburgh at last had their chance to shine, a chance which they
seized all too literally, as descriptions of their dresses make
clear. The ubiquitous eye-witness, who was later to accumu-
late all his impressions in *A Historical Account of His Majesty's Visit to Scotland*, an admirably serious volume of 336
pages and including five folding panoramas, was more charitable, though less truthful: "The demeanour of the ladies was
extremely characteristic, as they moved towards the State
apartments, sedate almost to demureness,—their eyes motionless, yet keen with intelligence,—dignified, but betraying, by
the timidity of their advances, the invincible modesty of their
nature." Modesty or otherwise, the ladies did not stint themselves in outward extravagance. The Marchioness of Queensberry set the tone: "White tulle petticoat, over rich white
satin, handsomely ornamented with embroidery; train of lilac
silk, trimmed with tulle shells. Headdress, black velvet, with a
profusion of lilac and white feathers, band and sprig of diamonds." The Countess of Morton favoured purple and gold,
and Lady Belhaven chose a "rich embroidered steel dress,
trimmed richly with blond; embroidered train to match, lined
with satin." Lady Pringle was more ambitious: "Rich gold
sprig lama dress, with French white satin train, trimmed round
with rich gold lama, and Highland bonnet, particularly rich
and novel, embroidered with a gold thistle intermixed with
heath; with an elegant plume of ostrich feathers, and a diamond star in the middle." Toques and petticoats, trains and
tassels, turbans and manteaux, the art of the couturier, the
milliner and the jeweller was on display in every colour in the
spectrum and, in the cases where the ladies had opted for tartan, far too many for all but the short-sighted. The King,
though, was delighted. At last he felt at home, surrounded by
women gathered in their hundreds to do him honour.

Thursday had been set aside for George's procession to
Edinburgh Castle. The weather was worsening once more,
with an overcast sky, and intermittent drizzle. But the crowds

were undaunted, and the various trade guilds began to assemble with their banners; the gardeners had constructed three Prince of Wales feathers out of hollyhocks, and the officer at the head of the society of glass-blowers wore a glass hat, and carried a glass sword and target. The three chief participants in the procession had also opted for something out of the ordinary, though they seemed a trifle uncertain about historical conformity: Sir Alexander Keith, the Knight Marischal, had Tudor inclinations, with a white and gold doublet, cloak and plumed hat; the Duke of Hamilton, who was carrying the Crown of Scotland, was definitely Stuart in his preference, with a black satin suit slashed with white and a Van Dyke collar; the Lord Lyon, the Earl of Kinnoull, clearly decided that colour was the main prerequisite, and must have presented a rainbow picture in a green and gold velvet surcoat, white and gold pantaloons, a long crimson velvet mantle, a gold crown and a crimson cap edged with ermine. Sir Walter Scott, who was cheered by the crowd, was faithful to his Windsor uniform.

In spite of the rain, the occasion passed off well enough. The King was in a closed carriage, but he bowed energetically and, once he was inside the walls of the Castle, decided that he should be seen properly:

One of his attendants expressed an apprehension, that the King would get wet. "O, never mind," replied his Majesty, with great animation, "I must cheer the people"; and taking off his hat, he waved it repeatedly, and gave three cheers, which were heard at some distance. The people, whose enthusiasm was now wound up to the highest pitch, again made the air resound with their loudest acclamations. The thick fog that brooded over the landscape deprived his Majesty of the full enjoyment of a prospect unequalled, perhaps, in variety and magnificence. But the same circumstance cast an air of sublimity over the wide expanse; and the broken outlines of crags, and cliffs, and stupendous buildings, peered out from amidst the incumbent gloom with a wild and most romantic effect. The King surveyed this singular prospect

with the most marked interest; and, turning to his attendants, exclaimed, "This is wonderful!—what a sight!"

George was damp but impressed, a combination which may
have induced unsteadiness on the staircase at Holyrood when
he was saved from a nasty fall by the shoulders of a stout
baronet.

And so the festivities continued. The cavalry review on the
sands at Portobello on the Friday was blessed with fine
weather and the sight of George on horseback; 50,000 spectators turned out to watch "the grandest military spectacle ever
witnessed in Scotland, in modern times." And, that evening, a
great ball was given in the King's honour in the Assembly
Rooms, which had been transformed under the direction of
Mr. Roberts and Mr. Murray from the Theatre Royal.
Wreaths and banners and obelisks, pillars and canopies and
candelabra, were strewn about with reckless abandon, and the
front of the building in George Street was brilliantly illuminated. The conglomeration of carriages and sedan-chairs was
so vast, and the swearing of the Highland chair-men so pro-
vocative, that a contingent of dragoons and some police were
needed to maintain some sort of order. Inside, though, all was
splendour:

The ladies were in most elegant white dresses, richly bespangled,
and had on plumes of white ostrich feathers. The gentlemen
were in every variety of elegant dress, the usual full court dress,
of course, greatly predominating. The Duke of Argyll was conspicuous in the dark-green plaid of the clan Diarmid; and other
noblemen and gentlemen gayly disported themselves in the
mountain garb. The scene was one of such extraordinary splendour as almost to entrance, at least to bewilder, the faculties in
the contemplation of it. The surpassing beauty of the ladies—
their plumage, in constant undulation, appearing to the eye like
an ocean of foam;—the glitter reflected from a profusion of jewels;—the throng of noble personages;—the room itself;—altogether presented a scene which more than realized all previous
conceptions of grandeur and magnificence.

George arrived at a quarter to ten and stayed for an hour and a half, watching with some amusement the reels and country dances, smiling at the band, snapping his fingers in time to the music, and applauding a demonstration strathspey: "His Majesty appeared highly gratified with the arrangements that had been made for him, and with the appearance of the company, particularly of the ladies, whose naiveté and genuine cordiality of manner were only tempered, but not suppressed, by their reverence for the royal presence." The ball continued long after the departure of the royal presence; "It was rich, it was beautiful, it was orderly," decided the editor of an Edinburgh periodical.

Perhaps, though, the centrepiece of the royal visit was the banquet given by the Lord Provost in the great hall of the Parliament House the following evening. Again the expenditure had been on a lavish scale. One candelabrum alone cost £2,000, and Mr. John Ranken's Flint-Glass Manufactory in Leith Walk had supplied goblets and wine-glasses for the King's table, each one in the shape of a thistle. Gow's band, inescapable during the previous days, was ensconced in a niche, and room was also found for the gentlemen of the press. Two kitchens were set up in the vaults of the Parliament House, and the catering was entrusted to Mr. George Steventon of the Albyn Club. Seats were provided for 295, but the food, profuse and rich to the point of exhaustion, would have satisfied four times that number. George himself consumed turtle and grouse soups, stewed carp and venison, grouse and apricot tart, but even then could not resist a dish of raspberries, some water and cream ices, and a great many candied orange chips; he drank Moselle, claret and champagne. One representative of the press commented:

It is a rare and most gratifying sight to behold a King indulging the sympathies of our common nature, and convivially engaged with his subjects in the free interchange of thought and of sentiment. To do so, and sustain at the same time the regal character at its proper elevation, is an attainment of no ordinary difficulty.

"Eulogy," he added somewhat hypocritically, "is altogether out of our province, as it is foreign to our inclination."

Walter Scott's son Charles and his nephew Walter held a silver ewer and a salver with a damask napkin respectively for the King's hands, and George joined in the singing of "Non nobis Domine." Then the real business of the evening began: an interminable string of toasts interspersed by glees and airs from the vocal band. No one could be left out. The Lord Provost toasted the King. The King responded (he "placed his hand upon his heart, and expressed himself with powerful emphasis"). The Lord Provost moved on to the Duke of York and the army, the Duke of Clarence and the navy. The King returned to the Lord Provost, announcing that he had just created him a baronet (Glee: "Glorious Apollo"). Thoroughly carried away, George rose again and spoke with deep fervour: "I shall simply give you, All the chieftains and all the clans of Scotland, and may God bless the Land of Cakes!" Massive applause, the playing of "The Garb of old Gaul" and "Highland Laddie," and after more bumpers the King departed leaving the Lord Provost to preside over the continuing entertainment and verbiage. Inspiration began to wane as the guests desperately tried to consider whom or what they might toast next. The King was fair game, perhaps even August 14, when the *Royal George* dropped anchor off Leith, August 15, when the King entered Edinburgh, and August 24, when he had honoured the Corporation with his presence, were reasonable. Lip-service had to be paid to Robert Peel, absent through illness diplomatic or otherwise, Lord Melville, the Duke of Hamilton, Lord Erroll, the Lord Provost's wife, the Church of Scotland, the Duke of Buccleuch, the Duke of Wellington (Air: "See the Conquering Hero Comes"), the memory of Nelson and Pitt, Wellington's companions in arms, and, inevitably, Walter Scott. Scott himself could think of nothing better than both sides of St. George's Channel; Glengarry broke into Gaelic, toasting the King of the Isles; Captain Napier R.N. became muddled over his friend, Sir

Michael Shaw Stewart, and the yeomanry of Scotland; Lord Ashburton added a literary note with "the author of *Waverley*, whoever he may be and his works"; Sir W. Maxwell fell back on the Lord Provost but coupled with his name, for no very apparent reason, "the rest of the company not yeomen" (Song: "Scots Wha Hae Wi' Wallace Bled," by Mr. Magrath); and the Lord Provost ended with a rag-bag of anything previously omitted, including the Cities of London, Dublin and Glasgow ("Prosperity to its Trade and Manufactures"), the Rose, the Thistle and the Shamrock, and George the Fourth.

Everyone began to retire at ten o'clock, but the party was not finally over until midnight. "The wines which were of the finest vintages and in great variety, were furnished by Messrs Lyall and Cargill, Edinburgh, and Messrs Cockburn and Co., Leith." It was noticeable that certain gentlemen present at the banquet were not in their places in the High Church of St. Giles, when the King attended divine service the following morning, but the compiler of the *Historical Account* was readily available and in excellent form:

There did not reign in the most sequestered glen of Scotland a more profound stillness than was now observed in the heart of the city of Edinburgh! Nor is this to be wondered at. The spectacle of a monarch proceeding to humble himself, in adoration, before the King of Kings, could scarcely fail, with a rational people, to act as an example—as an incentive to devotion, rather than as the signal of clamorous rejoicing.

George contributed £100 to the collection, and appeared to listen to the sermon with profound attention.

The King's visit to Scotland was drawing to an end. He made a private inspection of Holyrood on August 26, and was particularly impressed by the condition of the blanket in which Mary Queen of Scots had slept; he was presented with a silver knife, fork and spoon, said to have belonged to Charles Edward Stuart; he attended a ball given by the

Caledonian Hunt, and saw a performance of *Rob Roy* at the Theatre Royal; he gave a dinner party, visited the houses of Lord Melville and Lord Lothian, received more presentations of cloaks and panoramic views, and drank numerous glasses of Atholl brose. August 29 was set as the day for his departure, and as Port Edgar near Queensferry was considered a suitable place to board the *Royal George*, he decided to visit the superb Hopetoun House *en route*. Having distributed gold watches and silver breakfast services to the Dalkeith staff, he drove through Edinburgh, past the men, boys and girls of the Asylums for the Industrious Blind, past the Knight Marischal's residence of Ravelstone where a halt had originally been scheduled ("the gate was very tastefully decorated with flowers, and the King nodded approbation as he passed it"), past Lord Rosebery's house at Dalmeny ("He waved his hand three times to its noble proprietor"), and on to Queensferry.

The rain by this time had ceased; and though the sky continued to lour, the scene was one of the most animated description. The whole line of road, notwithstanding the badness of the day, was covered by crowds of spectators, mostly honest rustics, who accumulated as the royal carriage advanced. The vessels composing the royal squadron, in full view, were all (with the exception of his Majesty's yacht) decked out with a profusion of flags and streamers, as various as the rainbow in colour.

The Earl of Hopetoun awaited his royal guest at the top of the grand staircase, which was spread with scarlet cloth. A fork luncheon was devoured, and the King demonstrated his own brand of slightly heavy-handed gallantry. He asked Lady Hopetoun how many children she had. She vouchsafed that she had ten sons and an infant daughter. His Majesty, either struck by the number of male children, or by the beautiful and youthful appearance of the mother, exclaimed, "Good God! is it possible?" He also knighted Captain Adam Ferguson and Henry Raeburn the portrait-painter before departing for Port Edgar. Soon after three o'clock, the King

was safely on board the royal yacht, accompanied by ham-
pers of fruit sent by Lord Hopetoun and Lord Dalhousie.
The royal squadron passed Yarmouth on the last day of August, and George landed at Greenwich on September 1. By a
quarter-past five he was back at Carlton House.

Sir Walter Scott was exhausted. He had made two requests
of the King, that the cannon Mons Meg should be returned
from the Tower of London to Edinburgh Castle, and that
those peerages which had lain forfeit since the Jacobite risings
of 1715 and 1745 should be restored, and George had agreed
happily enough. The King had clearly been converted into a
good Scot, perhaps even into a good Jacobite. Sir Walter
wrote to Lady Abercorn on September 13:

We have had a singular scene in Scotland the visit of the King to
Edinburgh which was like the awaking of Abou Hassan to a
dream of Sovereignty . . . A number of Highland clans came
down of whom I got an especial charge which was rather an anxious one when you consider they were armed to the teeth with
sword and target pistol and dagger and full of prejudices and
jealousies concerning their particular claims of distinction. They
all behaved very well however and from their wild and picturesque appearance added prodigiously to the effect of the various
processions.

It had all been a great strain, though in reality Scott had enjoyed every minute of his glory: "I myself had nearly died in
the cause as I took an inflammatory complaint owing to fatigue and overexertion and anxiety which might have been serious but that it broke out in what is called a rash on my skin
and so relieved itself." He had made a rapid departure to
Abbotsford, "where I have lived the life of a *cow* that is eating, drinking and lying on the grass." There were naturally
criticisms of Scott and the emphasis laid on the romance of
the Highlander, but Croker, who greeted George at Greenwich, was able to report back that he was "in every respect
pleased and gratified and *grateful* for the devoted attention
paid him."

George was probably never in the future to enjoy such rapturous popularity. He did not travel again, indeed he retired increasingly into a private existence. Radicalism and reform were in the wind, the time for banquets and balls was past. But it had all been very splendid and amazing and more than faintly comic while it had lasted.

XI

Bucks and Dandies

What a routine we have had of everything disgusting, in the name of Fashion! Slouched hats, jockey waistcoats, half-boots, leather breeches, cropped heads, unpowdered hair . . . the present race of Bucks without blood, Beaux without taste, and Gentlemen without manners!

The Oracle, 1804

The Oriental, the Mathematical, the Osbaldeston, the Napoleon, the American, the Mail Coach, the Trône d'Amour, the Irish, the Ball Room, the Horse Collar, the Hunting, the Maharatta, the Gordian Knot, the Barrel Knot . . . to many men in 1818, and none more so than the Prince Regent himself, the precise choice of neckwear was of far greater importance than the latest political crisis or the death of Queen Charlotte. Perhaps at no other time in history have so much time, care and expense been lavished on the male form and its embellishment as during the first decades of the nineteenth century. Suddenly, taste, or rather good taste, seemed less desirable than flamboyance, elegance all too often gave way to vulgarity. The 1822 edition of *The Hermit in London* paints a vivid, though no doubt exaggerated picture of that phenomenon of post-Napoleonic society, the Dandy:

A being in regard to appearance of very doubtful gender, laced up like a young lady, with a pair of cossacks resembling a petticoat, a crop like a pouting pigeon, a painted face looking over a wall of starch and muslin, a patch at the corner of the mouth, its hair like the feathers of a Friesland hen, and a gold chain and glass dangling from a neck like a gander's. It was reserved for the exquisite polish of our present enlightened day for the men's trenching upon the petticoats, paints, stays, starched handkerchiefs, and pouting pigeon bosoms of the female. A Dandy is now so bolstered up in collars, so lost in trowsers, so pinched in the middle, than he can neither have bowels of compassion, expansion of heart, nor fair use of his limbs. To have a glass fixed in the socket of the eye is no longer a defect but rather a perfection; and the wide walk, from fixed spurs, resembling the stride of a felon, is quite the go . . . A young merveilleux accosted me. He is the son of a plain honest citizen though he smells like a civet cat, speaks like a young milliner, and is more affected than any stage character . . . The made up male doll who when wig, dyed whiskers, stiff cravat, padded breast, corset, paint, and perfume are taken away, sinks into something worse than nothing.

Plus ça change . . . As so often happens after a long and bloody conflict of arms, a levelling of class was in motion. Men, that is fashionable young men, because their older relations are rarely struck by the same lightning, yearn to forget the hard, military, masculine images of war. Therefore, inevitably, they borrow from the female sex. Fashions are taken to extremes of narrowness or wideness, looseness or tightness. Colours become flamboyant, the everyday adornments of the woman—scent, jewellery, cosmetics—are borrowed. And an industry is born. One fashion soon becomes unfashionable, change and more change and ever-faster change is the prerequisite of a self-regarding society. And nothing did society after Waterloo enjoy more than gazing at itself in the mirror.

With the changes in fashion came a change in manners. The elaborate courtesies of the eighteenth century were no longer the thing. The *Universal Magazine* had looked disapprovingly on this reprehensible state of affairs as early as 1810:

The manners of the men have undergone a complete revolution, particularly as they regard the fair sex. From a formal, precise, and ceremonious demeanour, constituting good breeding, a mode of conduct almost the reverse is becoming a distinguishing mark of high life. An indifference to the convenience and accommodation of the softer sex has taken place in our public assemblies . . . the extreme of the fashion is little short of brutal rudeness.

Not that the "softer sex" comported itself any less freely:

The ladies, from a degree of reserve and strictness of behaviour, have adopted a freedom of manners, a boldness of look and scantiness of apparel which had often occasioned women of character and condition to be taken for members of a body they affect to look down upon with pity or contempt. Indeed, such has been the revolution in this point that when it was attempted to exclude the Cyprian Corps from a theatre . . . the doorkeepers were so far misled by appearances that they were very near conveying a *nude* of high rank to the watchhouse.

Ladies were also fortifying themselves, perhaps in order to compensate for the extreme flimsiness of their costumes: "Instead of one, two, or three glasses of wine which used to be the ordinary stint of females, six, seven, and even eight glasses of Madeira have been tossed off by ladies scarcely out of their teens."

It was all very scandalous, no doubt, but the point must be made that such goings-on were confined to the wicked metropolis. Miss Austen's young heroines were not incipient drunkards, nor would such behaviour have been tolerated in the stiff surroundings of the Assembly Rooms throughout the country. Nor indeed were young men of the *haut ton* advised to essay the delights of rural Britain. Picture an unhappy exquisite, shooting, or attempting to shoot, in Scotland: "I endeavoured to ascend some mountains but my staylace gave way, my morocco boots burst, and my dowlas trousers got wet through . . . might I trouble you to tell my man to get me a new Cumberland corset?" The *Beau Monde* deprecated any attempt at countrification of dress:

Many gentlemen in their morning walks have attempted to introduce a sort of shooting dress, parading in a short coat of any light colour, and with drab-coloured cloth or kerseymere gaiters coming up to the knees; but we do not think such a dress adapted to the Promenade of Bond Street.

Bond Street had its own snares and delusions, for here the unwary might be deluded by a race of men possessed of more determination and gall than breeding. The *Spirit of the Public Journals* places a "Bond Street gemman," in other words someone who was far from being a gentleman, before our eyes: "A coat smartly cut with a high collar and scarcely any skirts, three or four waistcoats of different colours, and nankin pantaloons covering military boots. Round his neck he had a halter of many-folded muslin in which was buried the extremity of his chin."

But he might have been considered a passably sober dresser, compared with the more *outré* exquisites. The range of styles and the spectrum of colours were both startling. Jean de Bry coats, with absurdly padded shoulders and short tails; striped trousers ending well above the ankles; nankeen inexpressibles, moschettos and cossacks, Wellington pantaloons and *peau de pendu* pantaloons which were so tight that they fitted without a wrinkle; greatcoats with innumerable capes, morning gowns made of chintz, and banyans: anything and everything seemed possible. One year, scarlet waistcoats might be all the rage, another year violet would be the fashionable colour, or what was called the parsley mixture, an amalgam of greens and brown. Boots, too, received earnest attention. Should one don Hessians or Hussar boots, military

long-boots or top-boots, half-boots or highlows? And were
spatter-dashes or gaiters quite the thing?

Hats came in all shapes, tall, round flat, crescent-shaped;
there was the Wellington hat, the Turf, the Elastic, even the
Patent Travelling Hair Cap, "particularly well adapted for
Officers and Travellers who are obliged to wear either a
Welch wig or a nightcap." And great care was lavished upon
the hair. The Brutus wig was fashionable during the first decade of the century, but wigs in general were considered ex-
traordinarily *vieux jeu*. Instead hair was worn *á la* Titus, and
young beaux spent many hours making their locks appear
carefully dishevelled. As the century progressed, hair became
shorter and tidier, and whiskers made their appearance;
macassar oil was greatly valued.

Various artificial aids were by no means despised. Rouge
was applied, and hands were whitened with enamel, corsets
and stays were recommended by modish tailors. That inveterate observer of fashion, *The Hermit in London,* saw a
dandy walking in the park who "came up perfumed like a
milliner, his colour much heightened by some vegetable dye,
his breath savoured of myrrh." A quizzing glass or a spotted
Belcher handkerchief, rings and fob-seals, a tasselled cane or
even an umbrella might complete the ensemble.

Laundresses had never enjoyed such custom. Prince von
Pückler-Muskau, writing in 1827, recorded the necessities of
a London dandy:

An elegant requires per week twenty shirts, twenty-four pocket
handkerchiefs, thirty neck-handkerchiefs (unless he wears black
ones), a dozen (washing) waistcoats, and stockings "à
discrétion." A dandy cannot get on without dressing three or four
times a day: 1st. In breakfast toilette, a chintz dressing-gown and
Turkish slippers. 2nd. Morning riding dress, frock coat, boots
and spurs. 3rd. Dinner dress, dress coat and shoes. 4th. Ball dress,
with "pumps"—a word signifying shoes as thin as paper.

It was the final parade of the peacock before Victorian
drabness set in and vivid colours were left to the military. It

was also the culmination of a development in men's fashion
which had been gathering pace during the eighteenth century. In 1714, as the last of the Stuart rulers died and George
I prepared to launch the Hanoverian dynasty, a dandy's
clothes were certainly more vibrant in colour, if not as
outlandish in form, than his descendant's 100 years later.
That year, a Mr. John Osheal was robbed of

a scarlet cloth suit, laced with broad gold lace, lined and faced
with blue; a fine cinnamon cloth suit, with plate buttons, the
waistcoat fringed with a silk fringe of the same colour; and a rich
yellow flowered satin morning-gown, lined with a cherry-
coloured satin, with a pocket on the right side

—scarcely, one would have imagined, the most inconspicuous
haul for a burglar to carry through the streets. A decade
later, a beau was described as wearing

a fine linen shirt, the ruffles and bosom of Mechlin lace; a small
wig, with an enormous *queue*, or tail; his coat well garnished
with lace; black velvet breeches; red heels to his shoes, and gold
clocks to his stockings; his hat beneath his arm, a sword by his
side, and himself well scented.

It was small wonder that the worthy Dr. John Harris, a
disapproving divine with patriotic if puritan leanings,
launched himself into a resounding denunciation of such frip-
peries. Understandably, and correctly, he suspected a French
plot, and composed his *Treatise upon the Modes, or A Farewell to French Kicks.* English style was correct, because it
was English, but it was much disfigured by all the extras imported from Paris, "the shoulder-knot . . . the beads which
are fastened to the ends of their cravats . . . the ten thousand
kinds of buttons . . . the different magnitude of pleats, which
differ also from time to time in number, but always agree in
the mystic efficacy of an unequal number . . ." A more
knowledgeable commentator, Grosley, agreed:

A mode begins to be out of date at Paris, just when it has been
introduced at London by some English nobleman. The Court and

the first-rate nobility immediately take it up; it is next introduced about St. James's, by those that ape the manners of the Court; and by the time it has reached the city, a contrary mode already prevails at Paris, where the English, bringing with them the opposite mode, appear like the people of another world.

Beaux, or macaronis as they were later in the century called from their habit of frequenting Almack's, where the dish of macaroni was first invented, were everywhere. Richard Steele wrote:

The town swarms with fine gentlemen. A nimble pair of heels, a smooth complexion, a full bottom wig, a laced shirt, an embroidered suit; a pair of fringed gloves, a hat and feather; any one or more of these and the like accomplishments ennobles a man and raises him above the vulgar in a female imagination. On the contrary, a modest, serious behaviour, a plain dress, a thick pair of shoes, a leathern belt, a waistcoat not lined with silk, and such like imperfections degrade a man, and are so many blots on his escutcheon. The gilt chariot, the diamond ring, the gold snuffbox and brocade sword-knot are no essential parts of a fine gentleman, but may be used by him, provided he casts his eye upon them but once a day.

There was a constant change in the style of wig thought most fashionable. In 1760, Monsieur de la Papillon arrived from Paris and took an extremely grand advertisement in the *Grand Magazine*. He announced with justifiable pride that

he fabricates all kinds of perukes for churchmen, lawyers, physicians, military, mercantile, and country gentlemen, in a new, exquisite, curious, and extraordinary taste. As, for example, to ecclesiastical perukes he gives a certain demure, sanctified air; he confers on the tye-wigs of the law an appearance of great sagacity and deep penetration; on those of the faculty of physick he casts a solemnity and gravity that seems equal to the profoundest knowledge. His military smarts are mounted in a curious manner, quite unknown to every artist but himself. He throws into them what he calls the animating buckle, which gives the wearer a most war-like fierceness. He has likewise invented a species of Major or Brigadier for the better sort of citizens and

tradesmen which, by adding a tail to them that may be taken off
or put on at pleasure, may serve extremely well when they do
duty in the militia. He also flatters himself upon hitting the taste
of country gentlemen and fox-hunters by his short-cut bobs of
nine hairs of a side.

He was a wig-maker for all sorts and conditions of men, and
his ingenuity knew no bounds:

For young gentlemen of the law who are not troubled with
much practice, he has invented a peruke, the legs of which may
be put into a smart bag during the time of vacation, and which in
term time may be restored to its pristine form . . . For such as
love to save their cash, he will have perukes made of calves' tails,
which he engages will last a long time. He has by long study and
labour discovered and invented a commodious machine, called
the night basket, by which ladies and gentlemen may have their
heads dressed while they divert themselves at cards without loss
of time.

Wigs, selling as they often did at up to fifty guineas, were
big business. The Master Peruke Makers were an influential
body, always complaining about the arrival of so many
French hairdressers, let alone the alarming new fashion
adopted by gentlemen of wearing their own hair, even if it
was dressed and powdered. Other objectors came from the
lower echelons of society, for wigs were also much sought-
after by thieves. A favourite trick was for the practised wig-
snatcher to walk through the streets with a basket on his
head, pretending to be a baker. Inside the basket lurked a
small boy who, at the given moment, would lift the lid, lean
out, denude a passing gentleman's head, and retire back into
the safety of his lair. Bolder spirits would merely cut a hole in
the back of a slow-moving carriage and withdraw the wig.

It was only at the time of the French Revolution that the
wig really went out of fashion, and when Pitt imposed a
powder tax in 1795, unpowdered hair inevitably became the
accepted norm. But even then the habit died hard. The tax
brought in as much as £200,000 in the first year, and tradi-

tional Tory politicians continued to powder their heads, in marked contrast to the more revolutionary Whigs, who wore their hair cut short *à la guillotine*. Finally, though, only lawyers and churchmen persisted, though the latter were inconsistent. George IV would not allow an unpowdered bishop in his presence, and the Bishop of London was once barred simply because he wore his own hair.

As the eighteenth century moved into its second half, the beau still dominated the scene. He was a creature of both interest and scorn, as can be seen by an anonymous lampoon in verse which appeared in 1753, entitled "Monsieur A-la-Mode":

Take a creature that nature has formed without brains,
Whose skull nought but nonsense and sonnets contains;
With a mind where conceit with folly's allied,
Set off by assurance and unmeaning pride;
With commonplace jests for to tickle the ear,
With mirth where no wisdom could ever appear;
That to the defenceless can strut and look brave,
Although he to cowardice shews he's a slave:
And now for to dress up my beau with a grace,
Let a well-frizzled wig be set off from his face;
With a bag quite in taste, from Paris just come,
That was made and tied up by Monsieur Frisson;
With powder quite grey—then his head is complete;—
If dress'd in the fashion, no matter for wit:
With a pretty black beaver tuck'd under his arm—
If placed on his head, it might keep it too warm;
Then a black solitaire, his neck to adorn,
Like those of Versailles, by the courtiers there worn;
His hands must be covered with fine Brussels lace,
With a sparkling brilliant his finger to grace;
Next a coat of embroidery, from foreigners come,
'Twould be quite unpolite to have one wrought at home;
With cobweb silk stockings his legs to befriend,
Two pair underneath his lank calves to amend;
With breeches in winter would cause one to freeze,
To add to his height, must not cover his knees;

A pair of smart pumps made up of grain'd leather,
So thin he can't venture to tread on a feather;
His buckles like diamonds must glitter and shine—
Should they cost fifty pounds, they would not be too fine;
A repeater by Graham, which the hours reveals,
Almost overbalanced with knick-knacks and seals;
A mouchoir with musk his spirits to cheer,
Though he scents the whole room that no soul can come near;
A gold-hilted sword, with jewels inlaid—
So the scabbard's but cane, no matter for blade;
A sword-knot of riband to answer his dress,
Most completely tied up with tassels of lace:
Thus fully equipp'd and attired for shew,
Observe, pray, ye belles, that famed thing call'd a beau!

It is little more than doggerel, but it is good social observation, Lord Foppington or one of his ilk to the life. Nine years later, the *London Chronical* passed judgment on the latest excesses:

Surtouts have now four laps on each side, which are called dog's ears; when these pieces are unbuttoned, they flap backwards and forwards like so many supernumerary patches just tacked on at one end, and the wearer seems to have been playing many hours at back-sword, till his coat was cut to pieces. When they are buttoned up, they appear like combcases, or pacquets for a penny postman to sort his letters in. Very spruce *smarts* have no buttons nor holes upon the breast of these their surtouts, save what are upon the ears, and their garments only wrap over their bodies like a morning-gown: a proof that dress may be made too fashionable to be useful.

Beau Nash, the arbiter of fashion in Bath, would have agreed. No man strove more energetically to curb some of the excesses of the dandies, or to introduce some degree of elegance and manners into everyday social intercourse. He had his own brand of eccentricity. He always wore a white hat, so that it should not be stolen, and he favoured a mixture of styles rather than his own particular one. He was also insistent that the boorish country squires and supposed gentlemen should not appear at the Assembly Rooms as if they had just come in from a day's hunting, in topboots instead of shoes. According to Oliver Goldsmith, who wrote the first biography, Nash devised a puppet show, in which the Punch character appeared booted and spurred, and refused all requests to remove the offending articles:

My boots! Why, madam, you may as well bid me pull off my legs! I never go without boots. I never ride, I never dance without them; and this piece of politeness is quite the thing at Bath. We always dance at our town in boots, and the ladies often move minuets in riding-hoods.

"Thus he goes on," continues Goldsmith, "till his mistress, grown impatient, kicks him off the stage":

From that time few ventured to appear at the assemblies in Bath in a riding-dress; and whenever any gentleman, through ignorance or haste, appeared in the rooms in boots, Nash would make up to him, and bowing in an arch manner would tell him that he had forgot his horse.

But Nash, in spite of his complete command at Bath, would have seemed a mere anachronism to any self-respecting Regency buck, whose hero was George Bryan Brummell. Beau Brummell in more than one respect personified his age. His career and his influence were extraordinary. Approbation from him was as sought-after as a peerage, a snub could exclude the miserable recipient from society. He represented taste at its highest and least adulterated. He was never flashy. Lord William Pitt Lennox remembered him, and the effect he made:

Brummell, the undisputed *arbiter elegantarium*, was termed by the *ignorami* the King of the Dandies; with due submission, I beg to pronounce this is libel. He was anything but a dandy. The term "Dandyism" never could be applied with justice to him; it would be a profanation to couple his name with such an offensive distinction. Of all my acquaintances, he was the quietest, plainest, and most unpretending dresser. Those who remember him in his palmy days will bear testimony to the truth of this assertion; it was the total absence of all peculiarity, and a rigid adherence to the strictest rules of propriety in costume, which gained for him the homage due to his undisputed taste. He eschewed colours, trinkets and gewgaws; his clothes were exquisitely made, and, above all, adapted to his person; he put them on well, too; but for all this, there was no striving for effect—there was an unusual absence of study in his appearance.

George Brummell was born on June 7, 1778, and educated at Eton where, according to the Whartons' *Wits and Beaux of Society*, "he distinguished himself by the introduction of a gold buckle in the white stock, by never being flogged and by his ability in toasting cheese." He went on to Oriel College, Oxford, and then launched himself on society, via the army and a strong friendship with the Prince of Wales. George relied implicitly on his advice and, according to Tom Moore, once "began to blubber when told that Brummell did not like the cut of his coat." He also visited Brummell's apartment in Chesterfield Street almost every day, in time to see the Beau's valet Robinson emerge from the dressingroom, his arms full of discarded neckcloths which had not met with his master's exacting approval. The neckcloth was Brummell's chief concern, and his first biographer, Captain Jesse, has left a record of the method employed:

The collar, which was always fixed to the shirt, was so large that, before being folded down, it completely hid his head and face, and the white neckcloth was at least a foot in height. The first *coup d'archet* was made with the shirt collar, which he folded down to its proper size; and Brummell then standing before the glass, with his chin poked up to the ceiling, by the gentle and gradual declension of his lower jaw, creased the cravat to reasonable dimensions, the form of each succeeding crease being perfected with the shirt which he had just discarded.

This was Brummell's art, painstaking and perfectionist. He chose his tailors with care, moving from the Prince of Wales's Schweitzer & Davidson, to Mayer in Conduit Street, and finally to Weston in Old Bond Street. He had considerable affection for Weston, and gave an excellent reason in conversation with Tom Raikes:

That fellow Weston is an inimitable fellow—a little defective perhaps in his linings, but irreproachable for principle and buttonholes. He came to London, sir, without a shilling, and he controls more realised thousands than our fat friend [the Prince of Wales] does "frogs" on his "Brandenburg." He is not only rich, but brave; not only brave, but courteous; not only courteous, but candid.

Harriette Wilson, the entertaining though unreliable courtesan and diarist, gave an interesting view of Brummell:

He was extremely fair, and the expression of his countenance far from disagreeable. His person, too, was rather good; nor could anybody find fault with the lustre of all those who, for years, had made it a rule to copy the cut of Brummell's coat, the shape of his hat, or the tie of his neckcloth: for all this was in the very best possible style. No perfumes, Brummell used to say, but very fine linen, plenty of it, and country washing. If John Bull turns round to look after you, you are not well dressed: but either too stiff, too tight, or too fashionable. Do not ride in ladies' gloves, particularly with leather breeches. In short, his maxims on dress were excellent. Besides this, he was neither uneducated nor deficient. He possessed, also, a sort of quaint, dry humour, not amounting to anything like wit; indeed he said nothing which would bear repetition; but his affected manners, and little absurdities, amused for the moment. Then it became the fashion to court Brummell's society, which was enough to make many seek it who cared not for it, and many more wished to be well with him, through fear, for all knew him to be cold, heartless, and satirical.

He was, of course, a poseur, as he knew only too well. He once admitted as much to Lady Hester Stanhope, but considered that there were extenuating circumstances:

It is my folly that is the making of me. If I did not impertinently stare duchesses out of countenance, and nod over my shoulder to

a prince, I should be forgotten in a week; and if the world is so
silly as to admire my absurdities, you and I may know better, but
what does that signify?

He was right, but eventually the Prince grew tired of Brummell's nods and his condescension. The celebrated quarrel between the Beau and the Prince of Wales is hedged about
with supposition and gloss. Certainly, Mrs. Fitzherbert disap-
proved of his influence, and did not care for being referred to
openly as George's mistress. Then there was the idiotic affair
of the snuff box. The Prince of Wales had asked for one of
Brummell's, and had suggested in return that the royal jeweller should design a replacement to Brummell's own design. The Beau took great trouble in his choice, only for the
Prince to forbid the jeweller to hand it over.

The final episode in the drama came when George cut
Brummell at a ball in the Argyle Rooms, and Brummell
riposted with his celebrated rhetorical question to Lord Alvanley, "Who's your fat friend?" The Prince of Wales, notoriously conscious of his increasingly corpulent frame, was
not amused. Nor did Brummell's proud boast, duly relayed to
Carlton House—"I made him what he is, and I can unmake
him"—help to heal the breach. The two protagonists met once
more, at the Opera:

The Prince of Wales, who always came out rather before the
performance concluded, was waiting for his carriage. Presently
Brummell came out, talking eagerly to some friends, and, not seeing the Prince or his party, he took up a position near the check-
taker's bar. As the crowd flowed out, Brummell was gradually
pressed backwards, until he was all but driven against the Regent,
who distinctly saw him, but, of course, would not move. In order
to stop Brummell, therefore, and prevent actual collision, one of
the Prince's suite tapped him on the back, when he immediately
turned sharply round, and saw that there was not more than a
foot between his nose and the Prince of Wales's. I watched him
with intense curiosity, and observed that his countenance did not
change in the slightest degree, nor did his head move; they

looked straight into each other's eyes, the Prince evidently amazed and annoyed. Brummell, however, did not quail or show the least embarrassment. They receded quite quietly, and backed slowly step by step till the crowd closed between them, never once taking his eyes off those of the Prince.

Brummell's famous sang-froid never deserted him. In 1817, he left England, ruined by gambling for the highest stakes. For the last twenty-three years of his life he remained an exile, collecting *objets de vertu*, receiving visits from friends, acting as British Consul at Caen, hoping in vain for some sign of reconciliation from his erstwhile friend and admirer on his ascent to the throne as George IV. In 1829, Prince von Pückler-Muskau saw him in Calais:

I found him at his second toilette, in a flowered chintz dressing-gown, velvet night-cap with gold tassel, and Turkish slippers, shaving, and rubbing the remains of his teeth with his favourite red root. The furniture of his rooms was elegant enough, part of it might even be called rich, though faded; and I cannot deny that the whole man seemed to me to correspond with it. Though depressed by his present situation, he exhibited a considerable fund of good-humour and good-nature. His air was that of good society, simple and natural, and marked by more urbanity than the dandies of the present race are capable of. With a smile he showed me his Paris peruke, which he extolled at the cost of the English ones, and called himself, "le ci-devant jeune homme qui passe sa vie entre Paris et Londres" . . . Surely the English nation ought in justice to do something for the man who invented starched cravats! How many did I see in London in the enjoyment of large sinecures, who had done far less for their country.

In 1835, Brummell was imprisoned for debt and, though he was soon released, he never really recovered. Tom Moore saw him in 1837 and was appalled by the ravages of age and poverty: "The poor Beau's head was gone, and his whole looks so changed that I should never have recognised him." Alvanley wrote to Tom Raikes the same year: "Poor Brummell is become imbecile . . . He is grown slovenly and dirty;

is, however, otherwise well, and lives on what we subscribe for him." Even the news of George IV's death did not move him. His memory had gone. On March 29, 1840, he died. It was a pathetic end for the great arbiter of fashion. He had never taken anything to excess. Faults he had in abundance. He could be accused of conceit, of coldness, of emptiness. But he possessed style. His best obituary—and one which he himself would have appreciated—was supplied by Charles Whiteley:

Brummell was so finished a master of his craft that he could always elude notice between Chesterfield Street and White's. And he eluded notice because he fitted the landscape with delicate exactitude. In Regent Street his pantaloons might have cried aloud. They belonged to the scenery of Piccadilly.

As Beau Brummell died, so passed too the age of the dandy. Women, who had themselves been far from idle in fashionable excesses, took the centre of the stage. But the peacock had enjoyed a long reign—as had the tailors and cutters, the peruke-makers and hair-dressers, the jewellers and bootmakers. But then, as they were the first to realise, soberness of cut and style and colour did not necessitate a reduction in charges. As Brummell himself knew, the simpler the clothes, the more expensive.

XII

A Dream of the Orient

Beautiful and tasty. . . though it looks very much as if
St. Paul's had come down to the sea and left behind a lit-
ter of cupolas.

> *William Wilberforce to William Muncaster*

Oh, this wicked Pavillion! were we there till ½ past one
this morng., and it has kept me in bed with the headache
till 12 to-day.

> *Mrs. Creevey to Thomas Creevey*

Domes, minarets and cupolas; serpents, palm-trees and dragons; scarlets and golds and greens. The Royal Pavilion at
Brighton is an oriental fantasy, a magnificent folly, a description from Marco Polo's travels in Xanadu. It is wholly *sui
generis*, a unique confection which defies accusations of bad,
or vulgar, taste, and whose incongruity in such an English
setting actually reinforces its splendour. As Osbert Sitwell
and Margaret Barton remarked: "As for the alleged discord-
ance with its surroundings, Brighton, it is true, actually
overlooks the English Channel: but every English town has,
or should have, a view of the Indian Ocean." The Pavilion is

abiding proof of George IV's sense of style and architectural adventurousness, and its contents in their absolute sureness of choice underline the fact that he was one of the few connoisseurs of the arts who has also sat on the British throne.

Brighton, or Brighthelmston as it was originally called, had been growing in popularity during the latter half of the eighteenth century. Ever since the arrival of Dr. Richard Russell, and the publication in 1853 of his *Dissertation Concerning the Use of Sea Water in Diseases of the Glands*, the fortunes of the small, broken-down seaside town were established. The cult of sea-bathing, coupled with the less pleasant practice of drinking the sea-water, became all the rage. Selina, Countess of Huntingdon, brought her youngest son for a course of bathing; Dr. Johnson and his friends the Thrales were frequent visitors; and in 1765 George III's brother, the Duke of Gloucester, came, the first in a long line of royal patrons who included the Duke of York and the Duke of Cumberland. It was with the latter that George, Prince of Wales stayed at the beginning of September 1783, within weeks of his coming-of-age. George suffered from swollen glands in his neck, which necessitated his wearing a high stock, and the fashionable sea-water cure was thought to be the correct remedy. So began what almost amounted to a love-affair with Brighton which was to last, off and on, for nearly half a century, until he left the Pavilion for the last time in 1827.

It was Louis Weltje, the Clerk of the Prince of Wales's Kitchen, who set about finding a suitable residence for his royal master. Weltje was a remarkable man, a Brunswicker who had climbed the commercial ladder of London, from pastry-cook to owner of a club in St. James's Street to his position as the Prince of Wales's confectioner. Samuel Shergold, the owner of the Castle Tavern in Brighton, gave a vivid pen-portrait of Weltje and his wife:

He was of true German caste—certainly more like Silenus than he was to Antinous; and, what is more remarkable, he had a wife as like to him as the one yolk of a double egg is to the other. After a residence of thirty years in England they knew as little English as an elephant. How Weltje contrived to meet a wife so like himself, I know not, whether by advertisement or proclamation! I think it must have been by proclamation; for two such ugly persons would never otherwise have come together, but they were as good as gold.

The house which Weltje chose was Grove House, where George had stayed with his uncle Cumberland the previous year.

The sojourn of the Prince of Wales was not entirely taken up with the sea-water cure. A rumour was spread that his eye had fallen upon "the angelic figure of a sea-nymph whom he one day encountered reclining on one of the groins on the beach," an incident, imaginary or otherwise, given reality in Rex Whistler's witty picture of plump royal nudity about to have its way with the innocent Spirit of Brighton. A London newspaper also alluded to George's amorous propensities:

The visit of a certain gay and illustrious character at Brighton, has frightened away a number of old maids, who used constantly to frequent that place. The story of the gallantries of last season, which is in constant circulation, has something in it so voluminous, and tremendous to boot, that the old tabbies shake in their shoes whenever his R-L H-ss is mentioned.

The old tabbies had good reason for their nervous trepidation. For, that same year, the Prince of Wales met Maria Fitzherbert at the opera and fell passionately in love with her. She was, of course, totally unsuitable as the future Queen of England. She had been married twice previously, both husbands dying, and she was a devout Catholic, therefore barred by the provisions of the Royal Marriages Act. After a fervently romantic courtship on the part of the infatuated George, they were married secretly—in much the same way as Louis XIV had married Madame de Maintenon.

George was now consumed with good intentions. In debt to a sum of approximately £¼ million, on the worst possible

terms both with his father and with William Pitt's administration, he decided to opt for the simple life. Work on Carlton House ceased, his fine stud of racehorses was sold, and the
happy couple departed for the provincial attractions of
Brighton in a hired coach. They probably set up their establishment first at Grove House and subsequently at a near-by
farmhouse, again acquired by Louis Weltje (though Mrs.
Fitzherbert always spent the night in her own house).

The Prince of Wales's attempt at economy did not last. He
was determined to have something grander and more personal
as a residence, and Henry Holland, a brilliant young architect
who had been introduced to George by Charles James Fox
and who had already worked on Carlton House, was commissioned to draw up the requisite plans. The farmhouse was
converted, and the first Pavilion, or Marine Pavilion as it was
generally called, was built in under four months. Holland's
design was basically neo-classical, with a dome, Ionic pillars
and statues, but also making admirable use of Robert Adam's
invention, the bow-window. A house for Weltje was constructed in the grounds, and there were also stables, coach-
houses, and an ice-house. The interior decorations were very
much in the French style, and most of the furniture was obtained by Weltje also from France. One particular feature of
the Pavilion was George's bedroom, which gave him a splendid view over the Steyne; the room set aside for games of
chance was of ample proportions.

Opinions as to the architectural worth of the Pavilion
varied. Rowlandson considered it "correctly designed and
elegantly executed . . . The *tout ensemble* of the Building is,
in short, perfect Harmony." On the other hand, the anonymous "Antony Pasquin" writing in the *New Brighton Guide*
had nothing but contempt for it:

The Pavilion is built principally of wood; it is a nondescript
monster in building, and appears like a mad house, or a house run
mad, as it has neither beginning, middle nor end . . . The room
in which the Prince usually dined may be compared to a sort of

oven: when the fire is lighted the inmates are nearly baked or incrusted.

The total cost of the Pavilion and the various outbuildings was under £25,000.

The Prince of Wales's set was undoubtedly raffish, though hardly as wicked as it has been so often portrayed. His acquaintances included whips, jockeys, boxers and gamblers, but also politicians, men of letters, and a number of French émigrés fled from the perils of the Revolution. There were race-meetings to attend, routs and balls were given in the season, and George's birthday was celebrated every year with firework displays, mock military and naval contests, and the invariable roasting oxen. It was all mildly naughty and titillating, but for George himself an idyllic period. The blow fell when George III refused to pay his son's debts unless the latter agreed to marry. There was no refusal possible. George showed himself completely indifferent to the identity of his future wife. It was his cousin, Caroline of Brunswick, an unrefined, dirty, buxom girl, who was yoked to the reluctant royal bull—no longer the handsome young Prince, but an over-indulgent, corpulent man, who preferred strong waters to the marriage bed. Even so, a daughter, the ill-fated Princess Charlotte, was duly and dutifully produced. But that was enough for George. He elected to live apart from his embarrassing wife, discarded his very temporary mistress Lady Jersey, and resumed his relationship with Mrs. Fitzherbert.

He also turned his attention to matters architectural. The Marine Pavilion was not large enough for what was tantamount to a court in exile, and Henry Holland was asked to consider plans for elaboration. But it was Holland's nephew, P. F. Robinson, who actually undertook the work. He was a devotee of the new "picturesque" style (later, he would be responsible for the Swiss Cottage near St. John's Wood) and he added the metal canopies to all the windows, joined on two new oval wings to the main house, and removed his uncle's classical statues. Then, in 1802, an event of far-reaching significance took place. Edward Brayley has left a description:

Several pieces of a very beautiful Chinese paper were presented
to the Prince, who for a time was undecided in what way to
make use of them. As the Eating Room and the Library, which
were between the Saloon and the new northern wing, were no
longer required for their original purposes, Mr. Robinson, on
being consulted, advised the Prince to have the partition removed
and the interior formed into a Chinese Gallery. This was immediately agreed to; the walls were hung with the paper described
and the other parts of the Gallery were painted and decorated in
a corresponding style. About the same time, the passage room between what was then called the Small Drawing-Room and the
new conservatory, or Music Room, at the south end of the Pavilion, was constructed in a singular manner. A space was enclosed
within it, measuring twelve feet by eight, the sides and upper
parts of which were entirely formed of stained glass, of an orien-
tial character, and exhibiting the peculiar insects, fruit, flowers,
etc. of China. It was illuminated from without; and through it, as
through an immense Chinese lantern, the communication was
carried on; its effect is stated to have been extremely beautiful.

George had already had a Chinese room at Carlton House,
and indeed the concept of *chinoiserie* was by no means new.
Sir William Chambers had published his *Designs for Chinese
Buildings* as long before as 1757, and had followed this with
the *Dissertation on Oriental Gardening*. Robert Adam had
been using wallpapers bearing Chinese designs for some years,
and some of Chippendale's furniture displayed a marked oriental influence. Even the Royal Family had embraced the
style, commissioning Chambers to design a series of Chinese
temples for Kew, culminating in the Great Pagoda. But the
English *chinoiserie* had become highly delicate and simplified,
adapted to accommodate the neo-Palladian lines of Adam and
Wyatt, and the philosophical leanings of the French with
their great admiration for Confucius. The hectic colouring of
genuine Chinese art had been watered down, the vibrant lac-
quers given a silken finish, highly attractive but unauthentic.

The Prince of Wales, never one to imitate fashion when he could improve on it, began to experiment in the Music Room with dragons painted on the columns, and soon the Pavilion was a riot of bamboo patterns, Chinese wallpapers, lacquer cabinets, miniature pagodas, and full-size wood carvings of Chinese men and women. At this stage, most of the additions were imported direct from the East, and it was only later that English craftsmen were used to keep pace with George's demands.

So infected was the Prince of Wales with ideas of a completely Chinese palace, that he contemplated an entirely new exterior for the Pavilion. Holland prepared a few sketches, but it was William Porden who became most involved. He produced a set of five designs, enchanting in their lightness, with a Palladian sense of balance artfully elaborated with serpentine dragons, wrought-iron balconies, delicate pillars and pagoda-shaped roofs, a supremely elegant symphony in green and gold. Alas, the idea was considered too fanciful, and the designs were never used. The Prince of Wales's fertile imagination had moved on to grapple with an entirely different concept, the construction of the Royal Stables and Riding House. The abandonment of the East was, however, purely temporary.

The building of the Royal Stables began in 1803 and was to last for five years; the cost eventually ran to £54,000. The design was based on the Paris Corn Market and was dominated by a massive cupola sixty-five feet high and eighty feet in diameter. There was a fountain in the middle of the floor, and around the walls were forty-four stalls for the horses. The west wing was for the Riding House, and the east wing was originally intended for an indoor tennis court, although the work was never completed and the empty space was given over to coaches and further stabling. It is hardly surprising that George boasted of providing his horses with a palace to live in, and Clifford Musgrave, formerly Curator of the Pavilion, had no doubts about the success of the building:

The conception . . . was a magnificent one, and must rank as one of the Prince of Wales's important architectural achievements. Indeed it is one of the most impressive architectural compositions in Britain, with the immense dome crowning the central angular bay, the flanking wings crowned with pinnacles, and the whole possessing long dignified lines giving a sense of harmony and repose.

The Pavilion was now about to enter a period of massive reconstruction. Two very different visitors to Brighton in 1805 give some flavour of the atmosphere. Lady Bessborough thought the *chinoiserie* "in *outré* and false taste, but for the kind of thing as perfect as it can be" but found the tenor of life pleasant enough:

In the Morning he gives you horses, Carriages etc., to go where you please with you; he comes and sits *rather too long*, but only on a visit. Everybody meets at dinner, which, *par parenthèse*, is excellent, with the addition of a few invitations in the evening. Three large rooms, very comfortable, are lit up; whist, backgammon, Chess, trace Madame—every sort of game you can think of in two of them, and Musick in the third. His band is beautiful. He has Viotti and a Lady who sings and plays very well.

Sheridan endeavoured to liven up the proceedings. Thomas Creevey looked back:

His point of difference with the Prince [over politics] being at an end, Sheridan entered into whatever fun was going on at the Pavilion as if he had been a boy, tho' he was then 55 years of age. Upon one occasion he came into the drawing-room disguised as a police officer to take up the Dowager Lady Sefton for playing at some unlawful game; and at another time, when we had a phantasmagoria at the Pavilion, and were all shut up in perfect darkness, he continued to sit upon the lap of Madame Gerobtzoff, a haughty Russian dame, who made row enough for the whole town to hear her.

The Prince of Wales meanwhile had had an Indian vision. Probably inspired by Sezincote, a house designed for a retired Indian nabob, Sir Charles Cockerell, and spurred on by the consummation of his plans for the Royal Stables, George summoned Humphrey Repton, who had laid out the gardens at Sezincote in the Indian style, to advise him. Repton proceeded to lavish much ingenuity on plans both for the grounds and for the new house, involving such conceits as "a perpetual garden," a central bulbous dome and what Clifford Musgrave has called "two grotesquely clumsy columns copied from an excavated Indian temple." The Prince of Wales announced himself delighted with the plans: "Mr. Repton, I consider the whole of this work as perfect, and will have my part carried into immediate execution; not a tittle shall be altered—even you yourself shall not admit any improvement." But nothing happened. Repton was paid for preparing the designs and they were published in 1808. They were never acted upon, for the almost inevitable reason that George's debts had once more reached astronomic proportions. There would be no more money available for building until the Regency—and until after the departure of Mrs. Fitzherbert to the calm of Battersea. Poor Repton had been treated most shabbily and he never really recovered.

In 1812, Wyatt was commissioned to redesign the Pavilion, but he died in a carriage accident the following year, and the work passed to John Nash, who had already converted Cumberland Lodge in Windsor Park for the Prince Regent, and had also done work at Carlton House. Nash was entirely in sympathy with George's Indian vision, and worked for ten years to bring it to reality. Nash made his plan eminently clear:

It was therefore determined by H.M. that the Pavillion should assume an Eastern character, and the Hindoo style of Architecture was adopted in the expectation that the turban domes and lofty pinnacles might from their glittering and picturesque effect, attract and fix the attention of the Spectator, and the superior magnitude of the Dome of the Stables cease to be observed.

At first, it was only intended to rebuild the Eating Room and the Conservatory, to widen the passage which was to become a gallery, to add a Hall of Entrance, and to convert the old Stable offices into domestic offices. "H.M.," added Nash,

was induced by a strong dislike to the absurd and perverted taste which universally prevailed of introducing the simplicity which is the charm of the Great Temples into every structure, whether suited or not to the purpose of the building and even into the interior of our houses and to the furniture itself. H.M. knew also that the forms of which the Eastern structures are composed were susceptible more than any other (the Gothic perhaps excepted) of rich and picturesque combinations.

The Prince Regent oversaw the progress of the work and was displeased at the slightest indication of delay. Slowly, Nash's concepts began to materialise. The corridor was transformed into the New Gallery, with the imitation bamboo staircase made of cast-iron leading out of the pink and blue vista dominated by a huge waterlily chandelier. The tentlike Octagon Hall and the pale green and white, dragon-festooned Vestibule took shape. The splendid Kitchen, with its great open fireplace with bronze canopy, cast-iron columns like palm-trees, the stoneware barrels and flour bin, the roasting spits and bottle-jacks, and the *batterie de cuisine* of more than 500 pieces, was presided over by Carême, and was satisfactorily close to the Banqueting Room. This amazing room had a huge domed ceiling, which represented "an Eastern sky partially obscured by the broad and branching foliage of a luxuriant and fruited plantain tree," and which held a silver dragon at its centre from which hung an enormous gasolier, weighing almost a ton, and costing £5,613 9s. On the walls were landscape paintings *à la chinoise*, one figure said to represent George's mistress Lady Conyngham; fringes and tassels, lotus-flowers and dragons were everywhere.

The Saloon and two Drawing Rooms were perhaps less startling, but no one could deny the overwhelming effect of the Music Room, all scarlet, green, gold and blue, with its rampant dragons and serpents, its nine-foot pagodas, its huge central chandelier, and the enormous simulated-bamboo canopy at the far end. All this had been completed by 1818, and by that date Nash had also finished the major part of his work on the exterior, a brilliant pattern of minarets and domes with the great Indian cupola towering above but without dwarfing the other excrescences.

Visitors and sightseers poured in, and were by no means ecstatic in their approbation. William Hazlitt was matter-of-fact: "The Pavilion at Brighton is like a collection of stone pumpkins and pepper boxes. It seems as if the genius of architecture had at once the dropsy and the megrims. Anything more fantastical, with a greater dearth of invention was never seen." Princess Lieven, the wife of the Russian Ambassador, detected more than a whiff of unwholesome decadence:

I do not believe that, since the days of Heliogabalus, there have been such magnificence and such luxury. There is something effeminate about it which is disgusting. One spends the evening half-lying on cushions; the lights are dazzling; there are perfumes, music, liqueurs . . . We were shown a chandelier which cost eleven thousand pounds sterling—I write it out in full because it is really incredible. The chandelier is in the form of a tulip held by a dragon . . . How can one describe such a piece of architecture? The style is a mixture of Moorish, Tartar, Gothic and Chinese, and all in stone and iron. It is a whim which has already cost £700,000; and it still is not fit to live in.

The Princess, though extremely inaccurate in her assessment, represented the popular attitude. But it was Croker, in a famous passage which deserves to be quoted in full, who gave one of the best descriptions after a visit in 1818:

We went to look at the Pavilion. It is not so much changed as I had been told, and affords me a new proof how inaccurate people are . . . But in the place of the two rooms which stood at angles of 45° with the rest of the building—one of which I remember, a dining-room and which was also a kind of music-room, and the other, next the Castle Inn, a Chinese drawing-room, which was hardly ever opened—have been erected two immense rooms, sixty feet by forty; one for a music-room and the other for a dining-room. They both have domes; an immense dragon suspends the lustre of one of them. The music-room is more splendid, but I think the other handsomer. They are both too handsome for Brighton, and in an excessive degree too fine for the extent of His Royal Highness's premises. It is a great pity that the whole of this suite of rooms was not solidly built in or near London. The outside is said to be taken from the Kremlin at Moscow; it seems to be copied from his own stables, which perhaps were borrowed from the Kremlin. It is, I think, an absurd waste of money, and will be a ruin in half a century or more.

Croker was, however, impressed by the kitchen:

The kitchens and larders are admirable—such contrivances for roasting, boiling, baking, stewing, frying, steaming and heating; hot plates, hot closets, hot air and hot hearths, with all manner of cocks for hot water and cold water, and warm water and steam, and twenty saucepans all ticketed and labelled, placed up to their necks in a vapour bath.

Visitors to Brighton were equally critical of the general atmosphere at the Pavilion. A great dullness had settled over the court since the departure of Mrs. Fitzherbert. Lady Conyngham was plump and respectable, summed up devastatingly by Princess Lievens:

Not an idea in her head; not a word to say for herself; nothing but a hand to accept pearls and diamonds with, and an enormous balcony to wear them on. Is it really possible to be in love with a woman who accepts diamonds and pearls?

The answer was that George was not really in love with her, she was more of a companion than a mistress. Indeed, the Regent's amorousness was grossly exaggerated, to the point where the celebrated underground passage was rumoured to be the means for his secret descents on the town in search of unbridled licence and nameless vice. On the contrary, life at the Pavilion was far from exciting. William Wilberforce, on a visit in 1815, and fearing that the stories of terrible goings-on would be proved true, was almost dismayed by the domestic atmosphere:

It is sad work. Dinner comes on table at six, at nine the dinner party goes into the other rooms, in one of which is music, in another cards, in others, and a long gallery 160 feet long, walking about, till about quarter or half-past twelve, and then, on the Prince's retiring, all of us depart. But really it is a large part of existence from six to half-past twelve daily, or rather nightly.

Heliogabalus would hardly have enjoyed himself in such company.

Three years later, little had changed when Croker dined at the Pavilion:

The etiquette is, that before dinner when he comes in, he *finds* all the men standing, and the women rise; he speaks to everybody, shakes hands with new comers or particular friends, then desires the ladies to be seated. When dinner is announced, he leads out a lady of the highest rank or when the ranks are nearly equal, or when the nominal rank interferes a little with the real rank, as yesterday, with Lady Liddell and Mrs. Pelham, he took one on each arm. After dinner the new dining-room was lighted and he took the ladies to see it. It is really beautiful, and I liked it better than the other, if I can venture to say that I prefer either. Everybody was comparing them and the praise of one was always, as is usual in such cases, expressed by its superiority over the other. I ventured to say that this was not a fair way of judging of them; that though different they were, perhaps, both equally beautiful in their respective kinds, like a "handsome man and handsome woman." The poor little phrase had great success.

George's passion for music was always gratified, but supper was often no more than a tray with sandwiches and wine, and a few hands of patience the sole wickedness.

That inveterate complainer, Charles Greville, noted in his diary for December 18, 1821:

The gaudy splendour of the place amused me for a little and then bored me. The dinner was cold and the evening dull beyond all dullness. They say the King is anxious that form and ceremony should be banished, and if so it only proves how impossible it is that form and ceremony should not always inhabit a palace. The rooms are not furnished for society, and, in fact, society cannot flourish without ease; and who can feel at ease who is under the eternal constraint which etiquette and respect impose? The King was in good looks and good spirits, and after dinner cut his jokes with all the coarse merriment which is his characteristic . . . I was curious to see the Pavilion and the life they lead there, and I now only hope I may never go there again, for the novelty is passed and I should be exposed to the whole weight of the bore of it without the stimulus of curiosity.

Greville was writing in the first year of George IV's reign. George's father had died, tragic and misunderstood, on January 29, 1820, and he was close on sixty years of age, a portly, dropsical figure, given to bursts of self-congratulatory imagination. He moved into the completed Pavilion on January 2, 1821, six months before his coronation. The decorations were not finished but he could not tolerate any further wait. While his own set of apartments was under construction, he had stayed in a number of houses in Marlborough Row, much to the delight of Princess Lieven, who reported to Metternich:

In the middle of all this, the King occupies a little house (houses would be more exact) two hundred yards from his palace or pavilion, or Kremlin, or mosque—for it bears all these names and deserves them—quite alone, without means of receiving anybody, since his lodging is no bigger than a parrot's cage.

The years of the great reconstruction had brought George little joy. He missed Maria Fitzherbert, his corpulence and gout prevented him from taking any exercise, he was unpopular in the country at large, and he suffered a great personal tragedy with the death in childbirth of his daughter Charlotte. The unveiling of his apartments, a ground-floor suite consisting of an Ante-Room, a fine Library, a Bedroom and Bathroom, and his long-awaited inheritance of the crown were his only consolations. He had even quarrelled with Nash and commanded his Private Secretary, Sir William Knighton, to communicate his displeasure to the architect:

It has been represented to His Majesty that the Dihl Mastic employed on these Roofs [those of the Music Room and the Dining

Room] has *completely failed;* that the covering of the
magnificent Dining Room, the interior of which has cost so large
a sum, is now in that state that to secure it from injury, pans are
obliged to be placed over the surface, to guard the Interior from
the Influence of the Rain, and that when it rains, from day to
day, two men are under the necessity of watching this part of the
building night and morning. The flat Roofs belonging to the Pavilion are even in a worse state than those I have already named.

The case of the faulty Dihl Mastic dragged on until, in February 1823, Sir William was able to write: "I am very happy
& *much satisfied* that Mr. Nash's account is brought to a close
. . . I think it will be right to allow him his commission."
Nash was indeed paid, the sum of £4,646 13s 10d, but he
avoided the Pavilion until after George's death in 1830.

Additions to the royal collection continued to pour in: furniture, carpets, books, ornaments, bric-à-brac and orientalia
of every description; and Frederick Crace and his hard-
worked assistants painted and gilded and papered in a fever of
activity. But, perhaps because Lady Conyngham was never
enthusiastic about Brighton, the King made his final visit to
the Pavilion in January 1827. He had been expected at
Christmas, but his brother the Duke of York was ill and died
on January 5. Four pianofortes had arrived in four carriages,
and one of Brighton's characters, Sake Deen Mahomed, the
King's Shampooing Surgeon and proprietor of the Indian
Baths, was seen to enter the Pavilion, but an air of melancholy hung around the oriental palace. Then on January 22,
the King's bed arrived—"a Couch Bedstead Stuffed Head and
Foot with side cheeks and Crimson Coloured Chintz Damask
Cases"—as well as "four Bath Blankets," "a Machine for
Gouty uses in a satin case," and "a Gouty cradle from Carlton House stores." The following day, the Gouty King himself appeared. He stayed for six weeks, and on March 7 drove
along the sea-front to catch a last glimpse of his extraordinary
creation. Then he departed to Windsor, to supervise Jeffrey
Wyatt's reconstruction and to immerse himself in the novels
of Walter Scott. He died at Windsor on June 26, 1830.

The Pavilion did not quite die with its progenitor. William IV made regular visits, and was markedly kind to Mrs. Fitzherbert, who had revealed her secret marriage to George, inviting her to all the receptions and parties. But Victoria never really cared for the Pavilion, dismissing it in her usual forthright manner: "A strange, odd Chinese looking thing, both inside and outside; most rooms low." It was too public, too urban, and far too fanciful. The Queen was happier at her new acquisition, Osborne, and she took a practical decision. The Pavilion was sold to the Town Commissioners for £53,000, and the interior was immediately gutted. As for the furniture, vanloads of carpets, clocks, porcelain, glass and pictures were removed, the contents to be shared out between Windsor, Buckingham Palace, and Kensington Palace. Their restoration to their rightful home would not take place for many decades, and the whole Pavilion was to lie an empty shell virtually until the end of the nineteenth century. It was ironic that, at the very moment when all George's dreams and ideas reached a splendid flowering, the mists of Victorian England began to seep in. William Cobbett, no Georgian, summed up the indifference, even hostility, which surrounded Brighton's Xanadu:

As to the "palace," the apartments appear to be all upon the ground floor; and when you see the thing from a distance, you think you see a parcel of cradle-spits, of various dimensions, sticking up out of the mouths of so many enormous squat decanters. Take a square box, the sides of which are three feet and a half, and the height of a foot and a half. Take a large Norfolk-turnip, cut off the green of the leaves, leave the stalks 9 inches long, tie these round with a string three inches from the top, and put the turnip on the middle of the top of the box. Then take four turnips of half the size, treat them in the same way, and put them on the corners of the box. Then take a considerable number of bulbs of the crown-imperial, the narcissus, the hyacinth, the tulip, the crocus, and others; let the leaves of each have sprouted to about an inch, more or less according to the size of the bulb; put all these pretty promiscuously, but pretty thickly, on the top of the box. Then stand off and look at your architecture. There! That's "a Kremlin." Only you must cut some church-looking windows in the sides of the box. As to what you ought to put into the box, that is a subject far above my cut.

But one of the most charming descriptions of the Pavilion came from the pen of Charles Westmacott in 1825:

There is really something very romantic in the style of its architecture, and by no means inelegant, perhaps it is better suited for the peculiar situation of a marine palace than a more classical or accredited order would be. It has been likened, on its first appearance, to a chess-board; but, in my thinking, it more nearly resembles that soul-inspiring scene, the splendid banquet table, decorated in the best style of modern grandeur and covered with the usual plate and glass enrichments: for instance, the central dome represents the water magnum, the towers right and left, with their pointed spires, champagne bottles, the square compartments on each side are exactly like the form of our fashionable liqueur stands, the clock tower resembles the centre ornament of a plateau, the various small spires so many enriched candelabra, the glass dome a superb dessert dish.

A feast for the eyes and the senses the Pavilion undoubtedly was. It is George IV's greatest monument.

Epilogue

The King Is Dead

The anthem, besides being immeasurably tedious, would have served as well for a nuptial.

Horace Walpole on the funeral of George II

That ceremony was very well managed, and a fine sight, the military part particularly, and the Guards were magnificent.

Charles Greville on the funeral of George IV

"The crisis was now fast approaching," wrote Huish, "yet the death of the King was not expected till Friday night, the 25th. The physicians, however,

had been aware that it would probably be sudden, and the royal sufferer was prepared to receive the awful summons with resignation and submission. His Majesty's phrase was when this intimation was given to him a fortnight previously, "God's will be done." Within the last week he spoke but little, and in a tone quite faint, and sometimes almost inaudible and inarticulate. To speak so as to be heard in the chamber appeared to give him pain, and to require an effort beyond the remaining strength of his

shattered constitution. Business of any kind became irksome to
him and affected his temper.

George IV had been ill since the beginning of 1830.
Dropsy had been diagnosed, and he suffered from bilious attacks, hiccups, some difficulty in breathing. In early May, his
brother the Duke of Sussex had sent him "a chair of a peculiar construction, adapted to the circumstances of the case"
(the King had sent in return the ribbon of the order of St.
Patrick, a somewhat peculiar *quid pro quo*), and the physicians were busy puncturing the royal swollen legs. By June
he was clearly worse, and everyone prepared for the end.
Robert Huish, George's first biographer, waxed eloquent:

The death-bed scene of a monarch is one of the most impressive
lessons that humanity can be taught. It shows the nothingness—
the emptiness of earthly grandeur, and that a king after all is
nothing more than a mere human being, subject to a common des-
tiny as the meanest beggar of the country. Let us view George
IV, in the most splendid palace of the Kings of England, surrounded by elegance and luxuries unknown to his predecessors,
lying on his couch of anguish. A life of prosperity was near its
close; the poisonous dregs of the cup of pleasure "gnawed his in-
wards" . . . A poor old man, the wreck of a fine person, loaded
with more than the infirmity of age and sickness, he was the object of painful contemplation to his attendants . . . George IV
had long been the envy of his people; how different were the
feelings which the scene we are now about to describe was calculated to excite.

On June 25, the physicians reported that they could do
nothing more:

From eleven to three o'clock his Majesty appeared to be suffering what is commonly called restless sleep. He opened his eyes
occasionally, and when he coughed he appeared to suffer more
than the usual pain, but nothing occurred until three o'clock to
indicate any particular change.

George motioned to one of the pages in attendance that he
wanted to be moved to the Duke of Sussex's chair. It was his

last sign: "A great alteration overcast the royal countenance; the King's eyes became fixed, his lips quivered, and he appeared to be sinking into a fainting fit." The physicians rushed in, and the attendants applied sal volatile and eau de Cologne:

At this moment his Majesty attempted to raise his hand to his breast, faintly ejaculating, "Oh, God, I am dying"; and after two or three seconds of time, he uttered the following words, which were his last, "This is death!"—his expiring condition barely enabling him to announce the fatal sensation, so as to be heard by the page, on whose shoulder his Majesty's head had fallen.

George IV died at thirteen minutes past three on the Saturday morning, in the presence of the Bishop of Chichester, Lord Conyngham, the husband of the King's mistress, the physicians and various gentlemen of the household:

The stroke of death, it was manifest, had fallen lightly on the King; the features were neither drawn nor distorted, but appeared in that serene and tranquil state which would have induced the belief that his Majesty still slept, and reminded the beholder, that "sleep is elder brother to death." The King, it was observed, looked comparatively well; the cheeks, however, appeared rather sunk and the abdomen much raised.

The King's body was covered by a linen sheet and left on view until eight o'clock, when the sergeant-surgeon, Sir Astley Cooper, arrived to conduct the post-mortem and the embalming:

The result was that his Majesty's disorder was an extensively diseased organization of the heart; this was the primary disorder, although dropsical symptoms subsequently supervened, and in fact there was a general breaking up of his Majesty's constitution. The heart was uncommonly enlarged, but there was no effusion of water on the thorax cavity. The valves of the heart had become partially ossified, and there was a considerable degree of fatness about that organ generally. The liver was not diseased, the lungs were ulcerated, and there were dropsical symptoms of the skin in various parts of the body, but not of a nature necessarily to produce death. They appeared rather the eventual consequence of the impeded circulation of the blood, owing to the disorganization of disease of the bones, arising from the primary disorder; indeed the debilitated circulation of the vital fluid had everywhere left the traces of its long existence.

George IV had endured a considerable degree of pain, and been forced to drug himself with brandy and water, eau de Cologne, and other spirits: "The torture which the King suffered during the paroxysms of his disorder must have been excruciating, since it is said that his moans were at times even heard by the sentinels on duty in the quadrangle."

A complete silence descended on Windsor. The royal standard flew at half-mast, every window was tight shut, and the terrace and public apartments were closed. Everything and everyone was plunged into deep mourning, while preparations for the lying-in-state and funeral went ahead.

Wednesday was the day set aside for the lying-in-state:

Shortly after ten o'clock the iron gate was thrown open, and all persons indiscriminately admitted. The scene at this moment was by no means one of that solemnity befitting the occasion—the chimney-sweep and the bricklayer in their working dresses were seen pressing through the crowd, or overleaping the barriers; while the screams of the females, and the rude and indecent jokes of the blackguards, gave the whole scene more the appearance of a crowd hastening to some raree-show than to the chamber of death. The official order required all persons to appear in decent mourning, but there appeared to be a predominant feeling not to mourn at all, and it was only in the immediate presence of the body that the majority of the countenances put on a lugubrious show.

The sun was shining, the Castle looked magnificent, and it was more like a day's outing than the prelude to a funeral. The great British public, who had never loved George IV, were enjoying themselves.

The state apartment where the body lay was an impressive sight:

The richness of the purple canopy—the superbness of the coffin .
—the pall—the splendid masses of bright and flaming hues from
the golden drapery of the royal standard—the crowns and heralds' uniforms—imparted a death-like and spectral paleness to the
heads of the household mourners which had an intensely interesting effect. The mourners stood perfectly motionless, and like
statues upon a sepulchre. The atmosphere of the apartment rose
at times to a stifling heat. It was the chamber of mortality and
woe.

The funeral was to be the following day:

The road from London to Windsor was a full tide of busy life;
whilst thousands from the towns and villages around halted this
far in their pilgrimage to the tomb of royalty. The town itself
bore any thing but a just import of gloom. As the day advanced,
the wheels of carriages, and the to and fro anxiety of the people
almost induced us to disregard the mournful bells and guns. Before noon the town of Windsor felt all the profit and some of the
discomfort of ten or twelve thousand people squeezed into a place
not capable of comfortably accommodating as many hundreds.
The group resembled more the characters of a masquerade, than
spectators hastening to a funeral; white plumed field-officers and
their aide de camps, paupers, and professional pickpockets, heralds and pursuivants in their gorgeous tabards, gentlemen pensioners in all the pride of gold lace and black crape, and the
party-coloured multitude of the middle class mixed up in admirable confusion.

The new King, William IV, arrived with his Queen at
Frogmore soon after midday, and he proceeded to the Castle
with an escort of the Life Guards and the Blues in the extraordinary and fanciful uniforms designed by George. The
Duke of Wellington arrived, looking "much fatigued, jaded,
travel stained, and dusty." The scene outside St. George's
Chapel was one of pandemonium:

As the multitude gained ground, and poured in with redoubled
energy, the screams of distress and fright, and pain, became
more and more frequent, yet happily neither lives were lost nor
limbs broken; but several ladies fainted, and many were com-

pelled to give expression to their sufferings in a very audible manner . . . The hum of voices engaged in loud and animated conversation, continued for some time, but sank by slow degrees in a low murmur, and before the approach of the procession, was hushed into the deepest silence.

The funerals of Hanoverian monarchs were hardly notable for decorum or a sense of occasion. When George II had been buried, Horace Walpole gave a shocking account of the proceedings:

This grave scene was fully contrasted by the burlesque Duke of Newcastle. He fell into a fit of crying the moment he came into the chapel, and flung himself back in a stall, the Archbishop hovering over him with a smelling-bottle; but in two minutes his curiosity got the better of his hypocrisy, and he ran about the chapel with his glass to spy who was or was not there, spying with one hand, and mopping his eyes with the other. Then returned the fear of catching cold; and the Duke of Cumberland who was sinking with heat, felt himself weighed down, and turning round, found it was the Duke of Newcastle standing upon his train, to avoid the chill of the marble.

William IV behaved little better at the funeral of his brother, not that anyone expected better of him. Charles Greville was less than approving:

At the late King's funeral, he behaved with great indecency. That ceremony was very well managed, and a fine sight, the military part particularly, and the Guards were magnificent . . . With the exception of Mount Charles, who was deeply affected, they were all as merry as grigs. The King was chief mourner, and, to my astonishment, as he entered the chapel directly behind the body, in a situation in which he should have been apparently if not really, absorbed in the melancholy duty he was performing, he darted up to Strathnaven, who was ranged on one side below the Dean's stall, shook him heartily by the hand, and then went on nodding to the right and left.

Huish provides a more sober account:

The procession began to move from the Castle about a quarter before nine, and at a quarter before ten it entered the choir, and immediately the various heralds busied themselves, with distinguished activity and success, in marshalling the several individuals who formed the procession, and assigning to each his allotted position. The banners that were placed at the corners and sides of the canopy, under which the coffin was placed, were borne by Lords Verulam, Erroll, Cathcart, etc. The Duke of Wellington was on the right of his Majesty, bearing the sword of state. In their respective places were the Dukes of Cumberland and Sussex, Prince Leopold, and Prince George of Cumberland. The Knights of the Garter took their places in their respective stalls, on the south side of the choir; the Bishops on the north side; the two Archbishops, Canterbury and Armagh, were seated in stalls on the south side of the western entrance. The burial service was, for the greater part, chanted, and the anthem sung with splendid effect. Nothing could be more sublime or touching than was the whole of the service.

The body of George IV was borne to the royal mausoleum beneath Cardinal Wolsey's Tomb House and "lowered by machinery into the passage leading to the royal vault":

At five minutes to eleven o'clock, the whole of what fell to the officiating clergymen and choristers was concluded, and his Majesty who appeared much affected during the whole ceremony, retired through the door leading to the royal closet. Sir George Naylor proclaimed the style and various titles of his late Majesty, and thereupon the distinguished personages present quitted the chapel, without any regard to the order in which they entered it, and, therefore, not forming any returning procession. Sir George Naylor concluded his proclamation with the words, "God save King William IV," a rocket was let off, and the band outside played "God save the King."

It was all over. The last of the Hanoverian Georges, whose life had been such a strange mixture of magnificence and buffoonery, had been laid to rest in an entirely fitting manner.

Sources

Prologue

The Coronation Book (1902), by Jocelyn Perkins, sacrist and minor canon of Westminster Abbey, gives much information on coronations in general, and on the often bizarre ceremonial which accumulated over the centuries. W. J. Passingham's *A History of the Coronation* (1937) provides more precise details of both George I and George III's coronations. The first volume of Wolfgang Michael's *England Under George I: The Beginnings of the Hanoverian Dynasty* (1896, translated in 1936) has also been consulted.

Chapter I

I have again consulted *England Under George I: The Beginnings of the Hanoverian Dynasty* by Wolfgang Michael (1936). Sir H. M. Imbert-Terry's *A Constitutional King: George the First* (1927) is hardly complimentary to its subject, but it is difficult to find writers greatly attracted to the first George. J. H. Plumb's *The First Four Georges* (1956) is eminently balanced, whereas Thackeray's *The Four Georges* (1866) is predictably entertaining but misleading.

Chapter II

The various romantic novels about the Königsmarck affair should not be taken with any seriousness, but can be enjoyed simply as works of highly imaginative fiction. W. H. Wilkins's *The Love of an Un-crowned Queen* (1900 and 1903) and A. W. Ward's *The Electress Sophia and the Hanoverian Succession* (1909) are important sources for any assessment of Sophia Dorothea and the tangled affairs, political and sexual, of the Hanoverian dynasty. The best biography of Sophia Dorothea is by Ruth Jordan (1971) and I am indebted to her for her translations of letters between Königsmarck and Sophia Dorothea.

Chapter III

Sir Charles Petrie's *The Jacobite Movement* (revised edition, 1959) gives a full picture of events from the Jacobite point of view from James II's exile onwards. Other books which have been consulted include P. Hume Brown's *History of Scotland*, Volume III, 1689–1843 (1909); R. Campbell's *Life of the Most Illustrious Prince John, Duke of Argyle and Greenwich* (1745); R. Chambers's *History of the Rebellions in Scotland* (1829); the Comte de Forbin's *Mémoires* (Amsterdam, 1730); G. P. Insh's *The Scottish Jacobite Movement* (1952); the Chevalier de Johnstone's *A Memoir of the Forty-Five* (1820); R. Patten's *History of the Rebellion in the year 1715* (1745); John Prebble's *Culloden* (1961); P. Rae's *The History of the Late Rebellion* (1718); John, Master of Sinclair's, *Memoirs of the Insurrection in Scotland in 1715* (annotated by Sir Walter Scott, 1858); John Selby's *Over the Sea to Skye* (1973); and C. S. Terry's *The Chevalier de St George and the Jacobite Movements in His Favour: 1701–1720* (1901). Anyone seeking a wider list of sources should consult the bibliography in my own *Inglorious Rebellion: The Jacobite Risings of 1708, 1715 and 1719*.

Chapter IV

I have consulted three biographies of Frederick: Sir George Young's *Poor Fred: The People's Prince* (1937); Morris Marples's *Poor Fred and the Butcher* (1970) and John Walters's *The Royal Griffin* (1972). Lord Hervey's *Memoirs* are indispensable and extremely partial; there is an admirable one-volume edition, edited by Romney Sedgwick (1952, revised 1963). The Earl of Egmont's diaries were published by the Historical Manuscripts Commission in three volumes, in 1920 and 1923. Horace Walpole's *Memoirs of the Reign of King George II* were edited by Lord Holland (1847) and his *Letters* by Peter Cunningham (1891).

Chapter V

The definitive edition of the Letters of John Gay was prepared by C. F. Burgess (1966). Other useful sources are Lewis Melville's *Life and Letters of John Gay* (1921) and W. E. Schultz's *Gay's Beggar's Opera* (1923). There have been several biographies of Handel, of which Paul Henry Lang's (1967) is the most exhaustive, and Newman Flower's (1923, revised edition 1947) the more digestible. *The Reminiscences of Michael Kelly* (edited by Herbert van Thal as *Solo Recital*, 1972) are exceedingly entertaining and give a wonderfully vivid picture of musical life during the second part of the eighteenth century and the first decades of the nineteenth century.

Chapter VI

The intricacies of the Pragmatic Sanction and the War of the Austrian Succession are encapsulated in digestible though dry form in C. T. Atkinson's contribution to Volume VI of the *Cambridge Modern History* (Cambridge, 1909). J. W. Fortescue's *History of The British Army*, Volume II (1899), is invaluable for an account of the battle of Dettingen itself. William Biggs's *Military History of Europe . . . from the Commencement of the War with Spain in 1739, to the Treaty of Aix-la-Chapelle in 1748* (1755), and the interesting compilation of letters from Major Richard Davenport to his brother during service in the 4th Troop of Horse Guards and 10th Dagoons, 1742–60, edited by C. W. Frearson (1968), are also worth consulting. Last but no means least, there are the letters of Horace Walpole, and Voltaire's *Siècle de Louis XIV*.

Chapter VII

Morris Marples has written three admirable books which deal with the children of George III: *Princes in the Making* (1965), *Six Royal Sisters* (1969), and *Wicked Uncles in Love* (1972). I have also consulted Roger Fulford's *The Royal Dukes* (1933), the *Correspondence of George, Prince of Wales, 1770–1813*, edited by Arthur Aspinall (1963–7), and Dorothy M. Stuart's *Daughters of George III* (1939).

Chapter VIII

Andrew Steinmetz's two-volume compedium, *The Gaming Table* (1870), has a fund of anecdotes and curious facts about every aspect of gambling. A. L. Humphreys's *Crockford's* and Henry Blyth's *Hell and Hazard* (1953 and 1969 respectively) offer more specific information. Pierce Egan's *Boxiana* appeared in five volumes, in 1812, 1818, 1821, 1828 and 1829; there is also an excellent one-volume compilation, edited by John Ford (1976). Other valuable sources for the world of the prize fight include *Pugilistica* by Henry Downes Miles (1906), Renton Nicholson's *Boxing* (1837), and the handbook of rules, *Fistiana; or, The Oracle of the Ring,* by Vincent George Dowling, which went through twenty-four editions between 1840 and 1864. *The Reminiscences of Captain Gronow* are a constant delight and illumination. They appeared in four volumes (the final one posthumously), in 1861, 1863, 1865 and 1866. Nicolas Bentley recently edited an admirable selection for the Folio Society (1977).

Chapter IX

George III and the Mad-Business by Ida Macalpine and Richard Hunter (1969) is indispensable for any account of the King's illness, not only because it is intrinsically so convincing, but also because it assembles within the covers of one book a complete survey of medical practices at the end of the eighteenth and beginning of the nineteenth centuries. Other relevant works include *The Trade in Lunacy: A Study of Private Madhouses in England in the Eighteenth and Nineteenth Centuries* by William Parry-Jones (1972), and *Visits to Bedlam: Madness and Literature in the Eighteenth Century* by Max Byrd (Columbia, South Carolina, 1975). Volume IV of the *Diary and Letters of Madame d'Arblay* (1778–1840) offers Fanny Burney's particular view of George III at the time of his illness. Other books consulted include Sir Nathaniel Wraxall's *Historical and Posthumous Memoirs,* edited by H. B. Wheatley (1884), and *The Greville Diary,* edited by Philip Whitwell Wilson (1927).

Chapter X

The mainstay of this chapter was the often-quoted *A Historical Account of His Majesty's Visit to Scotland,* published with commendable speed by Oliver & Boyd in the year of George IV's visit; Robert Mudie, whose authorship is not revealed on the title page, had written a bestseller which must have pleased everyone and offended none, and which still affords entertainment, even though the modern reader will certainly laugh in the wrong places. I have also made use of Robert Huish's *Memoirs of George the Fourth* (1831); Volume VII of J. G. Lockhart's *Life of Sir Walter Scott* (1902); H. J. C. Grierson's edition of *The Letters of Sir Walter Scott: 1821–1823* (1934), and Carola Oman's *The Wizard of the North* (1973).

Chapter XI

Contemporary magazines and diaries are always the best source of material for observation on fashion, but if one were forced to rely on one book for the period of the Regency and the reign of George IV, one could do no better than choose C. Willett and Phillis Cunnington's marvellous *Handbook of English Costume in the Nineteenth Century* (second edition, 1966), which is a mine of anecdote, quotation, and expert opinion. James Laver's various books on costume are also indispensable, and F. W. Fairholt's *Costume in England: A History of Dress* (1846) and Georgiana Hill's *A History of English Dress*, Volume II (1893) contain interesting material. For Beau Brummell, one should consult Captain William Jesse's contemporary biography (1844), as well as Lewis Melville's *Beau Brummel: His Life and Letters* (1924).

Chapter XII

The indispensable book on the Pavilion is Clifford Musgrave's *Royal Pavilion: an Episode in the Romantic* (first edition, 1951; revised edition, 1959), a treasure-trove of elegant writing and fascinating detail. Musgrave's *Life in Brighton* (1970) is also well worth consulting, and a rapid picture can be obtained from Antony Dale's *History and Architecture of Brighton* (1950). *Brighton* by Osbert Sitwell and Margaret Barton (1935) was largely responsible for reawakening the general public's interest in the Pavilion, and its encrusted, somewhat mandarin prose is highly suitable for its subject. There is a most entertaining chapter devoted to the Pavilion in Philip Howard's *The Royal Palaces* (1970), and the Royal Pavilion itself produces an admirable and excellently illustrated brochure. I have also consulted John Gore's edition of *The Creevey Papers* (1963), Philip Whitwell Wilson's edition of *The Greville Diary* (1927), Peter Quennell's edition of *The Private Letters of Princess Lieven to Prince Metternich: 1820–1826* (1937) and Robin Furneaux's *William Wilberforce* (1974).

Epilogue

With the exception of the quotations from Horace Walpole and Greville, all the source material for this epilogue comes from Robert Huish's *Memoirs of George the Fourth* (1830).

Index

Fenton, Lavinia, 87
Ferguson, Sir Adam, 191
Figg, James, 140
Fitz Roy, Sir Charles, 128–29
Fitzherbert, Mrs., 122, 207,
212–13, 214, 218, 221, 223, 225
Flower, Newman, 92–93
Forbin, Comte de, 49–50
Forster, Thomas, 52
Fortescue, Sir John, 103, 105
Fox, Charles James, 115, 213
Fraser, Simon, *see* Lovat, 11th
Baron
Frederica, Princess of
Solms-Braunfels, 123
Frederick, Duke of York, 114,
116, 117, 119–20, 121, 123, 127,
163, 166, 167, 171, 189, 224
Frederick, Elector Palatine, 29
Frederick, Prince of
Hesse-Homburg, 126–27
Frederick, Prince of Wales,
69–82, 90–91, 95
Frederick, Prince of
Württemberg, 125–26
Frederick II, the Great, King of
Prussia, 98, 99
Frederick III, Elector of
Brandenburg, 41
Frederick V, Elector of
Hanover, 13
Frederick Augustus I, Elector of
Saxony, 39, 40, 41
Frederick William II, King of
Prussia, 43
Frescobaldi, Girolamo, 85

Gacé, Comte de, 49
Gainsborough, Thomas, 118
Gamble, boxer, 143
Garrick, David, 118
Garrod, Sir Archibald, 172
Garth, Captain Thomas, 128
Garth, General, 127–28, 165
Gay, John, 94–96; *The Beggar's
Opera*, 84, 85–88, 89, 91, 93, 96;
Polly, 88–89, 95

George, Prince of Cumberland,
233
George I, King, becomes king,
12–26; coronation, 2–3;
marriage, 30–32, 34–35, 37–38;
divorce, 42–43;
relationship with George II,
68; founds British Academy,
84; patronage of Handel, 95
George II, King, 12, 25, 88;
marriage, 43; and his mother,
44; relationship with the
Prince of Wales, 68–82;
patronage of Handel, 90–91,
93; and war of Austrian
Succession, 99–109; death,
231–32
George III, King, birth, 81;
coronation, 3–8; children, 68,
114–30; musical interests, 95;
ill-health, 150–72; relationship
with George IV, 118–19, 120,
213, 214; death, 171–72, 223
George IV, King, 129, 135–36,
194, 202; birth, 114; childhood,
115–16, 117, 118–19;
relationship with his father,
120, 213, 214; marriages, 122,
212; and George III's illness,
155, 156–59, 161, 163, 165–69;
Regency, 169, 170, 171;
coronation, 7, 146; and the
Jacobites, 63; visit to Scotland,
175–93; and Beau Brummell,
205, 206, 207–8; in Brighton,
216–26; death, 209, 224, 227–32,
233
George V, King, 68
George William, Duke of Celle,
29–30, 34, 42, 43
Gerobtzoff, Madame, 217
Gianetti, perfumer, 184
Gillray, James, 124–25
Gisborne, Dr. Thomas, 165, 166
Glenaladale, Macdonald of, 55
Glencoe, 56

55; proclaim James VIII, 56;
disagree on policy, 58;
confront Government troops,
59–60; defeated at Culloden,
60–61; final collapse of, 62
James I, King, 13, 29, 68
James II, King, 2, 3, 14–15, 68
Jennens, Charles, 91–93
Jersey, Lady, 214
Jesse, Captain, 205
John Frederick of Lüneburg, 28,
30
Johnson, Dr., 86, 91, 211
Johnstone, Chevalier de, 59–61
Jones, Dr. Robert, 164
Jordan, Mrs., 120, 153
Joseph, Archduke, 98

Keith, Sir Alexander, 186
Keith, George, Earl Marischal,
46, 55
Kendal, Cornet, 105
Kenmure, Lord, 52, 54
Keppoch, Macdonald of, 56
Ker, John, 48
Kielmansegge, Madame von, 26
Kilsyth, Viscount, 46
King, Sir Peter, 25
King's Theatre, London, 90, 91
Kinlochmoidart, Macdonald of,
55
Kinnaird, Lord, 48
Kinnoull, Earl of, 186
Kneseback, Eleonore, 35
Knighton, Sir William, 223
Königsmarck, Aurora von, 34,
40, 41
Königsmarck, Count Charles
John von, 32–33
Königsmarck, Countess von, 33
Königsmarck, Count Philip
Christopher von, 27–28, 32–42,
44
Kreyenberg, Hanoverian
Resident, 20, 22

Labourie, cook, 135
Lade, Sir John, 148
Lansdowne, Lord, 15
Leibniz, Gottfried Wilhelm, 13,
69
Lennox, Sarah, 115
Leopold, Prince, 233
Leopold I, Emperor, 30, 98
Lewenhaupt, Count, 34
Lewenhaupt, Countess Amelia,
34
Lewis, Erasmus, 17
Liddell, Lady, 222
Lieven, Princess, 133, 220, 221,
223
Linlithgow, Earl of, 46
Liverpool, Lord, 177
London Chronicle, 203
Londonderry, Lord, 177, 179
Lothian, Lord, 183, 191
Louis XIV, King of France, 3,
15, 16, 29, 30, 48, 212
Lovat, Simon Fraser, 11th Baron,
49
Luther, Martin, 29
Lyon of Auchterhouse, 46
Lytton, Bulwer, 137

Macalpine, Ida, 172
Macartney, General, 16
Macdonald, Alexander, 55
Macdonald of Sleat, 55
Macdonald of the Isles, 21
Macgregor, Rob Roy, 53, 54
Macintosh of Borlum, 50, 51
Macleod of Macleod, 21, 55
Madison, page, 135
Magrath, Mr., 190
Mahomed, Sake Deen, 224
Maintenon, Madame de, 212
Mann, Sir Horace, 133, 150
Mar, John, Earl of, 15, 45–47,
50–54
Maria Amalia, Electress of
Bavaria, 98
Maria Josepha, Electress of
Saxony, 98

Maria Theresa, Empress, 99, 100
Marlborough, Duke of, 16, 18, 20, 22, 25, 100–1
Mary, Princess, 114, 124, 127, 129–30
Mary, Queen of Scots, 190
Mary of Modena, 49
Mason, A. E. W., 28
Master Peruke Makers, 201
Matilda, Duchess of Saxony, 14
Maxwell, Sir W., 190
Mayne, John, 180
Melville, Lord, 179, 189, 191
Mendoza, Daniel, 142
Metastasio, Pietro, 84
Milton, John, 91, 92
Minshull, magistrate, 177
Modena, Duke of, 13
Mohun, Lord, 16
Molineaux, boxer, 142, 144
Montagu, Lady Mary Wortley, 69
Montalban, estate manager, 40
Moore, Tom, 205, 208
Morton, Countess of, 185
Mount Charles, 232
Murray, Lady Augusta, 121–22
Murray, Lord George, 57–59
Murray, John of Broughton, 56, 58, 59
Murray, Mr., 187
Musgrave, Clifford, 216–17, 218
Music Club, 90

Napier, Captain, 189
Napoleon I, 126
Nash, Beau, 134, 203–4
Nash, John, 218–20, 223–24
Naylor, Sir George, 233
Neal, William, 93
Neat, boxer, 144–45
Nelson, Admiral Lord, 176, 189
Newcastle, Duke of, 84, 232
Newton, Bishop, 5
Noailles, Maréchal Duc de, 102–4, 107
Normandy, Duke of, 3

North, Lord, 115
Northumberland, Duke of, 25
Nottingham, Earl of, 20
Nottingham, Lady, 3

O'Birne, gamester, 134
Octavius, Prince, 114
Ogilvy, Lord, 46
Ogle, Lady, 32
d'Olbreuse, Eléonore (Madame de Harburg), 29–30, 33, 42, 43
Old Dutch Sam, 147
Oliver, Tom, 142–43
Orford, Earl of, see Walpole, Sir Robert
Orkney, Lady, 2
d'Orléans, Louis Philippe, 126
Ormonde, Duke of, 15, 17, 21, 25, 52
Osheal, John, 199
Otho, Emperor, 13

Panmure, Lord, 48
Papillon, Monsieur de la, 200–1
Pargeter, Dr. William, 165
Pasquin, Antony, 213
Pearce, Henry, 139, 142, 143, 147
Peel, Robert, 178, 189
Pelham, Lord, 100
Pelham, Mrs., 222
Pepusch, John Christopher, 85
Pepys, Sir Lucas, 159, 163
Perceval, Spencer, 169
Perkins, Jocelyn, 3–4
Perrault, Charles, 78
Perth, Duke of, 58, 59
Philip V, King of Spain, 99, 108
Phipps, Sir Christopher, 22
Pitt, William, 151, 158, 161, 163, 165, 166, 167, 189, 201, 213
Pitt Lennox, Lord William, 204
Platen, Count, 31–32, 42
Platen, Countess Clara Elizabeth, 31–36, 38–43
Pope, Alexander, 85, 90
Porden, William, 216